Early Determination of Jurisdiction

International Arbitration Law Library

VOLUME 69

Editors

Professor Julian D.M. Lew QC has been involved with international arbitration for more than forty years as counsel, as arbitrator and as an academic. He is the founder and has been the Head of the School of International Arbitration, Centre for Commercial Law Studies, Queen Mary University of London since its creation in 1985. He is now an independent international arbitrator at 20 Essex Street, London.

Stavros Brekoulakis is Professor at Queen Mary University of London and an associate member of 3 Verulam Buildings (Gray's Inn). He is a leading academic in international arbitration and has led, or been involved in, several projects with ICCA, ICC Commission and ILA. He also acts as an independent arbitrator and has been appointed as chairman, sole arbitrator, co-arbitrator and emergency arbitrator under the rules of all the major arbitration rules.

Introduction

Since its first volume published in 1993, this authoritative practitioner-oriented series has published in-depth and analytical works on niche aspects of international arbitration, authored by specialists in the field.

Objective

This authoritative and established series covering in-depth analyses of niche areas appeals to both practitioners and academics. The series includes specific monographs and PhD dissertations of high quality, which are practical and cover issues not fully explored in general texts.

Frequency

A volume is published whenever an interesting topic presents itself.

The titles published in this series are listed at the end of this volume.

Early Determination of Jurisdiction

Fabricio Fortese

Wolters Kluwer

Published by:
Kluwer Law International B.V.
PO Box 316
2400 AH Alphen aan den Rijn
The Netherlands
E-mail: lrs-sales@wolterskluwer.com
Website: www.wolterskluwer.com/en/solutions/kluwerlawinternational

Sold and distributed by:
Wolters Kluwer Legal & Regulatory U.S.
920 Links Avenue
Landisville, PA 17538
United States of America
E-mail: customer.service@wolterskluwer.com

ISBN 978-94-035-0268-7

e-Book: ISBN 978-94-035-0278-6
web-PDF: ISBN 978-94-035-0288-5

Table of Contents

Foreword

Arbitration attracts users for a number of reasons, including its promise of efficiency and effectiveness, in terms of time and costs in resolving the dispute and enforcing the outcome. Through an agreement to arbitrate, users consent to refer their dispute to arbitration, thereby granting the arbitral tribunal jurisdiction to decide the dispute and, at the same time, restricting national court resolution of disputes that are within the scope of the agreement. Put simply, a valid applicable arbitration agreement bars court jurisdiction under the New York Convention on the Enforcement of Foreign Arbitral Awards (New York Convention) and the UNCITRAL Model Law on International Commercial Arbitration (Model Law). Over 170 countries are contracting states to the New York Convention, and many states have adopted the Model Law or have been influenced by it when adopting national arbitration legislation. These two key instruments seek to harmonise and promote global uniformity to ensure the integrity, efficiency and effectiveness of arbitration.

At the commencement of litigation or arbitration, a dispute may arise on the existence, validity, applicability, or scope of an arbitration agreement. This dispute about the proper forum and form for the dispute may be brought before a national court and may (or may not) appear before an arbitral tribunal at the same time. Such disputes over the enforceability of an arbitration agreement can relate to any number of issues and pose a multitude of threshold questions. A party may commence litigation in a court and the opposing party may raise the defence of a valid arbitration agreement that would require a court to refer the parties to arbitrate. A party may have commenced arbitration and the opposing party may apply to a national court to determine the validity and applicability of the arbitration agreement or may initiate litigation despite the pending arbitration. A party may go so far as to seek to enjoin the arbitration in courts that allow for such procedures. Pursuant to Articles 8(2) and 16 of the Model Law, the arbitrators have the power to address the objections to their jurisdiction and may continue proceedings despite parallel proceedings in a court relating to the validity and applicability of the arbitration agreement. Ultimately, the issue of jurisdiction may be decided by an appropriate court, a process that may be complicated if more than one court is asked to decide the jurisdictional dispute. A court's determination of jurisdiction could take place at an early stage or after an arbitral award is rendered and a party seeks to have it annulled or enforced by a court.

National courts have a crucial role in ensuring that valid arbitration agreements are effective, while they also have a role in ensuring the legitimacy of arbitration and protecting parties who have not consented to arbitrate the dispute. Ultimately, national courts will decide the 'gateway' jurisdiction issues, but the timing and degree of review for this determination remain controversial and divergent across jurisdictions. Early determination of jurisdiction triggers the tension between conflicting interests: facilitating efficiency and effectiveness of arbitration, ensuring the legitimacy of arbitration, respect for the widely accepted principle of the arbitrators' 'competence-competence' to determine their jurisdiction (subject to later court review), and protecting parties who have not consented to arbitration from being subject to the costly and potentially time-consuming proceedings until later court review.

Article 8(1) of the Model Law complements, and essentially replicates, Article II(3) of the New York Convention, both providing for early jurisdiction determination by a court. However, these provisions do not set out whether the early review should be 'prima facie' or a full and potentially final review, or something in between. The issue of the standard of court review remains open under the Model Law and the New York Convention, resulting in legal uncertainty and differing approaches, which may undermine the aim to harmonise international practice and provide predictability. The conflicting approaches rest upon significant theoretical and policy concerns that have practical implications. Although many courts and commentators have considered this issue, there remains lively debate in academia and practice.

With his book, *Early Determination of Jurisdiction*, Fabricio Fortese contributes to the debate and deepens understanding of the issues through his research and analysis of the background, interpretation, and application of Article 8(1). He frames his central research inquiry as 'whether national courts should (or could) conclusively settle jurisdictional disputes before or after the arbitrators have preliminarily determined that controversy'. His approach proposes an autonomous interpretative approach, detached from a given State's law, concepts, and rules and instead focuses on the international character and harmonisation aims of the Model law. Although focused on an interpretation of Article 8(1), this inquiry also has relevance to national arbitration laws and practices that are not based on the Model Law and, importantly, to the interpretation of Article II(3) of the New York Convention. His work not only provides a scholarly approach but also highlights how the ambiguity surrounding the matter leads to differing approaches in practice, creating challenges for courts, arbitrators, and users. The ambiguity opens opportunities for parties seeking to deploy strategies to delay and obstruct the resolution of a dispute through parallel proceedings that may unduly complicate a dispute and increase time and costs.

The uniqueness of Fortese's work lies in his developing a framework for approaching the legal interpretation of Article 8(1) of the Model Law through selected key legal interpretation methodologies. These methods include exploring and analysing the history and background of the Model Law, its context and aims, interpretative guidance of Article 2A, its relationship to the New York Convention, the element of good faith in the interpretation of international customary law to interpret treaties such as the New York Convention, textual interpretation, contextual and holistic interpretation, and court practice. His use of these methodologies provides a deeper understanding of the interpretation and application of Article 8(1), which may also be useful in interpreting Article II(3) of the New York Convention, as, despite the difference in the legal character of these two instruments, they are connected. Fortese's framework for interpretation, and his use of the methodologies underlying the framework, stand to inform and facilitate interpretation of other legal instruments intended to promote harmonisation and unification.

The book, which is an adaption of Fortese's PhD dissertation, addresses these issues in eight chapters, beginning with an introduction in Chapter 1, and ending with the conclusions. Chapter 2 introduces the relationship between the Model Law and the New York Convention as instruments intended to promote international arbitration. Fortese emphasises the international character, legitimacy, and flexibility of the Model Law and acknowledges the challenges to achieving international uniformity, particularly in interpreting Article 8 to achieve uniformity across diverse jurisdictions.

Chapter 3 focuses on analysing and applying interpretative methodologies specifically relevant to the Model Law. This chapter is divided into three parts. The first part analyses Article 2A(1), which provides that the interpretation of the Model Law should have 'regard ... to its international origin and to the need to promote uniformity in its application and the observance of good faith'. Article 2A(2) provides that any unsettled matters 'are to be settled in conformity with the general principles on which this Law is based'. The second part explores the rules of interpretation of the New York Convention. The third part proposes an 'autonomous' approach to interpreting the Model Law, including the national arbitration statutes based on it. The proposed approach focuses on the text of Article 8, its context, and legal purpose. Fortese argues that good faith as an element of legal interpretation plays a role, not only because Article 2A provides for it but also because it is embedded in international customary law to interpret treaties including the New York Convention.

Chapter 4 recognises the importance of national court decisions interpreting their national legislation based on the Model Law. It analyses cases drawn from a number of diverse civil and common law jurisdictions, illustrating the differing approaches to interpreting Article 8(1). Importantly, the case analysis reflects the case-based nature of the application of Article 8 and the need for the balancing of interests in facilitating arbitration and protecting the right to access to courts for litigants who exercise their right to contest having consented to arbitrate the dispute at all or in the form or forum claimed by the opposing party. Court decisions may clarify the ambiguity of Article 8(1) as implemented into national law, and may provide persuasive analysis which influences courts in other jurisdictions grappling with the same issues.

Chapter 5 is related to Chapter 3 as it examines the text of Article 8, with a focus on the legislative history (preparatory works) of the Model Law and, more particularly, Article 8. The legislative history of the Model Law is somewhat unique, (as compared to national legislation), in that it records the development of discussions, proposals, and draft text as the UNCITRAL Working Group evolves toward a commonly accepted text to present to the Commission for adoption. The relationship between the text of

Article 8(1) and Article II of the New York Convention is addressed in these discussions. This chapter notes some key issues underlying the application of Article 8, including the law applicable to the validity of the arbitration agreement and issues of arbitrability. In analysing the text of Article 8(1), the role of the national court and its obligations and powers are considered, including the timing of a court's conclusive determination on jurisdiction. Chapter 5 engages in an analysis of Article 8(2), insofar as it provides discretion for the parties to pursue arbitration and for arbitrators to continue arbitral proceedings in parallel with the court action.

Chapter 6 considers the interpretation of Article 8 in the overall context of the Model law, providing a contextual and holistic interpretative approach. In particular, it analyses Article 5, which provides that 'no court shall intervene except where so provided in this Law'. Article 16 specifically addresses the jurisdiction of the arbitral tribunal, providing for the principle of 'competence-competence' to enable the arbitrators to determine their own jurisdiction either as an early determination or in a final award, without having to await a judicial determination. Article 16(3) provides that if the tribunal 'rules as a preliminary question that it has jurisdiction', a party may within thirty days make a direct appeal to a specified court, which decision is not subject to an appeal. While this appeal is pending, 'the arbitral tribunal may continue the arbitral proceedings and make an award'. Chapter 6 analyses how these provisions of the Model Law work together to regulate early determinations of jurisdiction by courts and identifies the potential ambiguities.

Chapter 7 focuses on a teleological or purposive interpretation of Article 8(1) in the overall context of the Model Law's aims for international harmonisation and unification of international arbitration. This chapter circles the reader back to Chapter 2 of the book where the role of the Model Law was introduced, together with its relationship to the New York Convention, as instruments seeking to achieve harmonisation of international arbitration standards to promote international trade and business. National courts have an important role in ensuring this aim, while also fulfilling their obligation to ensure the legitimacy of the arbitral process, which rests upon the foundation of a valid applicable arbitration agreement binding the parties to arbitrate the particular dispute. This chapter concludes that: 'the Model Law's purpose can best be achieved by a well-balanced synergy between three critical components or factors: *legitimacy*, *efficacy*, and *efficiency*'.

Chapter 8 presents the conclusions of the academic study, presenting a comprehensive summary of the main arguments and highlighting the significance of the research. While it underscores the overarching objectives of the Model Law to achieve harmonisation, it concludes that Article 8 does not mandate either a prima facie or a full review standard of court review for early jurisdictional determinations. Instead, the study concludes that Article 8(1) permits either standard of review (or something between these two standards). In other words, courts may use their discretion when determining the standard of review. Fortese concludes that applying one or the other approach is a matter of court judgment, depending on the circumstances and factors involved, and aiming to achieve the fair and efficient resolution of the given jurisdictional dispute. However, he argues that this determination should be made in the light of the overarching purpose of the Model Law to harmonise internationally, rather than applying a State's national law, concepts, and rules.

This conclusion may leave some readers wishing for a more predictable, prescriptive approach to the interpretation and application of Article 8(1). The readers should keep in mind that the creation of the Model Law was based on the collaborative work of the members of the UNCITRAL Working Group. The Model Law seeks to provide a model for a national arbitration law which will be compatible with the New York Convention and which could be adopted by a wide range of jurisdictions as national law. This process requires finding solutions that are compatible with a range of national legal approaches and allow for reception into diverse legal systems. The regulation of the standard of review for court determination of its jurisdiction involves consideration of general policy and the facts and issues before the court in specific cases. On these, jurisdictions may reasonably disagree.

Fortese's book brings to the reader a carefully researched and deeply analysed study of Article 8(1) of the Model Law, applying different methodological approaches. This book will provide theoretical and practical insights valuable for policymakers, legislators, judges, practitioners, scholars, educators, and students. Drawing from selected cases, international arbitration practice, and legal scholarship, this book provides practical guidance on navigating the interpretation of national legislation based on the UNCITRAL Model Law as regards the early determination of arbitral jurisdiction. It engages with relevant theoretical and academic debates surrounding early jurisdiction determinations. The book is a welcome contribution to understanding the role of courts and arbitral tribunals in making early jurisdiction determinations. It also provides insights into drafting, interpreting, and applying international instruments seeking to promote harmonisation and unification of commercial law. Its structured approach will guide readers to a deeper understanding of the continuing debate over early jurisdictional decisions.

Prof. George A. Bermann
Gellhorn Prof. of Law & Jean Monnet Prof. of European Union Law
Director, Center for International Commercial and Investment Arbitration (CICIA)
Columbia University School of Law

Prof. Dr Stefan Kröll, LLM
Professor for International Dispute Resolution
Director, Center for International Dispute Resolution
Bucerius Law School

Dr Patricia Shaughnessy (JD, LLM, PhD)
Associate Professor for International Dispute Resolution
Stockholm University, Faculty of Law

CHAPTER 1

Introduction

[A] AN OUTLINE OF THIS BOOK

This book examines the timing of judicial determination of jurisdictional disputes in the presence of an arbitration agreement. The analysis focuses on Article 8(1) of the United Nations Commission on International Trade Law (UNCITRAL) Model Law on International Commercial Arbitration ('Model Law').[1]

This work does not question *who* has the authority to settle jurisdictional disputes (conflict of jurisdiction). The assumption is that both judges and arbitrators enjoy such decision-making power. This is because it is uncontroversial that national courts have the authority to decide, *conclusively*, disputes on arbitral jurisdiction. It is common ground that arbitrators, too, have the authority to rule on their own jurisdiction, subject to judicial control. This is known as the principle of competence-competence, which is widely recognised in arbitration legislation, institutional rules, and judicial practice.[2] Therefore, the critical question this book addresses is whether national courts should (or could) conclusively settle jurisdictional disputes before or after the arbitrators have preliminarily determined that controversy. Put differently, this study is about *when* (timing) a court should exercise its authority with conclusive effects.

Clarifying this matters because arbitration is not the default dispute resolution mechanism – not even for international commercial or investor-state disputes; litigation is. The legitimacy of arbitration stems from the parties' agreement, and so does the jurisdiction of arbitral tribunals. The parties' agreement to arbitrate displaces the authority of national courts to settle substantive disputes. It also draws the contours of

1. Resolution of the General Assembly at its Fortieth Session – Model Law on International Commercial Arbitration of the United Nations Commission on International Trade Law, A/RES/40/72 (11 December 1985).
2. A clear example of the codification of this principle is Article 16(1) of the Model Law. It provides that '[t]he arbitral tribunal may rule on its own jurisdiction, including any objections with respect to the existence or validity of the arbitration agreement.'

the tribunal's authority. The arbitrators' authority only extends to the parties who have empowered the tribunal, and over the disputes they have agreed, the arbitrators should determine. Such authority must be exercised in accordance with the parties' agreed procedures and applicable mandatory laws. In contrast, the authority of national courts does not emanate from private agreements but from the sovereign powers and structure of the legal system to which they belong.

Since arbitration limits access to ordinary courts, States have an interest in ensuring that such limitation is lawful and based on the valid agreement of the parties. It is natural, then, that objections to an arbitral tribunal's jurisdiction concern the very foundation and legitimacy of arbitration. Without jurisdiction, arbitrators do not enjoy the authority to resolve substantive disputes, and the parties should not be deprived of their fundamental right to court justice.

Given the effects that arbitration agreements produce, a court's opportunity to exercise its authority depends on the arbitration agreement's existence, validity, and enforceability. Deciding disputes over the arbitration agreement is crucial for the court because it will determine whether its authority has been displaced. For the arbitral tribunal, it is vital because it will determine whether its jurisdiction has been created.

This book's critical question arises because the interpretation and application of the competence-competence principle (under the Model Law) are not uniform across jurisdictions. There are divergent approaches to the extent and effects of the arbitral tribunal's competence-competence and the consequences of permitting an arbitral tribunal to decide initially on its own jurisdiction. There are also divergent approaches to the limitations of court involvement at the different stages where jurisdictional objections may arise. And there is minimal consensus on the proper timing for judicial involvement and the effects of the decisions made by national courts.

The conflicting approaches rest upon significant theoretical and policy concerns that have practical implications. As anticipated, they are addressed in this work in the context of Article 8(1) of the Model Law, which provides that '[a] court before which an action is brought in a matter which is the subject of an arbitration agreement shall, if a party so requests not later than when submitting his first statement on the substance of the dispute, refer the parties to arbitration, unless it finds that the agreement is null and void, inoperative or incapable of being performed.'

[B] THE FOCUS OF THIS BOOK

Although the focus of the study is Article 8(1) of the Model Law, it is vital to highlight that the starting point of the legal uncertainty addressed in this work is the 1958 United Nations Conventions on the Recognition and Enforcement of Foreign Arbitral Awards (the 'New York Convention').[3] The language of Article 8(1) was drafted to replicate Article II(3) of the Convention, which provides:

3. Convention on the Recognition and Enforcement of Foreign Arbitral Awards (1958), United Nations, *Treaty Series*, vol. 330, p. 3.

> The court of a Contracting State, when seized of an action in a matter in respect of which the parties have made an agreement within the meaning of this article, shall, at the request of one of the parties, refer the parties to arbitration, unless it finds that the said agreement is null and void, inoperative or incapable of being performed.

UNCITRAL designed the Model Law not only to improve and harmonise the treatment of arbitration across borders but also (and significantly) to promote uniformity in the interpretation of the New York Convention amongst States. Therefore, Article 8(1) of the Model Law is analysed here according to its interplay with other provisions of the same instrument and the New York Convention.

Given the textual similarities between Article II(3) and Article 8(1) and the intimate synergy between the Convention and the Model Law (discussed in Chapter 2), a closely related critical question arises: Has the Model Law dissipated the uncertainties around the role of national courts under Article II(3) of the New York Convention? Addressing this question is significant because a State party to the Convention may not invoke the provisions of its internal arbitration law to justify its failure to perform a treaty obligation.

The importance of focusing attention on the Model Law rests on its impact at the international level. The national legislation of eighty-eight States in 121 jurisdictions has formally adopted the Model Law,[4] and other countries have adapted their arbitration legislations to align them with the Model Law. In this book, the phrase 'Model Law jurisdiction(s)' refers to the jurisdictions that have formally adopted the Model Law.

Without an internationally consistent and predictable interpretation and application of the Model Law, parties to arbitral proceedings, arbitral tribunals, and national courts face uncertainties at different levels. The tensions surrounding these issues threaten to defeat the primary objective of the Model Law of promoting an internationally stable and predictable legal environment for international arbitration and contributing to the development of global trade.

One of the challenges in achieving global harmonisation and unification across cultural and legal stances is finding common ground for policy concerns. In general, lawmakers and courts in different jurisdictions appear to favour different interpretative results to reflect local interests in controlling the jurisdiction of arbitral tribunals. Paradoxically, jurisdictions that adopted the Model Law without textual deviations from Article 8 appear to diverge in its interpretation and application. This book tackles this issue and proposes an approach to avoid interpretative inconsistencies.

[C] THE FACTUAL AND LEGAL SCENARIO DISCUSSED

Although Article 8(1) of the Model Law addresses the scenario where a party seeks to litigate in court a dispute that should be arbitrated, there is uncertainty regarding its

4. *Source*: United Nations Commission on International Trade Law's webpage https://uncitral.un.org/en/texts/arbitration/modellaw/commercial_arbitration/status. Last accessed 23 October 2023.

interpretation and application. More specifically, the uncertainty relates to a matter of timing and extent of review: whether courts could or should comprehensively review and conclusively settle the contentions against the agreement to arbitrate *before* referring the litigants to arbitration.

According to Article 8(1), a court before which an action is brought in a matter covered by an arbitration agreement shall refer the parties to arbitration. The court shall do so under two conditions. The first condition is procedural, i.e., that a party requests such referral no later than when submitting its statement of defence. The second condition is that the arbitration agreement is not 'null and void, inoperative or incapable of being performed.'

The Model Law does not explicitly indicate whether courts should always postpone their conclusive decision on the validity and enforceability of the agreement to arbitrate until after the arbitrators have preliminarily decided the same controversy.

This question has not been answered consistently, and there is a split between two main approaches in both case law across jurisdictions and literature. According to one of the approaches, national courts should only undertake a '*prima facie*' review of the arbitration agreement and the objection to the arbitral tribunal's jurisdiction. The other approach is that national courts should undertake a '*full review*' of the existence and validity of the arbitration agreement and ultimately settle the jurisdictional dispute. Intermediate positions stem from these two approaches and operate as exceptions for these main propositions.

The comments in this section introduce those approaches, and the following chapters will delve more deeply and analytically into them.

The *prima facie* standard of review involves a decision based on the arbitration agreement's face value. It implies that the court will only look for clear, manifest and obvious signs that such an agreement suffers from a defect that makes it unenforceable. Where the arbitration agreement *appears* to be valid and effective, the court should discontinue the litigation in deference to arbitration. Because the *prima facie* approach imposes a rule of priority, the court gives way to the arbitration tribunal to decide the jurisdictional dispute, which the court will review at a later stage if one of the parties so requests.[5] The *prima facie* approach strengthens the arbitral tribunal's competence to examine and determine its jurisdiction.[6] This approach may also appear efficient and sensible when the jurisdictional issues are intertwined with the substantive disputes.

However, under the plenary or full merits approach, the court thoroughly hears the parties' case and examines the evidence to determine (fully and conclusively) the existence of a valid agreement to arbitrate and its scope. The court will only refer the parties to arbitration if it finds that the disputed arbitration agreement is valid, operative, and capable of being performed. The agreement must also bind the litigants, and the subject matter of the dispute must be capable of being settled in arbitration. Theoretically (and arguably), this approach might be more effective and efficient than the *prima facie* one. The court would make a final determination on its own jurisdiction and on the arbitral tribunal's jurisdiction at the outset of the dispute. At the very least,

5. According to Articles 16(3), 34(2)(a)(i) and 36(1)(a)(i) Model Law.
6. Article 16(1) Model Law.

this avoids the potential of expenditure in arbitral proceedings that lack the essential contractual basis. Under the *prima facie* standard of review, the court would defer the question to the arbitral tribunal at the risk of having the same question come back later.

As briefly introduced next, these approaches have found theoretical support.

[1] Some Theoretical Justifications

Some scholars are of the view that Article 8(1) of the Model Law only authorises courts to conduct a *prima facie* scrutiny of arbitral jurisdiction. This solution is perceived as the most arbitration-friendly approach. But even where the benefits of this approach might be desirable, the crucial question addressed in this book is whether the Model Law *imposes* that view.

According to its supporters, the legal architecture of the Model Law only permits the *prima facie* approach. Its Article 16 appears to give priority to arbitral tribunals to rule on their jurisdiction, subject to the possibility of an immediate judicial review and control of the arbitral decision. According to Professor Bachand, the opposite view would interrupt the internal coherence of the Model Law, as Article 8 would deny arbitral tribunals a priority that Article 16 recognises.[7] Professor Gaillard and Banifatemi add that the approach that gives priority to arbitrators would be coherent with the presumptive validity of the arbitration agreement that underlies the Model Law and the New York Convention.[8] It would also be the mirroring or negative effect of empowering arbitrators to rule on their own jurisdiction.[9]

That arbitrators enjoy the authority to determine their own jurisdiction is known as the *positive* effect of the competence-competence principle. The *negative* effect moves the spotlight away from the arbitral tribunal and focuses it on national courts.[10] In a nutshell, the negative effect encapsulates the idea that vesting arbitrators with competence-competence necessarily entails divesting national courts of the authority to conclusively determine jurisdictional questions at the threshold of an arbitration. Therefore, courts should only settle the jurisdictional challenge after the arbitrators have preliminarily done so. If Article 8(1) were intended to have the same meaning as Article II(3) of the New York Convention, then Professor van den Berg's conclusion

7. Frédéric Bachand, Does Article 8 of the Model Law Call for Full or *Prima Facie* Review of the Arbitral Tribunal's Jurisdiction?, 22 *Arbitration International*, no. 3 (2006), p. 473 DOI: 10.1093/arbitration/22.3.463; also, L. Yves Fortier, Delimiting the Spheres of Judicial and Arbitral Power: Beware, My Lord, of Jealousy, 80 *Canadian Bar Review* (2001), pp. 148-149.
8. Emmanuel Gaillard et al., 'Negative Effect of Competence-Competence: The Rule of Priority in Favour of the Arbitrators', in *Enforcement of Arbitration Agreements and International Arbitral Awards: The New York Convention in Practice*, ed. Emmanuel Gaillard and Domenico di Pietro (Cameron May, 2008), p. 258.
9. In a similar way, French authors have argued that the principle of competence-competence causes the negative effect, restricting court intervention at the outset of the arbitration to a prima facie level. *See* Philippe Fouchard et al., *Fouchard Gaillard Goldman on International Commercial Arbitration* (Kluwer Law International, 1999), paras 526, 660.
10. *See, e.g.*, Gaillard et al., *Negative Effect of Competence-Competence* (n. 8), p. 260. ('[A] court that is confronted with the question of the existence or validity of the arbitration agreement must refrain from hearing substantive arguments as to the arbitrators' jurisdiction until such time as the arbitrators themselves have had an opportunity to do so').

that courts should accept the unenforceability of the arbitration agreement in manifest cases would also apply to the Model Law. Referring to the broad language of Article II(3) of the New York Convention ('null and void, inoperative or incapable of being performed'), van den Berg concluded that: '[h]aving regard to the "pro-enforcement bias" of the Convention, the words should be construed narrowly, and the invalidity of the arbitration agreement should be accepted in *manifest* cases only'.[11] [Emphasis added]

Other authors do not recognise that the arbitrators' competence-competence produces a negative effect. For example, Professor Brekoulakis is of the opinion that, in general terms, arbitral competence-competence does not displace the court's powers to determine jurisdictional challenges preliminarily, at least not for certain types of jurisdictional disputes.[12] This resonates with Professor Bermann's opinion, who noted that '[t]here is, a priori, no reason why the court should not be entitled to assess its own jurisdiction. In another era, in which courts were thought to be hostile to arbitration, that may have been a dangerous recipe. But that era is behind us.'[13]

Further, it is important to correctly qualify the arbitrators' authority under the competence-competence principle as '*provisional*' or '*preliminary*'. A contextual reading of Article 16(1) of the Model Law impacts the arbitrators' competence-competence, which is not exclusive nor conclusive. At least regarding the decisions where the arbitrators decide against the objections and find they enjoy jurisdiction to resolve the substantive dispute.[14]

The arbitrators' decision on jurisdiction is provisional because it is reviewable at different stages and by different courts. At the seat of the arbitration, the judiciary could decide the issue immediately after the arbitrators have assumed jurisdiction in a preliminary ruling (Article 16(3) Model Law). This could also be done at the end of the proceedings, should the arbitrators have answered the jurisdictional question together with the award on the merits (Article 34(2)(a)(i) Model Law).

Courts other than the ones at the seat of the arbitration could also review the arbitrators' jurisdiction in an action for recognition and enforcement of the award (Article 36(1)(a)(i) Model Law and Article V(1)(a) New York Convention).

Born also rests relevance to the *prima facie* approach because the drafters of the Model Law rejected a proposal to amend Article 8(1) to require such a limited standard of review at that stage of the proceedings. However, the author notes that courts have the procedural discretion to conduct a *prima facie* assessment of a jurisdictional challenge if, for example, the party resisting the stay of the court proceedings had

11. Albert J. van den Berg, *The New York Arbitration Convention of 1958: Towards a Uniform Judicial Interpretation* (Kluwer Law International, 1994), p. 155.
12. Stavros Brekoulakis, The Negative Effect of Competence-Competence: The Verdict Has to Be Negative, *Austrian Arbitration Yearbook* (2009) at section III C, the author recognises and supports the positive effects of competence-competence, but finds theoretical, practical and policy reasons not to accord arbitral tribunals *exclusive* powers to decide every type of jurisdictional challenge.
13. George A. Bermann, The 'Gateway' Problem in International Commercial Arbitration, 37 *Yale Journal of International Law* (2012), p. 14 DOI: 10.1515/9783866539914.69.
14. The decisions whereby the arbitrators find that they lack jurisdiction are *usually* final, not provisional.

raised the jurisdictional challenge as a dilatory tactic.[15] Yet, as this study shows, when courts have applied the *prima facie* approach, they have concluded that that was the correct approach under the Model Law. In general, judges have not reasoned or concluded that they made a *prima facie* examination as a matter of discretion to prevent a dilatory tactic or because it was more efficient or just. Instead, they have concluded that the law required them to do so.

Although those and other publications[16] are insightful and useful as a starting step, the focus, the depth of the inquiry and the analytical framework in this work are different.[17] Different, because this work analyses and answers the *prima facie* versus *full review* question from an autonomous legal-interpretation perspective, detached from a given State's law, concepts, and rules. Its theoretical framework is specific to the Model Law and national arbitration laws that have adopted it without textual deviations – at least not from the wording of Article 8.

Following the theoretical framework explained in the next section, this work's conclusions differ from previous publications and theoretical justifications, many of which have based their conclusions on general policies favouring arbitration as a dispute resolution system. The text of Article 8 (analysed in Chapter 5 below), read in its context (Chapter 6) and in light of its purpose (Chapter 7), does not impose a strict rule of priority between courts and arbitral tribunals. It does not impose one approach (*prima facie*/full review) and excludes the other. The interpretative exercise proposed here affords the opposite outcome: no approach is imposed; both are permitted. Applying one or the other is a matter of judgment (rather than opinion), based on the particularities of the case, to achieve the fair and efficient resolution of the jurisdictional and substantive dispute.

[D] THE THEORETICAL FRAMEWORK

This study centres the analysis around the principles and rules that govern the powers of arbitral tribunals to determine their jurisdiction and their systematic interaction with

15. Gary B. Born, *International Commercial Arbitration*, 3rd ed., vol. 1 (Kluwer Law International, 2021), p. 1177.
16. For example, Professor Park reports, compares and discusses the approaches that courts have taken in Model Law jurisdictions (e.g., Germany, Canada) and non-Model Law jurisdictions (e.g., Switzerland, France, USA); *see*, William W. Park, 'The Arbitrator's Jurisdiction to Determine Jurisdiction', in *International Arbitration 2006: Back to Basics?*, ed. Albert Jan van den Berg, ICCA Congress Series, no. 13 (Kluwer Law International, 2007). Similarly, *see*, Stefan Kröll, 'Party Autonomy in Relation to Competence-Competence', in *Limits to Party Autonomy in International Commercial Arbitration*, ed. Franco Ferrari (Juris, 2016). In 2012, a doctoral study at Aarhus University compared how courts in Germany, Switzerland, and England address jurisdictional issues at the pre-arbitral award stage. But the only Model Law jurisdiction in that publication is Germany, which is excluded from this book because of its significant textual dissimilarity with Article 8 of the Model Law; *See*, Sandra Synková, *Courts' Inquiry into Arbitral Jurisdiction at the Pre-award Stage* (Springer, 2012).
17. The discussion perhaps most focused on Article 8 of the Model is found in Professor Frederic Bachand's 14-page journal article from 2006, though that had a limited discussion compared with the present work. *See*, Bachand, *Article 8 of the Model Law* (n. 7).

the norms that delimit the role of national courts when resolving jurisdictional disputes at the threshold of an arbitration.

This work is not concerned with a comparative analysis of different arbitration laws. It does not compare the *prima facie* or full review approaches under various laws. References to and examples from several Model Law jurisdictions are used to inform the reasoning behind the chosen approach and, in general, to elucidate the understanding of the Model Law. It would be pointless to compare those jurisdictions' national laws. Their text is (to a great extent) the same – at least regarding Article 8(1) of the Model Law. The assumption is that even if distinct national legislators formally adopt those arbitration laws, the 'intellectual originator' of the text is one and the same: UNCITRAL. Therefore, this work depersonalises the national identity of those laws because it sees them as part of the same community – the international arbitration community governed by the Model Law. Also, this work avoids discussing what approach (*prima facie* or full review) is best or preferred. It focuses on what obligations and powers the law affords to judges in the presence of an (even putative) arbitration agreement.

The goal is to synthesise meaning from the synergy between the multiple, seemingly conflicting principles at play – to uniformly apply Article 8(1) of the Model Law. In reaching its aim, Chapter 3 of this book proposes a distinct approach for interpreting the Model Law and the laws that implement it at the national level. The proposed interpretative approach for 'national (arbitration) law' of a 'transnational character and origin' aspires to contribute to an ongoing paradigm shift, away from state law and methodological nationalism[18] and towards transnational legal pluralism.

Despite hundreds of years of debate, philosophers have yet to reach a consensus concerning *what the law is*, and the realm of arbitration law is no exception. This work does not offer a general concept of international arbitration law or develop a comprehensive theory of arbitration. It does not aim to significantly contribute to the debate on the legal theories that present arbitration as an 'autonomous legal order'. Much discussion has been dedicated to this elsewhere. Professor Gaillard's 'Legal Theory of International Arbitration'[19] and Professor Lew's 'Achieving the Dream'[20] are two of the most significant propositions on the autonomy of international arbitration. But, their theories are not without controversies and criticism.[21]

18. Michaels explains and translates the social theory approach of methodological nationalism to the Westphalian model, in which national and international law find their ultimate point of reference in States; *see*, Ralf Michaels, 'Globalization and Law: Law Beyond the State', in *Law and Social Theory*, ed. Reza Banakar and Max Travers (Hart Publishing, 2013), pp. 4-5.
19. Emmanuel Gaillard, *Legal Theory of International Arbitration* (Brill Nijhoff, 2010).
20. Julian D.M. Lew, Achieving the Dream: Autonomous Arbitration, 22 *Arbitration International*, no. 2 (2006) DOI: 10.1093/arbitration/22.2.179.
21. *See, e.g.*, Stavros L. Brekoulakis, International Arbitration Scholarship and the Concept of Arbitration Law, 36 *Fordham International Law Journal* (2013); Ralf Michaels, Dreaming Law Without a State: Scholarship on Autonomous International Arbitration as Utopian Literature, 1 *London Review of International Law*, no. 1 (2013), pp. 37, 39 DOI: 10.1093/lril/lrt008; Michael Reisman et al., 'The Present – Commercial Arbitration as a Transnational System of Justice: Tribunals and Courts: An Interpretation of the Architecture of International Commercial Arbitration', in *Arbitration: The Next Fifty Years*, ed. Albert Jan van den Berg (Kluwer Law

Although this book does not aim to discuss, confirm, or refute Lew's or Gaillard's postulates, it shares some of their foundations. It grapples with the idea that arbitration laws based on an internationally developed model (the Model Law) are laws of a distinct nature and character. As such, they must be interpreted in an autonomous way. This work builds upon the premise that those national arbitration statutes are particular legal instruments, different from purely domestic, state-born laws. Not because those domestic laws are part of an 'autonomous legal order' or because arbitration constitutes a 'delocalised' system,[22] but because international arbitration laws belong, in part, to a national legal system in which their interpretation and application require special consideration. This book recognises a given arbitration law (based on the Model Law) as *national law of an international origin and character*.

State laws are not the only binding norms in the arbitration community. International arbitration regulation is not limited to state and interstate-centred legal positivism. International arbitration law (and practice) is not defined exclusively by national borders and is monopolised by traditional state-centred (national and international) laws. They are influenced by guidelines, rules, recommendations, models, and protocols emanating from arbitration institutions and associations of practitioners, and academics researching and exploring the development of arbitration law. Legislators use foreign and soft law instruments to draft new legislation, and national courts also draw inspiration from these sources.[23]

The law and practice of arbitration are characterised by the interaction of hard and soft law, in the understanding that international law's principles, rules, standards, and policies aim for uniformity. This is especially true in Model Law jurisdictions, as they deliberately seek textual and applied cross-border uniformity.

[E] BOOK DESIGN

This work is divided into eight chapters. Chapter 1 has introduced the topic and challenges surrounding the uniform interpretation and application of a uniform legal text. Chapter 2 refers, more generally, to the unification and harmonisation of

International, 2012), p. 747. *See, also*, Jan Paulsson, Arbitration in Three Dimensions, *International and Comparative Law Quarterly* (2011), pp. 301-306 DOI: 10.1017/s0020589311000054; and Jonathan Mance, Arbitration: A Law Unto Itself?, 32 *Arbitration International*, no. 2 (2016), p. 63 DOI: 10.1093/arbint/aiv072.

22. *See, e.g.*, Jan Paulsson, Delocalization of International Commercial Arbitration – When and Why It Matters, 32 *International and Comparative Law Quarterly*, no. 1 (1983) DOI: 10.1093/iclqaj/32.1.53, and William W. Park, The Lex Loci Arbitri and International Commercial Arbitration, 32 *International & Comparative Law Quarterly* (1983) DOI: 10.1093/iclqaj/32.1.21. Perhaps insisting on arbitration as not belonging to any state keeps fuelling the criticism of the autonomous and delocalised theories. Furthermore, it does not seem to echo the unified framework shaped by the legal instruments that the arbitration community so highly regards as the basis for the current success of international arbitration: the New York Convention and the Model Law.
23. For example, the International Bar Association (IBA)'s Rules on the Taking of Evidence in International Arbitration, the IBA Guidelines on Conflicts of Interest in International Arbitration, the Chartered Institute of Arbitrators (CIArb)'s Guidelines on Jurisdictional Challenges, the UNCITRAL Secretariat Guide on the Convention on the Recognition and Enforcement of Foreign Arbitral Awards, amongst many other.

arbitration laws under the United Nations and UNCITRAL's family of instruments. This chapter highlights the significance (and need) of an internationally shared interpretation and application of Article 8(1) of the Model Law. Chapter 2 paves the way for the distinct interpretative approach proposed in Chapter 3. The latter starts by examining the interpretative guidance in the Model Law and briefly considers that of the New York Convention. It concludes by proposing a nuanced, uniform approach to the legal interpretation of domestic statutes that incorporate the Model Law. One that contemplates the uniform interpretation and uniform application of uniform law (the Model Law) and is inspired by customary international law.

Chapters 4 to 7 follow the components of the interpretative approach proposed in Chapter 3. Chapter 4 examines case law. Decided cases provide insights into the development and the *status quo* of the issue at hand. It highlights the controversies in interpreting and applying the concepts, principles and rules found in the Model Law. The sampling and analytical approach of case law is explained in the introduction to Chapter 4. Rather than comparing practices between specific countries, it examines judicial decisions that illustrate the reasoning behind the *prima facie* and the full review approaches. The study of case law also tests in practice the concepts of unification and harmonisation of laws examined in Chapter 2.

Chapters 5 to 7 analyse the text of Article 8 of the Model Law (Chapter 5) in its context (Chapter 6) and in accordance with its purpose (Chapter 7). Scholarly opinions are also considered. The Model Law's drafting history will be analysed throughout these chapters too. This accepts and reflects the understanding that the interpreter learns about the context and purpose of the law from extrinsic sources. Especially because UNCITRAL recognised the significant role of its preparatory works when adopting and distributing the Model Law.

But before addressing the controversies around the interpretation of Article 8 of the Model Law, the next chapter highlights UNCITRAL's role in the harmonisation process for the unification of international arbitration law.

Chapter 8 contains the concluding remarks.

CHAPTER 2

Harmonisation and Unification of Arbitration Laws

[A] INTRODUCTION

Understanding legal harmonisation and unification is critical for this study because of their weight in drafting, interpreting, and applying the Model Law and the New York Convention. Although the language of the specific provisions studied here[24] is textually uniform across jurisdictions, their interpretation and application at the national level are not.

This book accepts the proposition that unification refers to the adoption of the same legal rules to govern particular aspects of, for example, international arbitration or international trade.[25] Uniformity seeks to provide legal certainty, not simply certainty of legal texts. That is why the two components of uniformity are textual and applied uniformity. This is the basis for addressing a *how* question, i.e., how to achieve a high degree of uniformity of the Model Law (in Chapter 3).

This book also accepts the proposition that harmonisation refers to the process through which discrepancies in domestic laws are eliminated (or reduced) to achieve greater similarity across jurisdictions.[26] That is why harmonisation is not a product or

24. Article 8 Model Law, and Article II(3) New York Convention.
25. Faria and Angel note that a convention is an international instrument that is adopted by States for the unification of the law at an international level. A model law would be an example of a legal instrument that is drafted to harmonise domestic law; Jose Angelo Estrella Faria et al., 'Legal Harmonization Through Model Laws: The Experience of the United Nations Commission on International Trade Law (UNCITRAL)', (United Nations Office of International Affairs – Working Group on Electronic Commerce, 2011), p. 2, n. 6.
26. David W. Leebron, Claims for Harmonization: A Theoretical Framework, 27 *Canadian Bussiness Law Journal*, no. 1 (1996), pp. 64-67 DOI: 10.2307/2686123. Also, Konrad Zweigert et al., *An Introduction to Comparative Law*, 3rd ed. (Clarendon Press, 1998), p. 24.

result but a process of making rules similar.[27] Therefore, some scholars see uniformity as a sub-category of harmonisation, where uniformity is the goal and harmonisation is the process to achieve it.[28] The harmonisation process may (or may not) result in the unification of law, but it is not its synonym.[29]

The legal harmonisation process acknowledges and accepts the existence of a diversity of results. That diversity is the reason for setting harmonisation in motion, as it aims to progressively eliminate legal disparities. Consequently, in the harmonisation process, uniformity is measured on varying degrees of similar results (rather than in absolute terms).[30]

More importantly, striving for 'harmonisation and uniformity' of laws across jurisdictions is not an end in itself. It is 'functional' because it serves to fulfil a (economic) purpose. For example, the uniformity of commercial law arose out of the need to increase international trade[31] by creating a legal environment with a high degree of certainty and predictability. Economic relations work better where the laws and policies of different jurisdictions are made more similar.[32] This creates a stable and level playing field for businesses, as they can predict the rules likely to apply to their contractual commitments.[33]

The unification of international arbitration law also has a purpose or function. It serves the needs of its users (the business community) by providing standards and predictable procedural tools to resolve international disputes effectively and efficiently.

The harmonisation process and the goal of unification of arbitration laws are not as ancient as the arbitration practice itself. Although arbitration has been used to resolve commercial disputes for centuries,[34] proceedings were based on national laws and domestic practices until the beginning of the twentieth century. The efforts to systematise international arbitration were a corollary of the need for the coordinated

27. Bruno Zeller, *CISG and the Unification of International Trade Law* (Routledge-Cavendish, 2008), p. 12; Loukas Mistelis, Is Harmonisation a Necessary Evil? The Future of Harmonisation and New Sources of International Trade Law, *Foundations and Perspectives of International Trade Law* (2001).
28. Camilla Baasch Andersen, Defining Uniformity in Law, 12 *Uniform Law Review*, no. 5 (2007), p. 15 DOI: 10.1093/ulr/12.1.5. This is what Andenas, Andersen and Ashcroft call 'procedural harmonisation', in Mads Andenas et al., 'Towards a Theory of Harmonisation', in *Theory and Practice of Harmonisation*, ed. Mads Andenas and Camilla Baasch Andersen, no., (Edward Elgar Publishing, 2012), p. 583.
29. Mistelis, *Is Harmonisation a Necessary Evil* (n. 27), para. 1-003.
30. Baasch Andersen, *Defining Uniformity* (n. 28) p. 42. In this sense, other authors describe uniformity as 'convergence' (of interests). *See, e.g.*, Helmut Philipp Aust, 'Between Universal Aspiration and Local Application', in *The Interpretation of International Law by Domestic Courts: Uniformity, Diversity, Convergence*, ed. Helmut Philipp Aust and Nolte Nolte (Oxford University Press, 2016), pp. 344-345.
31. Franco Ferrari, Uniform Interpretation of the 1980 Uniform Sales Law, 24 *Georgia Journal of International and Comparative Law*, no. 2 (1994) p. 183; William Tetley, Mixed Jurisdictions: Common Law v. Civil Law (Codified and Uncodified), 60 *Lousiana Law Review*, no. 3 (2000) DOI: 10.1093/ulr/4.4.877. Available at www.cisg.law.pace.edu/cisg/biblio/tetley.htm.
32. Leebron, *Claims for Harmonization* (n. 26), p. 67.
33. Richard Garnett, International Arbitration Law: Progress Towards Harmonisation, 3 *Melbourne Journal of International Law*, no. 2 (2002), pp. 400-401.
34. For a detailed overview of the history of international arbitration, *see* Derek Roebuck, Sources for the History of Arbitration: A Bibliographical Introduction, 14 *Arbitration International*, no. 3 (1998), pp. 237-344 DOI: 10.1093/arbitration/14.3.237. Also *see* Gary B. Born, *International Commercial Arbitration* (n. 15), Ch. 1; Michael John Mustill, Arbitration: History and Background, 6 *Journal of International Arbitration* (1989) DOI: 10.1093/arbitration/14.3.235;

growth of international trade in the aftermath of the First World War. A significant step in this sense took place in 1919 when the world's business community established the International Chamber of Commerce (ICC) to promote global trade and investment, open markets for goods and services, and the free flow of capital. In 1923, the ICC set up the International Court of Arbitration to provide a framework for an independent and neutral arbitration system to resolve commercial disputes. It has since been a driving force in promoting regulation to uphold and support the arbitration process.

The ICC promoted the adoption of the first two ground-breaking instruments aimed at achieving international recognition of arbitration agreements and awards, i.e., the 1923 Geneva Protocol on Arbitration Clauses and the 1927 Geneva Convention on the Execution of Foreign Arbitral Awards. These instruments cemented the foundation for replacing the formalistic and parochial arbitral regimes that had survived from previous centuries. However, the post-World War II increase in economic development and globalisation triggered the most revolutionary changes in the international arbitration scenario.

This publication does not aim to offer a detailed list of the establishment and development of each institution, practice, theory, and method in international arbitration. It should be enough to refer to the eloquent words of Lord Mustill, who stated that 'arbitration has been transformed more radically and abruptly in all its respects since the 1950s than in its entire recorded history.'[35]

The pivotal development in the international arbitration regime of the late 1950s was the adoption of the 1958 New York Convention. This instrument was established to address the shortcomings of the 1923 and 1927 Geneva Conventions, which ceased to have effect between contracting states when the New York Convention came into force in those States.[36]

Following its success with the New York Convention, the United Nations established the Commission on International Trade Law (UNCITRAL) in 1966.[37] In launching this new organ, the General Assembly recognised that disparities in national laws governing international trade had created obstacles to the development of world trade. It regarded UNCITRAL as the vehicle by which the United Nations could contribute to reducing or removing those obstacles.

Thus, UNCITRAL was explicitly established to promote the progressive harmonisation and unification of significant areas of international economic relations (arbitration being one of them).[38] As some authorities put it, UNCITRAL aims to help ensure national laws do not get in the way of doing business effectively and dissipate uncertainties in international trade.[39]

Michael J Mustill, 'The History of International Commercial Arbitration: A Sketch', in *Leading Arbitrators' Guide to International Arbitration*, ed. Lawrence W. Newman and Richard D. Hill (JurisNet, LLC, 2014), pp. 1-32.

35. Mustill, *The History of International Commercial Arbitration*, *ibid.*, p. 12.
36. Convention on the Recognition and Enforcement of Foreign Arbitral Awards (1958), Article VII(2).
37. United Nations, Resolution of the General-Assembly: Establishment of the United Nations Commission on International Trade Law A/RES/2205 (17 December 1966).
38. *Ibid.*, para. 14.
39. Timothy Lemay et al., 'Review of the Model Law's Implementation after Twenty-Five Years', in *The UNCITRAL Model Law after Twenty-Five Years: Global Perspectives on International Commercial Arbitration*, ed. Frédéric Bachand and Fabien Gélinas (JurisNet, LLC, 2013), p. 3.

When adopting the Model Law (in 1985), the United Nations reaffirmed UNCITRAL's mandate as its core legal body 'to co-ordinate legal activities to avoid duplication of effort and promote efficiency, consistency and coherence in the unification and harmonisation of international trade law'.[40]

With that aim, UNCITRAL develops legislative instruments, such as conventions,[41] model laws,[42] model provisions,[43] and legislative guides.[44] Others are non-legislative texts, such as contractual rules[45] that can be incorporated into commercial contracts; and legal and practice explanatory guides.[46]

The legitimacy of UNCITRAL texts stems from their (legal pluralistic) creation process and international reception. They are widely accepted in countries with different legal traditions and at different levels of economic development. They are of an international origin and character, the product of a negotiation process driven by the global epistemic community. That epistemic community includes UNCITRAL's Member States, non-Member States, inter-governmental and non-governmental organisations, and academics.

The General Assembly elects the seventy[47] Member States that compose UNCITRAL (for a six-year term), safeguarding an inclusive and diverse geographic representation and the world's main economic and legal systems. It is subdivided into six working groups. Working Group II is devoted to 'International Arbitration and Conciliation | Dispute Settlement'. Despite States' official membership to UNCITRAL, the General Assembly encourages and the Commission welcomes the participation in debates (without voting rights) of non-Member States, inter-governmental and international non-governmental organisations with expertise in the subject matter under discussion and drafting processes.[48]

---

40. Resolution of the General Assembly at its Fortieth Session – Model Law on International Commercial Arbitration of the United Nations Commission on International Trade Law, A/RES/40/71 (11 December 1985), para. 6.
41. For example, the United Nations Convention on Contracts for the International Sale of Goods (Vienna, 1980), amongst others.
42. For example, the Model Law on Electronic Signatures (2001); the Model Law on Public Procurement (2011), amongst others.
43. For example, the Model Legislative Provisions on Privately Financed Infrastructure Projects (2003); Unit of account provision and provisions for the adjustment of the limit of liability in international transport and liability conventions (1982).
44. For example, the Recommendations to Governments and international organisations concerning the legal value of computer records (1985).
45. For example, the Arbitration Rules (1976, revised in 2010) and the Rules on Transparency in Treaty-based Investor-State Arbitration (2014).
46. For example, the UNCITRAL Notes on Organizing Arbitral Proceedings (2016); the UNCITRAL Legal Guide on International Countertrade Transactions (1992); and the UNCITRAL Practice Guide on Cross-Border Insolvency Cooperation (2009).
47. According to the General Assembly Resolution A/RES/76/109 of 9 December 2021.
48. For example, the African Union, European Community, NAFTA Article 2022 Advisory Committee (NAFTA), Permanent Court of Arbitration, American Arbitration Association(AAA), American Bar Association (ABA), Arab Association for International Arbitration, Asia Pacific Regional Arbitration Group (APRAG), Association of the Bar of the City of New York (ABCNY), Center for International Legal Studies, Association Suisse de l'Arbitrage (ASA), Club of Arbitrators of the Milan Chamber of Arbitration, Forum for International Commercial Arbitration (FICA), International Chamber of Commerce (ICC), International Cotton Advisory Committee (ICAC), International Law Institute (ILI), Kuala Lumpur Regional Centre for Arbitration (KLRCA),

Generally, decisions at the Commission are adopted by consensus and, in its absence, by voting.[49] But, how a decision is adopted does not affect its legal status. As the Secretariat noted, '[o]nce adopted, it has the status of a legally adopted decision and the fact that it has been adopted by consensus or by means of a vote does not add to or diminish the legal value or significance of the decision in question.'[50]

The general practice of adopting decisions by consensus better contributes to achieving greater acceptance and cooperation amongst countries. It reflects the combination of public, private, and semi-private actors as the source of regulation and the driving force in developing international arbitration regulation and practice. These actors form a global community of knowledge[51] that affords legitimacy to the instruments they produce, and their harmonised adoption, interpretation and application at the national level, across jurisdictions.

As indicated earlier, the international arbitration world is a (transnational) epistemic community.[52] In general and basic terms, an epistemic community is a network of experts who share knowledge-based ideas about a specific field.[53] UNCITRAL Working Group II is representative of the transnational arbitration epistemic community, as it plays an influential role in furthering the law and practice of arbitration beyond national borders.[54] A prominent scholar identifies UNCITRAL's

School of International Arbitration (Queen Mary University of London), the Chartered Institute of Arbitrators, the European Law Students Association (ELSA), the London Court of International Arbitration (LCIA) and Union Internationale des Avocats (UIA).

49. Report of the Commission on its Forty-third session, General Assembly A/65 Supp. 17 (21 June-9 July 2010), Annex III, para. 2. In practice, most decision-making in the Commission takes place by consensus and very *exceptionally* by vote. In 2007, the Secretariat reported that until then, '[a] formal vote in the Commission took place only once ...' (in 1978); *see*, Notes by the Secretariat: UNCITRAL rules of procedure and methods of work, A/CN.9/638/Add.3 (17 October 2007), para. 57.
50. Notes by the Secretariat: UNCITRAL Rules of Procedure and Methods of Work, A/CN.9/638/Add.4 (18 October 2007), para. 2(b).
51. Interestingly, Ginsburg argues that the repeated interaction of the members of the epistemic community over time produce a culture, i.e., the culture of arbitration. Tom Ginsburg, The Culture of Arbitration, 36 *Vanderbilt Journal of International Law*, no. 4 (2003), p. 1337. Scholar Won Kidane has a critical view of the 'culture of arbitration'. The author recognises that international arbitration has developed its own culture, but without sufficient cultural diversity and at the expense of ignoring other cultures. *See*, in general, Won L. Kidane, *The Culture of International Arbitration* (Oxford University Press, 2017).
52. Roger P. Alford, The American Influence on International Arbitration, 19 *Ohio State Journal on Dispute Resolution*, no. 1 (2003) p. 69 ('[I]t is indisputable that the international arbitration world is an identifiable epistemic community that transcends national borders, and whose members are shaped by their own experience.').
53. Peter M. Haas, Introduction: Epistemic Communities and International Policy Coordination, 26 *International Organization*, no. 1 (1992) p. 3; ('[A] network of professionals with recognized expertise and competence in a particular domain and an authoritative claim to policy-relevant knowledge within that domain or issue-area.').
54. In Professor Kaufmann-Kohler's opinion, the members of the epistemic community play a dominant role in shaping the transnational consensus on arbitration law and practice, through a process of 'intellectual cross-fertilisation'; Gabrielle Kaufmann-Kohler, Global Implications of the FAA: The Role of Legislation in International Arbitration, 20 *ICSID Review: Foreign Investment Law Journal*, no. 2 (2005), p. 350 DOI: 10.1093/icsidreview/20.2.339.

vital role as a 'value provider'. The author of the paper 'Sociology of International Arbitration' highlights that UNCITRAL not only generates legal norms but also, notably, contributes to guiding the development of international arbitration and arbitral social life behaviour.[55]

Like in any epistemic community, the work and role of UNCITRAL Work Group II centre around identifying, analysing, and articulating the cause-effect relationship of arbitration problems. It also engages in collective debate to find specific coordinated-policy solutions resulting from shared knowledge and information based on shared values.[56]

The epistemic community contributes to the harmonisation and unification of international arbitration law.[57] Its authority influences individual states' behaviour and produces a domino-like effect, whereby individual states influence the interests and behaviour of other states. This chain of action and reaction snowballs the prospects of 'convergent state behaviour and international policy considerations.'[58]

Diversity in the community's membership enhances its legitimacy and the normative effects of the legal instruments it produces (soft and hard law).[59] Some of those legal instruments are central to this study and will be analysed in the next section. And, as it will become evident in the discussions throughout this work, the contributions and expert opinions of those involved in drafting such instruments influence their subsequent interpretation and application. This is particularly meaningful in the context of this book because the terms and phrases used in Article 8 of the Model Law evidence a drafting choice after skilful considerations and debate, agreement and compromise (Chapters 5-7 below).

[B] UNCITRAL'S EFFORTS TO HARMONISE AND UNIFY INTERNATIONAL ARBITRATION LAW

Three ground-breaking instruments have been created to promote a harmonised and unified legal framework for international arbitration: the New York Convention, the UNCITRAL Arbitration Rules[60] and the UNCITRAL Model Law.[61] This trilogy has been

55. Emmanuel Gaillard, Sociology of International Arbitration, 31 *Arbitration International*, no. 1 (2015), pp. 7-8 DOI: 10.1093/arbint/aiv021. In addition to 'value providers', Professor Gaillard identifies two other social actors that encompass the sociology of international arbitration: essential actors (the parties and arbitrators), service providers (e.g., arbitration institutions).
56. *See*, Haas, *Introduction: Epistemic Communities* (n. 53), pp. 2-3.
57. Gabrielle Kaufmann-Kohler, Soft Law in International Arbitration: Codification and Normativity, 1 *Journal of International Dispute Settlement*, no. 2 (2010), p. 295 DOI: 10.1093/jnlids/idq009 ('the global arbitration community is the driving force in international arbitration').
58. Haas, *Introduction: Epistemic Communities* (n. 53), p. 4.
59. Some authors have recognised that soft law is criticised because of its lack of democratic legitimacy. *See*, Kaufmann-Kohler, *Soft Law in International Arbitration* (n. 57), p. 298 (citing Klaus Peter Berger, *The Creeping Codifiction of the Lex Mercatoria* (Kluwer International Law, 1999), at 1964).
60. Report of the Commission on the Work of its Ninth Session, A/31/17 (15 December 1976).
61. General Assembly A/RES/40/72.

described as the 'most successful partnership' in the realm of international commercial arbitration[62] and as the principal pillar in the worldwide system of arbitral justice.[63]

[1] The 1958 New York Convention

The New York Convention is considered one of the most successful treaties in international trade law.[64] It was concluded in 1958 and entered into force on 7 June 1959. At present, 172 States have become party to it.[65] Veeder described the success of the New York Convention in colourful (yet accurate) language. He stated that the Convention was:

> The lubricating super-oil for the complex machinery which has made the explosion of global trade possible over the past 50 years, [as it] directly affects the lives of billions of people around the world, every minute of every day, in both seen and still more unseen ways. It is, therefore, a secular, sacred text of the greatest practical significance to every inhabitant of the 21st century's global village.[66]

The New York Convention is not a UNCITRAL text, as the United Nations adopted it in 1958 before UNCITRAL was established in 1966. However, monitoring and promoting the Convention is an integral part of UNCITRAL's work programme. For this reason, the New York Convention forms part of the CLOUT system. CLOUT, an abbreviation for Case Law on UNCITRAL Texts, is associated with free access to information. The UNCITRAL Secretariat established it to promote international awareness of the Commission's texts (and the New York Convention), and facilitate the uniform interpretation and application of those texts.[67] The Secretariat Guide on the New York Convention is another example of UNCITRAL's involvement in promoting a broader national adherence to the New York Convention and assisting its uniform interpretation and effective implementation.[68]

The New York Convention does not provide for a detailed regulation of the entire arbitration process. Although its title refers only to foreign arbitral awards,[69] it also

62. Fali S. Nariman, 'The Convention Contribution to the Globalization of International Commercial Arbitration' (paper presented at the Enforcing Arbitration Awards under the New York Convention. Experience and Prospects, New York), p. 11.
63. Lemay et al., *Review of the Model Law's Implementation* (Bachand, Gélinas eds, n. 39), p. 4.
64. VV Veeder, Is There a Need to Revise the New York Convention?, 1 *Journal of International Dispute Settlement*, no. 2 (2010), p. 500 DOI: 10.1093/jnlids/idq007.
65. *Source*: https://uncitral.un.org/en/texts/arbitration/conventions/foreign_arbitral_awards/status2. Last accessed 4 October 2023.
66. Veeder, *Is There a Need to Revise the New York Convention?* (n. 64).
67. Report of the Commission on the Work of its Twenty-First session, A/43/17 (11-22 April 1988), paras 98-109.
68. The Guide was initiated in 2010 on the basis of resolution 62/65 of 6 December 2007, when UNCITRAL commissioned the assistance of Professors Gaillard and Bermann to provide an insight on the application of the Convention by State courts. The Guide was published in 2016, and is available at https://newyorkconvention1958.org/.
69. United Nations Convention on the Recognition and Enforcement of Foreign Arbitral Awards.

deals with the recognition and enforcement of arbitration agreements in each State party.[70]

The Convention is generally identified as a foundational instrument of modern international arbitration. Due to its constitutional character,[71] the Convention provides the basis for most contemporary national legislation governing the arbitral process, other treaties, rules, guidelines, recommendations, and protocols. In particular, the New York Convention has explicitly and directly influenced the content of two crucial UNCITRAL instruments on arbitration: the Arbitration Rules and the Model Law.

The New York Convention has been implemented in different ways at the national level. Implementation depends on each State's constitutional procedures for incorporating international law into the national legal system.[72] In States that follow a monist approach, the New York Convention is considered a self-executing instrument. Its application is not subjected to further legislative action. For international and national law to coexist, this approach recognises a hierarchical order. If the provisions of the New York Convention conflict with national law, the Convention prevails.

Legislative action is needed in those States that, instead, follow a dualist approach to international law. The New York Convention gains legal force only via implementing legislation, i.e., either a new statute or an adaption of the existing one. Without an implementing action, the text of the Convention lacks legal significance in those States. According to a survey that UNCITRAL conducted, the implementing legislation in several States took the form of an 'Arbitration Act, to which the Convention is attached as a schedule', 'the enactment of a special act on Foreign Arbitral Awards', or the 'enactment of a legislative decree'.[73]

[2] The 1976 UNCITRAL Arbitration Rules

UNCITRAL adopted its Arbitration Rules in 1976.[74] They provide a model arbitral clause and set out the procedural aspects of the arbitral proceedings, including the composition of the tribunal. They also outline the form and effects of arbitral awards and their interpretation and corrections.

The Arbitration Rules were designed to serve all legal, economic, and social systems in practically all types of disputes and geographical regions. They become a

70. Article II of the New York Convention.
71. Thomas Carbonneau, The Reception of Arbitration in United States Law, 40 *Maine Law Review*, no. 1 (1988), p. 272 DOI: 10.1093/acprof:oso/9780199965519.003.0009. *See also* Born, *International Commercial Arbitration* (n. 15), p. 99 (The New York Convention 'provides what amounts to a universal constitutional charter for the international arbitral process, whose expansive terms have enabled both national courts and arbitral tribunals to develop durable, effective means for enforcing international arbitration agreements and arbitral awards.').
72. For a discussion on the monist and dualist approaches to international law, *see*, in general, James Crawford, 'The Relations of International and National Law', in *Brownlie's Principles of Public International Law* (Oxford University Press, 2019), pp. 45-104.
73. UNCITRAL Report on the Survey Relating to the Legislative Implementation of the Convention on the Recognition and Enforcement of Foreign Arbitral Awards, A/CN.9/656 (16 June-3 July 2008), paras 9-13.
74. *See* General Assembly A/31/17, paras 46-57.

part of the parties' contract by reference made therein as contractual obligations rather than compulsion by law.

The Rules have been widely used worldwide in the settlement of a broad range of disputes. These include controversies between private commercial parties where no arbitral institution is involved, investor-State disputes, State-to-State disputes and commercial disputes administered by arbitral institutions. In 2010, they were revised to accommodate the developments in arbitral practice that had taken place over the years. In 2013, as a result of the Rules on Transparency in Treaty-based Investor-State Arbitration, a new paragraph was added to the text of Article 1 of the UNCITRAL Arbitration Rules.[75] Its purpose was to incorporate the Rules on Transparency for arbitrations related to investment treaties concluded on or after 1 April 2014. In all other respects, the 2013 UNCITRAL Arbitration Rules remained unchanged from the 2010 revised version.

Though the Arbitration Rules influenced the drafting of the Model Law, they are not extensively addressed in this work. The core inquiry relates to a matter that the Rules do not directly deal with: the jurisdictional decision-making powers of national courts at the threshold of an arbitration. That role and effects on the arbitral process are governed and analysed here in light of the text of Article 8(1) of the Model Law.

[3] The 1985 UNCITRAL Model Law

UNCITRAL adopted the Model Law twenty-seven years after the New York Convention in 1985.[76] Experts on international commercial arbitration from member and non-Member States and international organisations extensively negotiated its text. It was envisioned to assist States in reforming and modernising their legislation to strengthen the global legal framework of international arbitration. Notably, the Model Law was also thought out to complement and supplement the New York Convention and assist its interpretation. The Model Law's ultimate aim is to contribute to the development of international trade by facilitating international arbitration as the proper and efficient means of dispute resolution.

The complexities surrounding the adoption or modification of a binding treaty motivated UNCITRAL to avoid amending the New York Convention when it was deemed desirable. In 1976, the Asian-African Legal Consultative Committee on International Commercial Arbitration (AALCC) invited UNCITRAL to consider adopting a protocol to annex to the Convention. This was a response to growing concerns regarding some uncertainties, ambiguities, lacunae, and the conflicting case law regarding its interpretation and application.[77] However, given the general success of the New York Convention, the type of changes needed, and the magnitude of the process, it was understood that amending the Convention was not the appropriate way

75. Resolution adopted by the General Assembly 68/109, A/RES/68/109 (16 December 2013).
76. Report of the United Nations Commission on International Trade Law on the Work of its Eighteenth Session, A/40/17 (21 August 1985), and *see*, General Assembly A/RES/40/72.
77. Notes by the Secretariat: Further Work in Respect of International Commercial Arbitration, A/CN.9/127 (20 October 1976).

forward. Instead, establishing uniform standards of arbitral procedure, in the form of a 'model law', was a better approach to solving the difficulties detected with the New York Convention.[78]

Therefore, the Model Law was deliberately designed to interplay with the Convention and other legal arbitration instruments. In fact, in 1979, UNCITRAL had already envisioned the future family ties between them when it requested its Secretary-General 'to prepare a preliminary draft of a model law on arbitral procedure, taking into account (...) the provisions of the 1958 Convention and the UNCITRAL Arbitration Rules.'[79] Ultimately, when adopting it in December 1985, the General Assembly recognised that the Model Law, together with those two earlier instruments, would significantly contribute to establishing a unified legal structure for the *fair and efficient settlement of disputes* arising in international relations.[80] This symbiotic relationship of legal instruments exposes the intricacies of UNCITRAL's continuous efforts to unify and harmonise international arbitration law.

'Fair and efficient settlement of disputes' is emphasised in the paragraph above to highlight the significance of this wording in the interpretation and application of the Model Law.[81] It represents and encapsulates the purpose of the instrument and the aim of UNCITRAL's work: 'to promote efficiency, consistency and coherence in the unification and harmonisation of international trade law.'[82]

The structure and content of the Model Law establish standards for the arbitral procedure, from its inception to the enforcement of the final award. Its immediate goal is to facilitate arbitration by unifying procedures across jurisdictions and provide its users with a high degree of legal certainty, predictability, and efficiency in dispute resolution. Truthful to its ideal, the Model Law was also designed to minimise the possible conflicts between national laws, the New York Convention and arbitration rules.[83]

At a more general level, those goals do not have an intrinsic value. They respond to the *what* question: what do the Model Law's provisions achieve? The purpose, i.e., the *why* the Model Law is drafted to accomplish those objectives, is utilitarian. The understanding is that by reaching a *fair and efficient settlement of disputes*, arbitration would fulfil its role as a *supporting tool* for bringing about *fairness and equality in*

78. *See* Report of the Secretary-General: Study on the Application and Interpretation of the Convention on the Recognition and Enforcement of Foreign Arbitral Awards, A/CN.9/168 (20 April 1979), and the Notes by the Secretariat: Further Work in Respect of International Commercial Arbitration, A/CN.9/169 (11 May 1979).
79. *See* Report of the Commission on the Work of its Twelfth Session, A/34/17, para. 81.
80. General Assembly A/RES/40/72 para. 4 [emphasis added].
81. Chapter 8 below addresses the 'Purpose' of the Model Law as an element of statutory interpretation.
82. *See* A/RES/40/71, para. 6.
83. UN Resolution 2205 (XXI), (1966); UN General Assembly Resolutions 40/71 and 40/72 (1985). *See also*, Howard M Holtzmann, and Joseph E Neuhaus, *A Guide to the UNCITRAL Model Law on International Commercial Arbitration* (Kluwer Law International, 1989), pp. 9-10. In developing a model arbitration law, UNCITRAL intended 'to bring about fairness and equality in business relationships'. General Assembly A/34/17, paras 76-81.

business relations. In turn, this would contribute to the expansion of international commerce and, with it, to *global prosperity*.[84]

The legal uniformity objective conditioned and focused the work of the drafters of the Model Law, for whom:

> [T]he paramount consideration in reviewing and revising the draft text should be the *efficient* functioning of international commercial arbitration. To that end, due account must be taken of the needs of those who, in day-to-day practice, would use the text and whom it was ultimately intended to serve.[85]

Hence, it is fair to conclude that the rationale behind the harmonisation and unification of arbitration laws is not purely legal but also economic. The Model Law was not adopted to benefit and develop the legal profession but the business community, whether it involves large, medium, or small enterprises. Businesses are the users of arbitration that UNCITRAL aimed to benefit from when drafting the Model Law. They have a direct interest and a (legitimate) expectation that its text means what it says. Adding nuances and complexities that do not plainly stem from the text negatively impacts the facilitation of international trade, for it would require expert legal advice that only increases the costs of doing business.

Access to the arbitration law carries little weight for its users if that law needs to be deciphered by legal counsel, not just any general legal counsel but an elite lawyer, expert on arbitration law and practice. And even then, the conflicting views amongst experts regarding what the text says or fails to say but still applies contradicts the very state of legal uncertainty and unpredictability that the Model Law intends to dissipate. It risks indulging arbitrary interpretations and, with it, shaking the rule of law. The effect of this would not be the intended expansion of international commerce but a shackling of its development.

As mentioned earlier, adopting a model law instead of a convention in international arbitration was based on practical reasons. Flexibility at the time of its national reception was one of those reasons. A model law (soft law instrument) becomes the law of a State when enacted by its legislature (hard law).[86] In passing legislation based on a model, States can adopt its text in whole or only in part, and adjust its language to be compatible with their legal tradition. The potential for swift implementation also influenced the decision to adopt a model law. States can draw guidance from model laws as soon as their draft is approved and adopted, rather than going through the costly and time-consuming business of diplomatic negotiations, followed by a (usually long) period to achieve the necessary number of ratifications for a convention to enter into force.[87]

84. General Assembly A/34/17, paras 76-81.
85. Commission Report A/40/17, para. 15 [emphasis added].
86. The hybrid character of international arbitration statues in Model Law jurisdictions does not fit easily with the categories of either domestic or international law. This will impact the approach applicable for their interpretation and application. *See*, Chapter 3 below.
87. *See, e.g.*, the Report of the Commission on the Work of its Tenth Session, A/32/17 (24 August 1977), Annex II, para. 31, which records different opinions on the type of instrument (model law, convention, etc.) to unify international arbitration standards. Also, the Report of the Secretary-General: Possible Features of a Model Law on International Commercial Arbitration,

Admittedly, model laws, like other instruments of soft law codification, carry a moderate normativity weight. Professor Kaufmann-Kohler calls this 'soft normativity' because soft law may be relevant and influential, but its application is not mandatory.[88] The soft normativity of the Model Law 'hardens' over time through its court deferential recognition[89] and, primarily, its worldwide reception in arbitration statutes (hard law).

Although flexibility in adopting the Model Law has contributed to its widespread reception, it has hindered, to some extent, one of the very purposes it intends to achieve: cross-jurisdiction uniformity; at least regarding the interpretation and application of its Article 8, which is the focus of this book.

In broad terms, this may jeopardise the relevance of model laws, which aim to eliminate differences and make national laws come close to one another so that it does not matter which national forum applies them.[90]

The question that emerges, then, is how judges should approach the interpretation of their national arbitration laws (based on the UNCITRAL Model Law) to achieve the highest degree of uniform application. The next chapter addresses that question.

[C] CONCLUSION

The harmonisation and unification of arbitration laws, particularly through the adoption of the UNCITRAL Model Law (and the New York Convention), have played a significant role in promoting the efficiency and effectiveness of international dispute resolution. The flexibility inherent in the Model Law has facilitated its wide acceptance and implementation across jurisdictions, providing a framework that adapts to various legal systems and cultures.

That flexibility also presents challenges in achieving uniformity across jurisdictions – at least regarding Article 8 of the Model Law, which is the focus of this book. This, in turn, may undermine the very purpose of the Model Law by failing to eliminate differences amongst national arbitration laws and impeding the desired uniformity.

A/CN.9/207 (14 May 1981), UNCITRAL Yearbook, para. 26, affirming that 'a model law is not necessarily less conducive to reaching uniform standards than a convention'.

88. Kaufmann-Kohler, *Soft Law in International Arbitration* (n. 57), pp. 295-297. The same author is of the opinion that the globalisation process of arbitration occurs 'primarily' under national statutes (hard law), in the classic fashion; Gabrielle Kaufmann-Kohler, Globalization of Arbitral Procedure (n. 54), p. 1333.

89. For example, a court decision acknowledged the Model Law's normative weigh and enforced one of the principles it codifies, even without local statutory reception: '[T]he principle of the autonomy of the arbitration clause is internationally accepted and, as such, incorporated in the Model Arbitration Law (article 16(1)). Although the Model Law has not been adopted in Argentina, it generally reflects accepted principles in the matter and can be considered to make up for the absence of a specific national norm.' *Enrique C. Wellbers S.A.I.C. A. G. v. Extraktionstechnik Gesellschaft für Anlagenbau M.B.M. s/ Ordinario,* La Ley, 1989-E-302, National Court of Appeals (Comm), Argentina, 26 September 1988.

90. Mustill, *The History of International Commercial Arbitration* (n. 34), p. 23. *See also*, Kaufmann-Kohler, *Globalization of Arbitral Procedure* (n. 54) (national arbitration laws are increasingly harmonized. As a result, they tend to become interchangeable. If … interchangeable, which one applies becomes irrelevant, at p. 1320).

Ultimately, the harmonisation and unification of arbitration laws remain an ongoing endeavour. While challenges exist, the potential benefits of achieving uniformity across jurisdictions in international arbitration are significant. As the next chapter of this book proposes, by adopting a principled and unified approach to interpretation, judges can contribute to advancing harmonised international arbitration practices and uphold the relevance and effectiveness of model laws in a rapidly evolving global legal landscape.

The next chapter of this book then addresses a matter of legal interpretation. The first part discusses the interpretative rules found in Article 2A of the Model Law (section [B]). The second explores the rules of interpretation of the New York Convention (section [C]). Lastly, the next part proposes an 'autonomous' approach to interpreting the Model Law and the domestic arbitration statutes based on it (section [D]).

CHAPTER 3

A Matter of Interpretation

[A] INTRODUCTION

This chapter delves into the hermeneutics of the Model Law. It primarily discusses the appropriate rules and methods for its interpretation. This is important because textual similarity and proper rules of interpretation influence applied uniformity. The following chapters build on the present one, addressing and applying the interpretative approach discussed here.

Interpreting and applying the law are discrete exercises, although almost impossible to dissociate. The application of the law inevitably requires a degree of interpretation. Interpreting the law involves a cognitive process and an epistemological inquiry into the interaction of several elements to give meaning to the text.[91] Applying the law, for its part, is the process of giving effect to the text in each situation; it materialises the actions and the consequences that the text commands or allows.

The interpretative technique followed delineates the elements considered in the interpretative process. For example, the *textualist* approach to legal interpretation adheres to the instrument's text. It infers meaning solely from the terms it uses. It is a context-independent approach that rejects the study of extrinsic material to assist the interpretation of the law. The words used in a legislative instrument represent and carry the legislative intent. In its purest form, the interpretative task begins and ends with the text of the legal instrument. The judge decides the interpretative quest by giving the words in the legal provision their plain (or more technical) meaning,[92] read

91. For a brief discussion on interpretation, syllogistic reasoning and the role of legal method, *see* Torben Spaak, Relativism in Legal Thinking: Stanley Fish and the Concept of an Interpretative Community, 21 *Ratio Juris*, no. 1 (2008), pp. 158-160 DOI: 10.1111/j.1467-9337.2007.00384.x. For a thorough exposition of the different methods of legal interpretation (whilst advocating for textualism), *see* Antonin Scalia et al., *Reading Law: The Interpretation of Legal Texts* (West, 2012).
92. *See, e.g.*, Scalia et al., *ibid.*, pp. 15-18.

in their context.[93] Instead, the *intentionalist* approach to legal interpretation seeks to unveil or reconstruct the lawmaker's intention when the law was adopted. This may be ascertained by studying historical facts and documents that recorded the original legislative intent. These are usually found in parliamentary discussions or drafting history reports, the instrument's preamble, or annexes. Under the *purposive* approach, the interpreter strives to achieve the goals and policies of the legal instrument. The text, historical records, case law, and scholarly work may be used to determine the law's purposive meaning.

The interpretative method followed also conditions the views on the interpreter's role. For example, one may conceive the interpreter's task as content determination rather than law ascertainment.

This publication does not intend to rehash that debate.[94] Nor does it intend to adopt one interpretative approach at a total exclusion of others. Instead, it proposes to follow a combination of textualist, intentionalist, and purposivist techniques. To advance such an approach, it is crucial to consider the existing interpretative rules in the Model Law and those applicable to the New York Convention. This is addressed next (in sections [B] and [C]), followed by a discussion and the proposition of an interpretative approach to national arbitration laws that is in line with those two international instruments (sections [D] and [E]).

[B] THE INTERPRETATIVE GUIDANCE IN THE MODEL LAW

Article 2 of the original version (1985) of the Model Law defines some terms and lays out rules of interpretation. For example, it clarifies that when a provision in the Model Law refers to 'claims', it also applies to 'counter-claims'. Where it refers to 'arbitral tribunal', it does not matter whether a case is before a sole arbitrator or a panel of arbitrators. It applies to both. Although Article 2 sheds light on the interpretation of specific terms and situations, it does not provide an overarching interpretative theme or principles for the entire instrument.

The Inclusion of Article 2A in the Model Law

The 2006 amendments to the Model Law incorporated further interpretative guidance in Article 2A. This article does not create a new interpretative framework. It simply aims to further assist in understanding the Model Law.[95] Article 2A codifies broad

93. *See, e.g.*, John F. Manning, Textualism and the Equity of the Statute, 101 *Columbia Law Review*, no. 1 (2001), pp. 106-107 DOI: 10.2307/1123509 ('Textualists ... reject purposive interpretation *only* when it requires them to assign the text a meaning that it will not bear in context. ... language has meaning only in its social and linguistic context.').
94. For a general discussion on this, *see*, for example, Jean d'Aspremont, 'The Multidimensional Process of Interpretation: Content-Determination and Law-Ascertainment Distinguished', in *Interpretation in International Law*, ed. Andrea Bianchi, Daniel Peat et al. (Oxford University Press, 2018).
95. Report of the Commission on the Work of its Thirty-Ninth Session, General Assembly A/61/17 (SUPP) (14 July 2006), paras 175-176. *See* the Explanatory Note by the UNCITRAL Secretariat on the 1985 Model Law on International Commercial Arbitration as amended in 2006, para. 4.

principles that existed implicitly in the original version of the Model Law,[96] especially its first paragraph. This means that the same guidance applies to the interpretative process even where the language of Article 2A is not included in the local arbitration statute that adopts the Model Law.

Article 2A provides:

> International origin and general principles
> (1) In the interpretation of this Law, regard is to be had to its international origin and to the need to promote uniformity in its application and the observance of good faith.
> (2) Questions concerning matters governed by this Law which are not expressly settled in it are to be settled in conformity with the general principles on which this Law is based.

The language of Article 2A requires some explanation. Though its drafting history is succinct, it explicitly reveals that Article 2A is based on Article 7 of the Convention on International Sales of Goods (CISG).[97] However, Article 2A of the Model Law replicates the language of Article 3 of the Model Law on Electronic Commerce (1996), which was also based on Article 7 of the CISG. In fact, Article 7 of the CISG inspired interpretative provisions in many other UNCITRAL texts.[98] It carries high relevance because it codifies the need to interpret international uniform law 'autonomously', independently from national law and concepts, and the interpretative approach appropriate to purely domestic legislation.[99]

In its drafters' view, including an article (Article 2A) akin to the one in the CISG would promote a uniform understanding of the Model Law.[100] Yet, the Model Law and the CISG are instruments of a distinct legal nature. On a basic-level comparison, a convention is an agreement between States, governed by international public law, and binding for those that become a party to it. When becoming a party, a State cannot amend the convention's language or exclude some of its provisions (other than the permitted reservations). A model law is precisely the opposite. It is a non-binding instrument that works as a 'suggestion', an 'example', or a 'prototype' to inspire

96. *See, e.g.*, Frédéric Bachand, 'Judicial Internationalism and the Interpretation of the Model Law: Reflections on Some Aspects of Article 2A', in *The UNCITRAL Model Law after Twenty-Five Years* (Bachand and Gélinas eds, n. 39), p. 233. Binder, however, seems to suggest that in contrast to a convention, laws based on a model law are correctly interpreted according to each state's accepted interpretative regime; Peter Binder, *International Commercial Arbitration and Conciliation in UNCITRAL Model Law Jurisdictions*, 4th ed. (Kluwer Law International, 2019), pp. 59-60.

97. United Nations Convention on Contracts for the International Sale of Goods (1980). The two articles have a similar, but not identical, wording. *See*, A/61/17 (SUPP), para. 174.

98. For example, Article 7 of the Convention on the Assignment of Receivables in International Trade (New York, 2001); Article 5 of the Convention on the Use of Electronic Communications in International Contracts (New York, 2005); Article 3 of the Model Law on Electronic Commerce with Guide to Enactment 1996; Article 4 of the Model Law on Electronic Signatures (2001); Article 2 of the Model Law on International Commercial Conciliation (2002).

99. *See*, amongst many others, Franco Ferrari, Autonomous Interpretation Versus Homeward Trend Versus Outward Trend in CISG Case Law, 22 *Uniform Law Review*, no. 1 (2017) DOI: 10.1093/ulr/unw057.

100. A/61/17 (SUPP) para. 175. *See also*, the Explanatory Note by the UNCITRAL Secretariat on the 1985 Model Law on International Commercial Arbitration as amended in 2006, para. 4.

national legislation. States draw guidance from the model and have the discretion to respect the language suggested or modify it.[101] The model gains the force of law when a parliamentary (or similar) act adopts it into the national legal system.[102]

Significantly, the approach to legal interpretation differs where the instrument is a convention or a national law. On the one hand, conventions are construed according to internationally accepted principles and goals[103] (they will be discussed in the next section). On the other hand, national laws are generally interpreted according to domestic concepts, definitions, and understandings of the given jurisdiction. They do not need to conform to other jurisdictions' concepts, definitions, or rules, even when the terms are the same.[104] Similarly, the method of interpretation of national laws may differ from jurisdiction to jurisdiction.[105]

Despite the legal differences between a convention and domestic statutes, laws that adopt or implement a UNCITRAL model law enjoy a distinct status from ordinary national statutes. Hence, they deserve special interpretative considerations. The distinction is primarily rooted in (i) the national law's international origin, (ii) their international unification objective, and (iii) the principles on which they are based.

The Significance of the Model Law's Origin and Goal

At first glance, Article 2A's declaration that the Model Law has an *international origin* may appear redundant or simply state the obvious. The Model Law is certainly an international instrument, regardless of its indication in an article. Its provisions were discussed and negotiated by delegates of member and non-Member States of the United Nations and non-governmental members of the epistemic community of international arbitration. Its text was adopted by an international organisation (UNCITRAL), not a national legislator. Therefore, the fact that a State adopts the Model Law by a parliamentary or similar legislative action does not make it the law's intellectual

101. For example, the arbitration laws of Germany, Denmark, and Peru deviate from the language suggested in Article 8(1) of the Model Law (amongst other provisions). *See* the discussion in Chapter 7, section 7.4 for further examples.
102. Schultz refers to this as the process of *formal positivisation* where 'shared principled beliefs' are 'translated into formal amendments or creations of regulations (...)'. The result is a global harmonization of the practice of arbitration; Thomas Schultz, Secondary Rules of Recognition and Relative Legality in Transnational Regimes, 56 *American Journal of Jurisprudence* (2011) p. 64 DOI: 10.1093/ajj/56.1.59. Michaels calls it 'incorporation' in Ralf Michaels, The Re-Statement of Non-State law: The State, Choice of Law, and The Challenge from Global legal Pluralism, 51 *Wayne Law Review* no. 3 (2005), p. 299; And Brekoulakis calls it 'institutional support'; Brekoulakis, *International Arbitration Scholarship* (n. 21).
103. Article 7 of CISG, for example, is based on those principles (A/61/17 (SUPP), para. 174). In brief, they refer to the legal instrument's international origin and uniform application, the observance of good faith, and an autonomous approach for their interpretation.
104. This is somewhat different in the context of political and economic unions like the European Union or MERCOSUR. For example, according to Article 288 of the Treaty on the Functioning of the European Union, Member States can choose the form and method for implementing a EU Directive, as long as the domestic instrument conforms with the content and achieves the result sought in the Directive.
105. In general terms, common and civil law jurisdictions are usually known for adopting different approaches on reading the law, whether they place decisive weight to either the text or the purpose of the law.

originator. The State activity is not one of 'creation' but of 'incorporation' of the norms created by the non-state actor.

Neither the brief drafting history nor the Secretariat Notes record any discussion on the meaning or purpose of the language of Article 2A. However, referring to Article 3 of the Model Law on Electronic Commerce (1996),[106] UNCITRAL explained that:

> The purpose of paragraph (1) is to draw the attention of courts and other national authorities to the fact that the provisions of the Model Law (or the provisions of the instrument implementing the Model Law), while enacted as part of domestic legislation and therefore domestic in character, should be interpreted with reference to its international origin in order to ensure uniformity in the interpretation of the Model Law in various countries.[107]
>
> UNCITRAL offers the same explanation in other instruments that mirror Article 3 of the Model Law in Electronic Commerce's language.[108] There is no reason to conclude that the same text in the arbitration Model Law has a different meaning and purpose.

In that understanding, Article 2A's reference to the instrument's international origin seeks to differentiate arbitration laws based on the Model Law from statutes of national origin. They are *national laws* of *international origin*.

An example of this understanding found ground in a decision of the Supreme Court of Bermuda, which explicitly recognised the special nature of its local arbitration law based on the Model Law. The Court held that the Model Law 'is essentially international legislation, the language of which largely reflects the compromises and negotiations conducted by expert representatives from a wide array of national legal systems'. Hence, the Model Law 'must ... be construed distinctively from the approach that would be adopted while construing ordinary domestic legislation'.[109] This reasoning is appropriate for the Model Law before and after its amendment in 2006 and whether Article 2A is present or not.

Interpreting laws of international origin requires an autonomous approach that carries two main consequences. One is that the interpreter should avoid giving its text

106. Which the Model Law in arbitration copied verbatim.
107. Guide to Enactment of the UNCITRAL Model Law on Electronic Commerce (1996), para. 42. Available at https://uncitral.un.org/sites/uncitral.un.org/files/media-documents/uncitral/en/19-04970_ebook.pdf.
108. For example, in the Guides to enacting the Model Law on Electronic Signatures (2001) and the Model Law on International Commercial Conciliation (2002/2018), at paras 109 and 40, respectively.
109. *Montpelier Reinsurance Ltd v. Manufacturers Property & Casualty Ltd*, [2008] SC (Bda) 27 Com, Supreme Court of Bermuda, 24 April 2008, para. 21. In more general terms, the decision of the Federal Court of Australia in *El Greco* case offered a similar explanation. It held that '[s]ubject to any contrary intention revealed by the domestic statute making an international instrument part of domestic law, the ascertainment of the meaning of, and obligations within, an international instrument that is made part of domestic law is to be ascertained by giving primacy to the text of the international instrument, but also by considering the context, objects and purposes of the instrument (...) The manner of interpreting the international instrument is one which is more liberal than that ordinarily adopted by a court construing exclusively domestic legislation; it is undertaken in a manner unconstrained by technical local rules or precedent, but on broad principles of general acceptation (...)', *El Greco (Australia) Pty Ltd v. Mediterranean Shipping Co SA*, [2004] FCAFC 202, Federal Court of Australia, 10 August 2004, para. 142.

the same meaning that similar terms have in laws of national origin. The High Court of Australia echoed this conclusion in the *TCL* case when it held that:

> [C]onsiderations of international origin and international application make imperative that the Model Law be construed without any assumptions that it embodies common law concepts, or that it will apply only to arbitral awards, or arbitration agreements that are governed by common law principles.[110]

The other consequence is that it frees the interpretative exercise from the method, rules and means commonly followed for construing laws of national origin. For this reason, courts would defeat the Model Law's objectives if they looked to their own legal order for interpretation and application purposes.

Article 2A's mandate to consider the *need to promote uniformity* in the application of the Model Law is linked to the instrument's international origin and its objective of bringing about international uniform standards of arbitral procedure.[111] That need did not arise out of the 2006 amendments. The Resolution that adopted the Model Law in 1985 had already made that need clear.[112] It is also consistent with the declarations of the UN General Assembly for establishing UNCITRAL in 1966: to advance international trade by preparing legal instruments, including model laws, and by promoting ways and means of ensuring their uniform interpretation and application.[113]

To contribute to 'the uniform interpretation and application' of the Model Law (and other UNCITRAL instruments), the Secretariat established the CLOUT database in 1988 and publishes its Digest.[114] Therefore, it cannot seriously be argued that the pre-2006 Model Law did not seek uniformity in its application but only textual uniformity.

The Model Law's reference to 'international origin' is also closely connected to the second paragraph of Article 2A:

> Questions concerning matters governed by this Law which are not expressly settled in it are to be settled in conformity with the general principles on which this Law is based.

Although this paragraph does not identify the *general principles* on which the Model Law is based, they transpire from the instrument's text, purpose, and drafting history. Those internal principles recognise that party agreement is at the core of arbitration.[115] It affords parties a myriad of choices, starting with the essential one that legitimises the entire process: 'to arbitrate or not to arbitrate'. It also entrusts parties

---

110. *TCL Air Conditioner (Zhongshan) Co Ltd v. The Judges of the Federal Court of Australia,* [2013] HCA 5, High Court of Australia, 13 March 2013, para. 8.
111. *See* Chapter 2, section [B][3] above.
112. Resolution of the General Assembly at its Fortieth Session – Model Law on International Commercial Arbitration of the United Nations Commission on International Trade Law, A/RES/40/72 (11 December 1985).
113. A/RES/2205 (XXI), para. 8(c), and (d).
114. Report of the Commission on the Work of its Twenty-First session, A/43/17 (11-22 April 1988), paras 98-109.
115. *See, e.g.,* Articles 4, 7 and 8 of the Model Law.

with the freedom to arrange and direct the proceedings[116] and limits the instances where court involvement is possible.[117] The Model Law is based on ideals of procedural fairness and efficiency in resolving international disputes.[118] Again, these are pervasive principles of international arbitration on which the Model Law is based, whether Article 2A is present or not. They have guided the interpretation and application of the Model Law since its adoption in 1985.[119]

Good Faith Interpretation

The interpreter's attitude to the specific law or field of law influences the interpretative result. This is why the *observance of good faith* steers the entire interpretative activity.[120] But, Article 2A's directive to observe good faith is vague. This is especially true for a subjective term that does not enjoy an internationally uniform definition and scope. In broad terms, good faith moderates arbitrariness and biases. In the realm of legal interpretation, the concept is a synonym for intellectual fidelity. It aims to avoid giving words or phrases a meaning that they do not bear. It also requires that meaning is not coloured by the interpreter's preconceptions or opinions of what the law should say or provide for.

This does not mean that interpretation is an entirely objective activity. If the text permits multiple meanings, the interpreter's values or preferences influence the interpretative outcome.[121] Still, the choice between permitted results requires a degree of 'impersonality' (objectivity) rather than the interpreter's notion of correctness.[122] Nor should the interpreter's ideas and ideals of the desired policy behind the legal instrument determine the meaning of its provisions. It would be contrary to good faith to attribute those personal ideas to UNCITRAL and characterise them as the Model Law's aim.[123] Good faith also limits the risk of misconceiving the role of the interpreter,

116. *See, e.g.*, Articles 3, 10, 11, 13(1), 15, 17, 19(1), 20-26 of the Model Law.
117. *See, e.g.*, Articles 5, 6, 34, 35-36 of the Model Law.
118. *See*, e.g., Articles 18 and 19(2) of the Model Law, and Resolution A/RES/40/72.
119. As well as the New York Convention, earlier instruments, and the uncodified arbitration practice throughout its development.
120. Interpreting legal texts through good-faith lenses is not new. For example, the rules of interpretation codified in the Vienna Convention require that '[a] treaty shall be interpreted in good faith ...', United Nations Vienna Convention on the Law of Treaties (1969), Article 31(31).
121. This reflects the general 'anchoring and adjustment' judgment process whereby decision makers first focus on anchors and then make a series of dynamic adjustments toward their final answer to a question or problem. *See*, in general, Nicholas Epley et al., 'Putting Adjustment Back in the Anchoring and Adjustment Heuristic', in *Heuristics and Biases: The Psychology of Intuitive Judgment*, ed. Thomas Gilovich, Dale Griffin, et al. (Cambridge University Press, 2002), pp. 139-149.
122. For a discussion on objective interpretation *see*, in general, Owen M. Fiss, Objectivity and Interpretation, 34 *Stanford Law Review* (1982), pp. 739-763 DOI: 10.2307/1228384.
123. Several courts have confirmed this understanding. *See, e.g.*, *TELUS Communications Inc. v. Welman*, 2019 SCC 19 (CanLII), Supreme Court of Canada, 4 April 2019, p. 79 ('Policy considerations cannot be permitted to distort the actual words of the statute (...). While policy analysis has a legitimate role in the interpretive process, the responsibility for setting policy in a parliamentary democracy rests with the legislature, not with the courts'). *See also*, *Australian Education Union v. Department of Education and Children's Services*, [2012] HCA 3, High Court of Australia, 29 February 2012, para. 28. *Henry Schein, Inc. v. Archer and White Sales, Inc.*, 139 S.Ct. 524, Supreme Court of the United States, 8 Januray 2019, paras 14-15.

who is not entitled to revise the language of the Model Law. Or to disregard elements that contradict the interpretative result that the interpreter considers to fit the instrument's legislative goals best. The interpreter's job is to give the text a logical and reasonable meaning that results from the established interpretative rules, method and means or sources.[124]

In this understanding, good faith calls for considering the *context* of the terms under analysis, the *uniformity* goal, the *purpose* of the Model Law and the general principles it is based on. That interpretative outcome, in turn, would likely reflect and give effect to the legislative intent that the drafters of the Model Law sought to record when formalising its wording.

The Missing Interpretative Rules

It is important to acknowledge that Article 2A only offers some interpretative guidance or direction. Its language does not provide the steps or method the interpreter should follow to 'promote uniformity in its application and the observance of good faith'. It is also silent on the materials the interpreter should consider and their hierarchy and weight. What Article 2A does is to: (i) highlight the Model Law's international origin, (ii) direct the use of its own general principles in gap filling, and (iii) crystallise two pre-existing goals, i.e., uniformity in its application[125] and observance of good faith.

The lack of a clear interpretative approach within the Model Law and its silence regarding the sources, material, and hierarchy leave room for undermining the instrument's uniformity objective. The approach advanced here addresses that matter, as it also proposes that judges adopt the same analytical framework for interpreting statutes based on the Model Law (section [E] below). This, in turn, contributes to achieving the highest degree of international applied uniformity. These words are chosen carefully to underscore that uniformity is a matter of degree; it cannot be measured in absolute terms.[126] In this understanding, adopting a single interpretative method does not necessarily guarantee attaining the same, unique result. However, adopting a uniform approach to legal interpretation fosters applied uniformity. It disciplines the interpretative process, provides a solid starting point, and maximises the possibilities of reaching (the highest possible degree of) uniform outcomes.

A uniform approach to legal interpretation endorses inter-judicial dialogue.[127] It is also coherent with the consistency and predictability goals in applying the Model

124. Richard K. Gardiner, *Treaty Interpretation*, 2nd ed., Oxford International Law Library (Oxford University Press, 2017), pp. 169-174. *See also* the commentary of the UN Special Rapporteur on the task of the interpreter of international law, who described it as one that calls for investigation, weighing of evidence, judgment, foresight, and the appreciation of a number of factors varying in each case. Humphrey Waldock, ILC Third Report on the Law of Treaties A/CN.4/167 and Add.1-3 Yearbook of the International Law Commission, p. 53, paras 51-52.

125. To unify the arbitral procedure across jurisdictions (goal), as a tool to support the needs of its users in the development of international trade (purpose); Report of the Commission on the Work of its Twelfth Session, A/34/17, paras 76-81.

126. *See, e.g.*, Andersen, Defining Uniformity in Law (n. 28), p. 42.

127. *See, e.g.*, Anne-Marie Slaughter, A Global Community of Courts, 44 *Harvard International Law Journal*, no. 1 (2003), whose vision on judicial cooperation in transnational litigation is 'a dialogue between the adjudicative bodies of the world community' would not be composed of US, French, German, Japanese courts and international tribunals but simply of adjudicative

Law throughout the jurisdictions that adopt it. Cross-jurisdiction consistency and predictability create a sense that forum shopping is not worthwhile.

The question that arises is how to interpret a national law of an international origin, which has a unification and harmonisation objective and is explicitly based on and bound to interact with and complement a convention (the New York Convention). A related question is whether interpretation could result in different meanings where the provisions of the New York Convention and the Model Law are the same, especially where Article 8(1) of the Model Law was designed to correspond to Article II(3) of the New York Convention.

Before addressing those points, the following section briefly identifies the approach to the interpretation of the New York Convention. The subsequent section proposes an interpretative approach to national arbitration statutes in Model Law jurisdictions that respects the guidance offered by its Article 2A. Also, it aligns it with the rules and means of interpretation applicable to the New York Convention.

[C] INTERPRETATION OF THE NEW YORK CONVENTION

The New York Convention does not include an interpretative provision like the Model Law, and its interpretation has not always been uniform. The approach that States have used to implement the New York Convention has sometimes affected their attitude to its interpretation. For example, depending on a state's dualist or monist approach to international law, different interpretative techniques have been followed to construe the Convention (international instrument) or the law that implements it at the national level (domestic statute). As mentioned earlier, a UNCITRAL survey revealed that some States interpret the New York Convention following the principles laid down in their Constitutions. Others follow the interpretative guidelines issued by their respective highest court.[128]

However, since the New York Convention is a legal instrument of international law, it must be interpreted autonomously, detached from a given State's law, concepts, and rules. The Vienna Convention[129] satisfies that need. The principles of treaty interpretation that the Convention codifies 'help to bridge the "gulfs in language, culture, and values that separate nations" by providing a set of definitive "conventions of description, argument, judgment, and persuasion" to facilitate inter-judicial dialogue.'[130]

entities engaging in resolving disputes, interpreting and applying the law as best they can. It is a vision of a global legal system, established not by the World Court in The Hague, but by national courts working together around the world.', at p. 204).

128. UNCITRAL Report on the Survey Relating to the Legislative Implementation of the Convention on the Recognition and Enforcement of Foreign Arbitral Awards, A/CN.9/656 (16 June-3 July 2008), paras 35-40.

129. Vienna Convention, Articles 31-33.

130. Evan Criddle, The Vienna Convention on the Law of Treaties in US Treaty Interpretation, 44 *Vanderbilt Journal of International Law*, no. 2 (2003) p. 498 (citing *Trans World Airlines, Inc. v. Franklin Mint Corp.*, 66 U.S. 243, 262 (1984) (Stevens, J., dissenting)).

Although the Vienna Convention (1969) entered into force twenty-one years after the New York Convention (1958), its retroactive application is accepted because it does not create innovative interpretative rules. It only crystallises the existing rules developed in international case law and doctrine over time. The International Law Commission (ILC) has confirmed that the rules of interpretation in Articles 31 and 32 of the Vienna Convention reflect customary international law.[131]

The International Court of Justice (ICJ) reached the same conclusion in several cases. For example, the ICJ recalled that the rules of interpretation reflected in the Vienna Convention had been applied to treaties concluded in 1955 and 1890.[132] And that they applied even where the States involved were not parties to the Convention. This was the situation of India and Pakistan in the *Jadhav* case.[133] India was not a party to the Vienna Convention, and Pakistan had signed but not ratified it.

In any event, it is accepted that the rule and means of interpretation in Articles 31-33 of the Vienna Convention (as an expression of public international law) apply to the New York Convention.[134] Adopting the Vienna Convention approach to interpret the New York Convention significantly contributes to achieving a higher degree of uniformity in its application.

The Vienna Convention sets forth a method that reflects elements of several approaches to legal interpretation. Article 31 describes the general rule of interpretation. Together with Article 32, it lists several primary and supplementary means of interpretation that *shall* (Article 31) or *may* (Article 32) be considered when interpreting treaties.[135] Article 33 recognises an equal authoritative value to treaties authenticated in multiple languages.[136]

Much has been written about the rule and means of interpretation in Articles 31-32 of the Vienna Convention, so there is no added value in examining them here. This publication is not about the theory of those rules. Instead, it assumes they apply

131. United Nations General Assembly, Report of the International Law Commission on its Seventieth session A/73/10 (30 April-1 June and 2 July-10 August 2018), p. 17. *See also*, the decision of the ICJ in *Sovereignty over Pulau Ligitan and Pulau Sipadan (Indonesia v. Malasia)*, [2002] ICJ Reports 625, International Court of Justice, 17 December 2002, para. 37.
132. *Arbitration regarding the Iron Rhine ('Ijzeren Rijn') Railway between the Kingdom of Belgium and the Kingdom of the Netherlands*, International Court of Justice, 24 May 2005 p. 62, para. 45. *See also*, *Pulp Mills on the River Uruguay (Argentina v. Uruguay)*, [2010] ICJ Reports 14, International Court of Justice, 20 April 2010.
133. *Jadhav* case *(India v. Pakistan)*, [2019] ICJ Reports International Court of Justice, 17 July 2019, para. 71.
134. *See, e.g.*, Reinmar Wolff, *New York Convention Articly-by-Article Commentary*, 2nd ed. (Beck – Hart – Nomos, 2019), pp. 19-20; Marike R.P. Paulsson, *The 1958 New York Convention in Action* (Kluwer Law International, 2016), pp. 43-51; Albert Jan van den Berg, *The New York Arbitration Convention of 1958* (n. 11), pp. 1-6. For the opposing view, *see* Filip J.M. De Ly, 'Uniform Interpretation: What Is Being Done?', in *Autonomous Versus Domestic Concepts under the New York Convention*, ed. Franco Ferrari and Friedrich Jakob Rosenfeld (Kluwer Law International, 2021), p. 24 ('[T]he application of the VCLT [Vienna Convention on the Law of Treaties] to New York Convention cases is in most instances to be avoided if not wrong and may expose States to liability for actions of their judiciary').
135. ILC Report on its 70th session (A/73/10).
136. The text of the New York Convention has been authenticated in Chinese, English, French, Russian and Spanish.

to interpret the New York Convention and uses them to support Article 2A of the Model Law. Therefore, it suffices to introduce only some brief remarks on their substance.

The Vienna Convention Rules of Interpretation

According to the *general rule* of interpretation in Article 31 of the Vienna Convention, treaties must be construed 'in good faith, according to the ordinary meaning given to the terms of the treaty in their context and in light of its object and purpose.'[137]

Like Article 2A of the Model Law, the first directive detaches the interpretative exercise from subjectivity. Instead, it focuses on the ordinary meaning of the words used. The second directive completes the first one. Because it is impossible to grasp the nuances of an isolated word without some contextual clues, Article 31 requires that the ordinary meaning be found against the background in which the words are used. Lastly, the purposive approach to legal interpretation sways the contextual, ordinary meaning of the terms used in a treaty.

The article further describes the *primary* means that the interpreter must consider in identifying the context of the treaty. Apart from the text of the treaty itself, it includes extrinsic sources: the treaty's preamble and annexes, and instruments and agreements made by all or some of the parties to the treaty in connection with its conclusion.

In addition to 'context', the interpreter should consider the agreements and the practice that develops after the adoption of the treaty. This permits a degree of dynamism in treaty interpretation. It acknowledges that some of the terms used in a treaty may have been given a meaning capable of evolving over time. Significantly, the ILC has clarified that subsequent agreements and practice should be taken as an interpretative source rather than an avenue to modify or amend the treaty.[138] In particular, the ILC observed that '[t]he possibility of amending or modifying a treaty by the subsequent practice of the parties has not been generally recognised.'[139]

The different elements of the general rule (text, context, good faith, object and purpose) balance out the interpretative exercise. They do not operate in isolation or in a sequential or hierarchical order. They operate as a whole – in a combined, integrated way. The different elements are assessed one at a time but weighed together.[140] Good faith and the ordinary meaning of the terms used in a treaty provision are influenced and conditioned by their context, object and purpose. The several means of interpretation in Article 31 are part of a single rule. No means of interpretation has priority over others.[141]

Because interpretation is an 'art, not an exact science', it involves a discretional appreciation of factors rather than a step-by-step rigid formula.[142] The combined

137. Vienna Convention, para. 1.
138. Conclusion 8 on the possible effects of subsequent agreements and subsequent practice in treaty interpretation. ILC Report on its 70th session (A/73/10).
139. *Ibid*. This is without prejudice to the rules on amendment of treaties under Part IV of the Vienna Convention.
140. Gardiner, *Treaty Interpretation* (n. 124), pp. 31-32.
141. ILC Report on its 70th session (A/73/10), pp. 20, 22.
142. International Law Commission, Draft Articles on the Law of Treaties with Commentaries, 2 *Yearbook of the International Law Commission*, no. 2 (1966) p. 218, para. 214.

analysis of the general rule and means produces the legally relevant interpretation of the treaty provision.[143]

The ILC made this point clear when addressing issues related to States' subsequent practice by asserting that '[t]he interpretation of a treaty consists of a single combined operation, which places appropriate emphasis on the various means of interpretation indicated, respectively, in Articles 31 and 32.'[144] For this reason, interpretation has been described as an open, inelegant and circular process towards the meaning of a treaty provision rather than a 'linear algorithm tied to a particular hierarchical sequence.'[145] This is also known as the 'crucible' approach.[146]

Article 32 of the Vienna Convention includes a non-exhaustive list of *supplementary* means of interpretation: preparatory works and the circumstances of the treaty's conclusion.[147] Their use is discretionary and serves to fulfil two purposes. One is to *confirm* the meaning resulting from the general rule. This implies that where the meaning of a treaty provision appears clear by reading it in good faith, in its context and in light of its purpose, the interpreter could not look into preparatory works to ascertain a different one.

The other purpose is to *determine* the meaning of a treaty provision when the interpretation according to the general rule leaves the meaning ambiguous, obscure, or leads to a manifestly absurd or unreasonable result.

The intention of the parties to the treaty, too, has a place in the interpretative process. Article 31(4) captures this idea, as it provides that '[a] special meaning shall be given to a term if it is established that the parties so intended.' Treaties interpreted according to Articles 31 and 32 of the Vienna Convention will reflect the *parties' presumed intention* to the treaty.[148] This appears consistent with the auxiliary status of a treaty's preparatory works as a means of interpretation. As indicated above, their recourse is discretionary and only supplements the general rule of interpretation where this, in theory, is insufficient.[149]

143. Gardiner, *Treaty Interpretation* (n. 124), pp. 10-11.
144. ILC Report on its 70th session (A/73/10), draft conclusion 2 (p. 13). *See*, in particular, the Commission's commentary on pp. 21-23.
145. Julian Davis Mortenson, The Travaux of Travaux: Is the Vienna Convention Hostile to Drafting History?, 107 *American Journal of International Law*, no. 4 (2013), p. 781 DOI: 10.5305/amerjintelaw.107.4.0780.
146. Commission, *Draft Articles on the Law of Treaties with Commentaries* pp. 219-220, para. 218 ('All the various elements, as they were present in any given case, would be thrown into the crucible, and their interaction would give the legally relevant interpretation.').
147. The Convention does not offer a definition of what constitute preparatory works (e.g., working papers, memoranda submitted for the discussion at the diplomatic conference, reports of the agreements reached at those conferences, etc.), nor what the circumstances of the conclusion of a treaty may entail.
148. Report of the International Law Commission on the work of its Sixteenth Session, A/CN.4/173 (11 July 1964), p. 204. *See also*, the decision of the ICJ in the *Dispute Regarding Navigational and Related Rights (Costa Rica v. Nicaragua)*, ICJ Reports 2009, p. 213, International Court of Justice, para. 48: 'A treaty provision (...) must be interpreted (...) in accordance with the intentions of its authors as reflected by the text of the treaty and the other relevant factors in terms of interpretation.'
149. In noting that preparatory works have in practice been relied upon as a regular, rather than supplementary, source of interpretation, Judge Schwebel recognised that the hierarchical structure of Articles 31 and 32 of the Vienna Convention is 'unreal'; Stephen Schwebel, May

Of significant importance for the interpretative approach suggested in the next section is the fact that the process of interpretation envisioned in the Vienna Convention is not a rigid one. As Waldock (the Special Rapporteur on the Convention) noted during the drafting of Articles 31-32, they have a character of 'guidelines' with a degree of flexibility.[150] Their application is mandatory to treaty interpretation but understood as 'regulations, principles, or guidelines, which are not exclusive of other compatible interpretative principles or techniques.'[151]

[D] UNIFORM INTERPRETATION AND UNIFORM APPLICATION OF UNIFORM LAW

A sound approach to legal interpretation is paramount in the international arbitration context, where legal pluralism dominates the creation of normative instruments. The term 'sound approach' translates here as a distinct, nuanced, and appropriate interpretative toolbox. And a process that considers the role of the individual interpreter but prefers the legal meaning relevant for the interpretative community.[152]

Considerations of legal interpretation require pondering the role of the interpreter. Given the cross-border breadth of the Model Law and the New York Convention, their coordinated uniform-application goal, the diversity of legal families they interact with and the divergent approaches to reading the law, the pin here drops beyond the individual interpreter. The focus is on the interpreters' sociological dimension as a cohesive group, i.e., as an interpretative community.[153]

In the context of this work, legislators, government legal advisers and judges are the primary members of the interpretative community called to construe the Model Law. The original members of that interpretative community were the members of the epistemic community[154] that participated in the *drafting* of the Model Law.[155] The

Preparatory Work Be Used to Correct Rather than Confirm the 'Clear' Meaning of a Treaty Provision?, 2 *Transnational Dispute Management (Previously published in Svensk Juristtidning, 1997, Häfte 10)*, no. 5 (2005), p. 799.

150. Humphrey Waldock, ILC Sixth Report on the Law of Treaties ILC Sixth Report, A/CN.4/186 andAdd.1-7 Yearbook of the International Law Commission, p. 94 (para. 91).
151. Gardiner, *Treaty Interpretation* (n. 124), p. 40.
152. Michael Waibel, 'Interpretive Communities in International Law', in *Interpretation in International Law*, ed. Andrea Bianchi, Daniel Peat, et al. (Oxford University Press, 2015), p. 149. ('[I]nternational legal rules acquire meaning only in the light of background norms common to particular interpretive communities.').
153. *Ibid.*, p. 147. ('Individual and group identity, the background and the shared understandings of interpreters are key ingredients in the interpretative process.').
154. According to Waibel, the term interpretative, rather than epistemic, communities is a less generic concept that concerns interpretation specifically. The term epistemic communities, instead, 'centres on networks of experts and their role in creating a regime, or in applying the regime on an ongoing basis'. For a brief discussion on the distinction between those concepts, *see*, *ibid.*, pp. 149-151.
155. This conforms with Fish's theory, for whom 'interpretative communities are made up of those who share interpretative strategies not for reading (...) but for writing texts, constituting their properties, and assigning their intentions. In other words, these strategists exist prior to the act of reading and therefore determine the shape of what is read rather than, as is usually assumed, the other way around. Stanley Eugene Fish, *Is There a Text in This Class?: The Authority of*

drafters shared a strategy for achieving uniform standards for arbitration practice. They thoroughly discussed and chose the Model Law's language based on the meaning that the epistemic community intended to assign to each provision.

For legislators and government legal advisers, the interpretation of the Model Law elicits better-informed legislative drafting. The interpretative exercise has a *regulatory* character and aims to understand its content when weighing its adoption. Implementing the Model Law at the national level (with or without deviations) is a *choice*. For that reason, making an informed decision requires first interpreting and understanding its language. The provisions of national arbitration legislation in Model Law jurisdictions that do not deviate from its text assume the same meaning as the model.[156]

National judges are members of the international arbitration interpretative community but from a different perspective. They engage in an interpretative decision-making exercise. They are charged with *applying* the Model Law through the domestic arbitration law that adopts it rather than interpreting it for general regulatory purposes. This is particularly evident in an Article 8 scenario. That provision speaks directly to judges, as it regulates their behaviour in any substantive action covered by an arbitration agreement. In that situation, the adoption of an interpretative method is also a choice,[157] which should be in line with or be 'the continuation of the decisions of states to create a distinct regime in the first place.'[158]

In this understanding, judges in Model Law jurisdictions are responsible for interpreting it with an eye on its international uniform application (Article 2A),[159] constituting what Slaughter calls a 'global community of courts'.[160]

Although national judges are grounded in a specific jurisdiction and a body of law, they are also part of a larger system (transnational dispute resolution). Talking about judges of 'one global legal system' might be a stretch; instead, they constitute a global *community of courts*. Slaughter believes that that community is formed by the

Interpretive Communities (Harvard University Press, 1980), p. 171. Also, for Fish, interpretative communities bear linguistic and contextual meaning. The instrument under interpretation (e.g., an arbitration statute) is an institutional (rather than natural) object. It is for this reason that Spaak notes that in Fish's position, 'a person will find in a text what he is looking for.' Spaak, *Relativism in Legal Thinking* (n. 91), pp. 160-161.

156. Article 2 of *International Arbitration Act* (South Africa) (19 December 2017) explicitly puts it in these terms: 'A word or expression used in Chapter 2 of this Act bears the same meaning as it has in the Model Law, unless inconsistent with the context and the Constitution.'

157. This highlights the 'desire', 'willingness' and 'determination' factor (rather than an obligation), to look beyond national boundaries and adopt a consistent interpretative approach.

158. Waibel, *Interpretive Communities in International Law* (n. 152), p. 164. Consequently, Waible also notes that '[w]hether national courts are a source of fragmentation or a source of integration depends partly on whether they use the same interpretative methodology, and what role interpretative communities along national lines play. Michael Waibel, 'Principles of Treaty Interpretation: Developed for and Applied by National Courts?,' in *The Interpretation of International Law by Domestic Courts: Uniformity, Diversity, Convergence*, ed. Helmut Philipp Aust and Nolte Nolte (Oxford University Press, 2016), p. 17.

159. Article 2A Model Law: '1. In the interpretation of this Law, regard is to be had to its international origin and to the need to promote uniformity in its application … .'

160. Slaughter, *A Global Community of Courts* (n. 127).

self-awareness of the role of national and international judges.[161] Waibel adds that to become a genuine community of courts, the members must 'share the common values and principles that constitute the normative understandings of a community'.[162]

In theory (and ideally), the outcome of these actors' interpretative exercise should not differ depending on the individual interpreter (e.g., judges sitting in different jurisdictions). That would ignore the very purpose for adopting the Model Law and the objectives for establishing UNCITRAL. Significantly, it would eclipse the internationally uniform regime that the interpreter's own State intended to contribute to by implementing the Model Law in the national framework. More generally, it would also undermine the value of certainty and predictability.[163] This is why there should be coherence in interpretative rules, be they the Vienna Convention rules or others. The point is that the uniform application of uniform law requires uniform interpretative rules.

With that in mind, the following section proposes a distinct strategy for interpreting the Model Law and the national arbitration laws that implement it. Emphasis is placed on internationality and uniformity.

[E] THE PROPOSED INTERPRETATIVE APPROACH

Relying on parochial methodologies to interpret a domestic arbitration law that incorporates the Model Law risks distorting the Model Law's double aspiration: to be both international and local.[164] It has an international origin but is intended for local application – in an internationally uniform fashion.

Its applied uniformity across jurisdictions would be better served by relying on the Vienna Convention's harmonised principles of interpretation to complement the interpretative guidance of Article 2A of the Model Law.

Understood correctly, this proposition is that Articles 31-32 of the Vienna Convention should inform, guide, or inspire the interpretative approach to the Model Law. In other words, the proposition should not be understood as stating that model laws fall within the scope of the Vienna Convention, which *applies* only to treaties.[165] And the Model Law is not a treaty. As indicated in more detail above, the Model Law is an international legal instrument resulting from the negotiating and drafting efforts of States members of the United Nations and relevant international arbitration organisations. It does not bind those States, but it guides national legislative actions

161. *Ibid.*, pp. 192, 194, 197.
162. Waibel, *Interpretive Communities in International Law* (n. 152), p. 215.
163. Helmut Philipp Aust, 'Between Universal Aspiration and Local Application', in *The Interpretation of International Law by Domestic Courts: Uniformity, Diversity, Convergence*, ed. Helmut Philipp Aust and Nolte Nolte (Oxford University Press, 2016), p. 343 ('[T]he rules of interpretation fulfil an important role in ensuring that those who will be affected by decisions can anticipate interpretative outcomes, at least within a range of permissible interpretative results.').
164. This is a characteristic typically recognised in international law, which should be interpreted uniformly regardless of geographical differences. At the same time, it aspires to have concrete local meaning and relevance. *See*, Helmut, *ibid.* pp. 333-336.
165. Vienna Convention, Article 1.

worldwide, whether or not a State participated in its drafting. However, treaties are binding agreements between contracting states and are governed by international law.[166]

Although model laws and treaties are of a different legal nature and character, they share essential features and goals. They are international instruments designed to create a normative synergy to regulate matters in a unified way. This is evident from the legal ecosystem that the United Nations and UNCITRAL created for international arbitration law. As described earlier, the Model Law was engineered to interplay with and complement the New York Convention.[167] These instruments, individually considered, form part of a unified legal framework and do not constitute compartmentalised, self-reliant legal instruments.[168] Consequently, the relationship between these instruments has a reciprocal bearing on their interpretation and application.

An illustration of the influence of the New York Convention on the interpretation of the Model Law can be found in a decision of the High Court of Australia. In the *TCL* case, the Court concluded that given their special relationship, the Model Law had to be construed in context and in light of the object and purpose of the New York Convention.[169]

Considering that the Vienna Convention must be applied to interpret the New York Convention, there is no plausible reason why its interpretative rules could not permeate the interpretation of the Model Law.

Admittedly, this proposition is not entirely novel. Bachand, for example, suggests that the interpretative rules of the Vienna Convention are suitable to guide the interpretation of model laws because they are 'transnational normative instruments that seek to unify the law governing certain matters through uniform legislative provisions'.[170] Similarly, Lewis' starting general proposition is that the Model Law's interpretative method can be compared with the one for treaty interpretation.[171]

In more general terms, Mann recognises that the Vienna Convention was designed primarily to regulate relationships between States under public international law. Yet, for legal interpretation, the author does not find a crucial difference between a treaty and an international instrument that governs relationships between private persons and has a legal uniformity objective. Mann, therefore, concludes that Articles 31 and 32 would apply to both types of instruments.[172] Although dealing with the

166. *Ibid.*, Article 2.
167. *See* Chapter 2, section [B][3] above.
168. UN General Assembly 40/72, para. 4. *See* Renaud Soriel, The Influence of the New York Convention on the UNCITRAL Model Law on International Commercial Arbitration, 2 *Dispute Resolution International*, no. 1 (2008).
169. *TCL Air v. Castel*, [2013] HCA 5, para. 8.
170. Bachand, *Judicial Internationalism* (n. 96), pp. 242-251.
171. Dean Lewis, *The Interpretation and Uniformity of the UNCITRAL Model Law on International Commercial Arbitration: Focusing on Australia, Hong Kong and Singapore* (Kluwer Law International, 2016), p. 53. However, the author suggests an internationalist approach to the interpretation of the Model Law which involves at least one of three standards or norms: (i) a conscious decision to adopt an internationalist attitude, (ii) regard to the Model Law's *travaux preparatoire*, and (iii) regard to international case law (*see* pp. 58-59).
172. Francis A. Mann, Uniform Statutes in English Law, 94 *Law Quarterly Review* (1983) p. 378 DOI: 10.1093/oso/9780198252474.003.0010. Rau suggests that principles of interpretation like those

Model Law on Cross-Border Insolvency and not arbitration law, the Full Federal Court of Appeal of Australia elucidated that it was 'unnecessary to express in any detail the principles governing the interpretation of international instruments. Reference must be made in the first instance to the Vienna Convention on the Laws of Treaties'.[173]

The usefulness of following the Vienna Convention's interpretative rules to guide the interpretation of the Model Law appears perhaps more evident where the New York Convention regulates the same legal issue. Take, for example, the case where a national court is seized of an action covered by an arbitration agreement. Both the Model Law and the New York Convention address this situation in the same way, as Article 8(1) of the Model Law echoes the language of Article II(3) of the New York Convention. According to the Vienna Convention, Article II(3) must be construed under its general rule, following the primary and supplementary means outlined in Articles 31 and 32. Given its relationship with the New York Convention, its international origin and its cross-borders unification objective, the Model Law could (and even should) be interpreted in accordance with the *same analytical framework*.[174]

This proposed approach is consistent with Article 2A(1) of the Model Law, according to which judges should approach the interpretation of national arbitration law, bearing in mind the international instruments behind it, rather than considering it as purely domestic legislation. By adopting the Model Law, national legislators give effect to an international instrument's substantive provisions, which seek a specific unification goal and a specific purpose. The terms, rights, obligations, values and policies set out in the domestic law assume the meaning and extent under the Model Law.[175] In turn, the internationally negotiated instrument (Model Law) is in strict alignment with the New York Convention. Therefore, the customary international interpretative guidelines codified in the Vienna Convention should assist in reading the Model Law and the domestic legislation that adopts it.

Again, as acknowledged a few paragraphs earlier, this publication is not about the theory of treaty interpretation and its suitability for interpreting the Model Law. To avoid lengthy discussions and justifications on that point, this work proposes an 'international arbitration' approach for interpreting the Model Law and laws that adopt it without deviations. A nuanced interpretative strategy rooted in Article 2A of the

in the Vienna Convention can be found also in statutory and contract interpretation; Alan Scott Rau et al., BG Group and Conditions to Arbitral Jurisdiction, 43 *Pepperdine Law Review*, no. Special Supp. (2016), pp. 148-149.

173. *De Akers as a joint foreign representative of Saad Investments Company Limited (in Official Liquidation) v. Deputy Commissioner of Taxation*, [2014] FCAFC 57, Federal Court of Australia, 14 May 2014.

174. Some authors have advanced a different opinion, indicating that where a Model Law has its own interpretative article, recourse to the Vienna Convention is not allowed; *see, e.g.*, Bruno Zeller et al., The Transnational Dimension of Statutory Interpretation–Tragically Overlooked in a Global Commercial Environment, 1 *Nordic Journal of Commercial Law* (2019), pp. 13-14.

175. A similar process takes place in jurisdictions that give effect to a treaty by passing national legislation adopting the words of the treaty itself, or by adapting it to their own legislative provisions. In either case, the interpretation and application is that of the international instrument, not the (domestic) implementing legislation. For a discussion on the monist and dualist approaches to international law, *see, in general*, Crawford, *The Relations of International and National Law* (n. 72), pp. 45-104.

Model Law and modelled on and inspired by the Vienna Convention. This approach is not textual, purposive, or any other method in a pure form. It is an 'autonomous' approach that combines various interpretative techniques (like the Vienna Convention does). It is an approach to legal interpretation that focuses on: (i) the text of the Model Law, (ii) the internal and structural context of each provision, and (iii) in light of their purpose and that of the legal instrument as a whole. This last point signals the need to keep an eye on the systemic coherence and consistency of the several provisions of the Model Law (and the New York Convention).[176] It also ensures that the interpretation will serve as a connection between the Model Law and the New York Convention, which creates the backbone of an efficient and effective international arbitration system.

Under this view, several sources inform the context and the purpose of the Model Law; these will be addressed below. Preparatory works have a special role in identifying the instrument's context, purpose, and the drafters' understandings and agreements when choosing its language. This does not turn the approach into a historical-intentionalist one.[177]

Naturally, interpreting the Model Law requires pondering the words UNCITRAL used,[178] considering the instrument's goal, purpose, and observance of good faith.[179] This directs the interpreter to exclude a pure textualist approach and embrace elements of the purposive one.[180] The purpose of the Model Law is a safe lighthouse that guides the interpretive process where the language used may allow conflicting meanings. Where the language is plain, clear, and unambiguous, the purpose supports and confirms the meaning of the text and should not override it.

[1] The Legal Text and Its Context

As a starting point, the text of Article 8 of the Model Law (and II(3) New York Convention) is of great importance. This positive element of the law sets the limits of

176. The synergy between the Model Law and the New York Convention requires the interpreter to view the Convention and the Model Law as part of the same 'distinct' system.
177. I do not claim this to be a novel proposition. An example of a comprehensive approach to legal interpretation can be found in the decision of the Canadian Supreme Court in the *R. v. Big* case, where the court reasoned that a statute should be construed by reference to the character and the larger objects of the statute itself, to the language chosen to articulate the specific provision, to the historical origins of the concepts enshrined, and where applicable, to the meaning and purpose of the other specific provisions with which it is associated within the text of the specific provision. *R. v. Big M Drug Mart Ltd.*, [1985] 1 SCR 295, 1985 CanLII 69 (SCC), Supreme Court of Canada, 24 April 1985, paras 116-117.
178. This was spelt out, for example, by the highest court of appeal in Australia for the process of statutory interpretation, indicating that '[t]he process of construction begins with a consideration of the ordinary and grammatical meaning of the words of the provision having regard to their context and legislative purpose'; *Education Union v. Department of Education* [2012] HCA 3, para. 26.
179. Article 2A of the Model Law.
180. It also avoids being content with the etymology of the word, but rather with the more technical meaning of the term.

its interpretation and provides the content of the text's purpose.[181] Because no provision or article of the Model Law stands alone, they must be read harmoniously with its context and overall purpose.[182]

The context requires consideration of other provisions in the Model Law and the instrument as a whole, including the preamble and annexes. As judge and philosopher L. Hand put it, '[t]he meaning of a sentence may be more than that of the separate words, as a melody is more than the notes, and no degree of particularity can ever obviate recourse to the setting in which all appear, and which all collectively create'.[183] The different provisions in a statute constitute integral parts of what Barak calls a 'legislative alignment', which, as a whole, influence the legislative purpose of the instrument.[184] In turn, the statute should be considered part of a legislative structure. It is influenced and influences the system's fundamental values.

The subject of the legislation, the way it is organised, and the interplay between them provide a foundation for inferring its purpose. The systematic layout and structure of its provisions, and the specific matters addressed, could suggest the goals that the law intends to accomplish.

In this understanding, the language of Article 8(1) of the Model Law is construed here considering the whole article, including its second paragraph, and its interaction with the principle of minimum curial intervention (Article 5), competence-competence (Article 16(1)), and court control of arbitral jurisdictional decisions (Articles 16(3), 34 and 36).

[2] Extrinsic Sources

The interpreter also learns about the context and purpose of the law from extrinsic sources.[185] In the Model Law framework, the records of its preparatory works are a rich source of information. They elucidate the meaning of the terms used and the purpose that UNCITRAL envisioned achieving. The Full Federal Court of Australia highlighted and accepted their relevance in *Comandate Marine v. Pan Australia,* where it held that:

> The proper construction and interpretation of the International Arbitration Act, in respect of its implementation of the New York Convention and the Model Law, requires an understanding of the context of those international instruments and an

181. *See* Aharon Barak, *Purposive Interpretation in Law* (Princeton University Press, 2007), pp. 92, 157-158.
182. For example, in the *Hunter v. Southam* case, the Supreme Court of Canada explained that the interpreter should first delineate the nature of the interest that a given legal provision is intended to protect, within the larger context in which the provision is found. *Hunter et al. v. Southam Inc.,* 1984 CanLII 33 (SCC), Supreme Court of Canada, 17 September 1984, pp. 154-157.
183. *Helvering v. Gregory,* 69 F. 2d 809, US Court of Appeals, 2nd Circuit, 19 March 1934, pp. 810-811.
184. Barak, *Purposive Interpretation* (n. 181), p. 160.
185. In the words of Chief Justice Marshall of the USA Supreme Court, '[w]here the mind labours to discover the design of the legislature, it seizes everything from which aid can be derived'; *The United States v. Fisher et al. Assigness of Blight, A. Bankrupt,* 6 US 358, 2 L. Ed. 304, US Supreme Court, p. 386.

understanding of the subjects of concern and debate in the Working Groups, meetings and other discussion leading up to their formation.[186]

In some legal traditions, a statute's legislative history cannot be considered during the interpretative exercise. In others, domestic law explicitly directs the interpreter to consider the instrument's parliamentary discussions and negotiations. For example, the arbitration legislation in Singapore, Bermuda, Australia, New Zealand, Mauritius, and Fiji provides that in interpreting the law, reference may be made to the working papers that led to the preparation and adoption of the Model Law.[187]

Preparatory works carry a distinctive weight in the interpretation of the Model Law. Bachand, amongst others, notes that courts should give them a more predominant role than the supplementary one indicated in Article 32 of the Vienna Convention. This is because the UN General Assembly specifically recommended sending them to the governments annexed to the text of the Model Law as an interpretative tool.[188] It can be argued, then, that they form part of the primary means of interpretation, in line with Article 31(2) of the Vienna Convention.[189]

When studying the Model Law's preparatory works, it is important to distinguish the type of information they record and their effect on the interpretative exercise. For example, preparatory works may reveal that the instrument's drafters reached an agreement on the exclusion of specific terms or the inclusion and intended meaning of the terms used. On the contrary, the records could simply reflect opinions but show that the issue was left without conclusion, to be shaped by national laws or subsequent practice. It appears almost intuitive that the first scenario is more influential in construing a provision, especially because the Model Law was drafted by experts in international arbitration law and practice.

Consequently, given the exceptional interpretative value of these preparatory works, it could be argued that the drafters' agreements form part of the context that the interpreter must consider in addition to the text of the instrument, in the sense of Article 31(4) of the Vienna Convention.[190]

In addition to the records of the discussions at each meeting of the Working Group and the Model Law's Explanatory Note, this work includes a study of the Analytical Commentary on the Draft Text of the Model Law prepared by the Secretariat. The Analytical Commentary provides a '*summary of why a certain provision has been*

186. *Comandate Marine Corp. v. Pan Australia Shipping Pty. Ltd*, [2006] FCAFC 192, Federal Court of Australia, 20 December 2006, para. 191.
187. Singapore International Arbitration Act, Article 4.1., Bermuda International Conciliation and Arbitration Act 1993, section 24; International Arbitration Act of Australia, section 17, the New Zealand Arbitration Act, Article 3, the Mauritius Arbitration Act, Article 3C, and the Fiji International Arbitration Act 2017, sections 5(1)-5(3).
188. Bachand, *Judicial Internationalism* (n. 96), pp. 249-250. *See also*, Resolution 40/72, para. 4.
189. Vienna Convention, 'General Rule of Interpretation', Article 31(2): 'The context for the purpose of the interpretation of a treaty shall comprise, in addition to the text, including its preamble and annexes … .'
190. Article 31(4) provides: 'A special meaning shall be given to a term if it is established that the parties so intended.' But this proposition contrasts with treaty interpretation, where the parties' intended 'special meaning' cannot be found in the preparatory works, but in the other documents referred to in Article 31(2). *See*, Gardiner, *Treaty Interpretation* (n. 124), pp. 335-337.

adopted and what it is intended to cover, often accompanied by explanations and interpretations of particular words...'.[191]

However valuable a source of information, preparatory works should not determine or impose a static reading of the law (and model laws), frozen at the time of its adoption.[192] The meaning and the context of the law advance with new realities. Therefore, the interpretation of arbitration law must be dynamic to serve and respond to the changing needs of modern societies and business practices.

The developments in arbitration practice[193] and scholarly works[194] can also be considered valuable sources for interpreting the Model Law. Many principles of international arbitration have arisen and evolved along with international arbitration practice. Practices developed by arbitration users reflect their dispute resolution needs in facilitating business transactions. When considering international arbitration practice, judges should be mindful of their responsibility in articulating and orienting the objectives of the law that they are called upon to interpret and apply.[195] This work considers scholarly works and the opinions of leading practitioners in international arbitration. Those authorities, however, are regarded and referred to only to confirm the interpretative results reached or to open a debate when it contradicts them. They are not relied on as a primary source to give meaning to the language of Article 8(1) of the Model Law.

[3] Case Law

Case law is a tool to give (a dynamic) meaning to the provisions of the statute under interpretation. To achieve the highest degree of applied uniformity of the Model Law, the interpreter can seek guidance in domestic and foreign judicial precedent and the international consensus that those decisions might form. This idea is reinforced by the Model Law's reference to its uniform-application objective, which is of an international dimension. To achieve that objective, it is almost expected for judges to consider how other courts interpret and apply the same text. Especially where '[j]udicial deference to

191. UN, Analytical Commentary on Draft text of a Model Law on International Commercial Arbitration: Report of the Secretary-General, 18th session A/CN.9/264 (25 March 1985), p. 4, para. 5 (emphasis added).
192. Emil Lask et al., *TheLlegal Philosophies of Lask, Radbruch, and Dabin*, Kurt Wilk, Reprint 2014 ed., Twentieth Century Legal Philosophy Series (Harvard University Press, 1950), pp. 141-142.
193. Authoritative commentators on the Model Law are of the same opinion. *See, e.g.*, Howard M. Holtzmann et al., *A Guide to the 2006 Amendments to the UNCITRAL Model Law on International Commercial Arbitration* (Wolters Kluwer, 2015), p. 25.
194. In *Fung Sang v. kai Sun*, for example, Judge Kaplan recognised that not only the preparatory works for the Model Law but also scholarly works aid its interpretation. In particular, the judge highlighted the usefulness of two books for that task: 'A Guide to the UNCITRAL Model Law on International Commercial Arbitration' written by Howard Holtzmann and Joseph Neuhaus, and Aron Broches' 'Commentary on the UNCITRAL Model Law'; *Fung Sang Trading Ltd v. Kai Sun Sea Products & Food Co. Ltd*, [1991] HKCFI 190, High Court of Kong Kong, 29 October 1991, paras 46-51.
195. *See, e.g.*, Fabien Gélinas, Peeking Through the Form of Uniform Law: International Arbitration Practice and Legal Harmonization, 27 *Journal of International Arbitration*, no. 3 (2010) at p. 323 DOI: 10.54648/joia2010018. Also, *see in general*, Stacy I. Strong, *Research and Practice in International Commercial Arbitration* (Oxford University Press, 2009), pp. 9-37.

foreign courts is based on efficiency, fairness, and the "ends of justice" rather than on sovereign prerogatives'.[196]

In general terms, foreign case law provides guidance and inspiration for the new interpreter to grasp the meaning and the purpose that the text is intended to accomplish.[197] Even more so where the legal provision is textually the same (e.g., Article 8(1)), the legal instrument it forms a part of is based on an international instrument of a unification and harmonisation nature (like the Model Law), and the identity of its intellectual originator is the same (UNCITRAL).

Case law from other Model Law jurisdictions can show the interpreter the result that may be accomplished by interpreting and applying the common text with a shared purpose. Those foreign decisions may dissipate interpretation and application uncertainties and help maintain the harmony and consistency of that legislative purpose. In this scenario, the national judge becomes an international judge in a matrix of courts that interpret and apply the Model Law. This reflects Dworkin's idea of each judge being a link in a continuous chain of case law but at a cross-border level.[198]

A court in a Model Law jurisdiction highlighted how crucial it is to consider foreign case law and other sources when construing local arbitration legislation. That court held that:

> ... it is not only appropriate, but essential, to pay due regard to the reasoned decisions of other countries where their laws are either based on, or take their content from, international conventions or instruments such as the New York Convention and the Model Law. It is of the first importance to attempt to create or maintain, as far as the language employed by Parliament in the I[nternational] A[rbitration] A[ct] permits, a degree of international harmony and concordance of approach to international commercial arbitration. (...) Where there has been extensive discussion and negotiation of the model law under the auspices of ... UNCITRAL, and where the Model Law has been adopted by the General Assembly of the United Nations with the recommendation of 'due consideration'... to advance a uniformity of approach, the same respect for, and where necessary, sensitivity or deference to, reasoned decisions of other countries, should be shown.[199]

196. Slaughter, *A Global Community of Courts* (n. 127), p. 210. Also, William Burke-White, International Legal Pluralism, 25 *Michigan Journal of International Law*, no. 4 (2003), p. 979 ('[A] pluralist system will operate most effectively if it is closely linked to ... interjudicial dialogue.'). As Zeller and Andersen put it, 'shared international laws, in convention format or springing from Model Laws (...) have to be interpreted with an eye to how others are applying and interpreting them, so this cannot happen purely in domestic settings'; Zeller et al., *The Transnational Dimension of Statutory Interpretation* (n. 174), pp. 7-8.
197. Slaughter, *A Global Community of Courts* (n. 127), p. 201. ([L]ooking abroad simply helps [judges] do a better job at home, in the sense that they can approach a particular problem more creatively or with greater insight. ... Evidence of like-minded foreign decisions could enhance the legitimacy of a particular opinion.).
198. Ronald Dworkin, Law as Interpretation, 60 *Texas Law Review*, no. 3 (1982), pp. 540-546. *See also*, Emmanuel Gaillard, *Legal Theory of International Arbitration* (n. 19), p. 59, where the author considers that status of 'international judge' that some courts accord to arbitrators illustrates the fact that arbitrators can today be considered to be the organs of a distinct (autonomous) legal order.
199. *TCL Air Conditioner (Zhongshan) Co Ltd v. Castel Electronics Pty Ltd*, [2014] FCAFC 83, Federal Court of Australia, 16 July 2014, para. 75.

Bearing in mind the close relationship between the Model Law and the New York Convention and that both instruments regulate certain issues in a harmonised manner and even with the same language,[200] court decisions based on one instrument become relevant for the interpretation of the other.

Authoritative commentary has also concluded that considering the Model Law's international origin and uniformity objective, courts should take heed of international and foreign sources.[201] This conclusion is coherent with UNCITRAL case law reporting systems developed to facilitate the uniform interpretation and application of its instruments.[202]

At a more general level, some authors advocate the use of 'global jurisconsultorium' to encourage courts, arbitrators, and practitioners to embrace a uniform and transnational interpretation and application of shared legal concepts.[203] Global jurisconsultorium refers to the *duty* to consider and find inspiration in foreign sources and judicial precedent.[204] Similarly, other authors indicate that judges should engage in what is known as judicial internationalism.[205]

But considering foreign court decisions is only one half of the equation. The decision-maker must then assign them a value. Given that no international arbitration stare decisis exists, examining foreign case law serves to benefit from the persuasiveness of reasoning and deliberations rather than to borrow outcomes.[206]

Some authors go a step further and suggest that the interpretation of domestic arbitration legislation in Model Law jurisdictions should follow a two-fold approach that gives pre-eminence to case law. Courts should first engage in a comparative analysis to determine whether there is an international consensus on the disputed issue.[207] If the question has been considered and consistently answered in a significant

200. For example, Articles II(3) and V of the New York Convention; and Articles 8(1), 34 and 36 of the Model Law.
201. *See*, Howard M. Holtzmann et al., *A Guide to the 2006 Amendments to the UNCITRAL Model Law* (n. 193) pp. 24-27; Gélinas, *Peeking Through the Form of Uniform Law*, p. 323.
202. CLOUT, the Digest of Case Law on the Model Law, and the Guide on the New York Convention. All of them are available online and access is free of charge. *See* https://uncitral.un.org/en/case_law.
203. Camilla Baasch Andersen, A New Challenge for Commercial Practitioners: Making the Most of Shared Laws and Their Jurisconsultorium, 38 *University of New South Wales Law Journal*, no. 3 (2015), p. 923.
204. Andersen's comments of the global jurisconsultorium approach are in the context of the CISG, not of a model law. Although the different legal nature of these instruments is relevant, the rules of interpretation under Article 7 of the CISG and Article 2A of the Model Law are similar. This reflects the common uniformity purpose of both UNCITRAL instruments, which, in turn, is in line with UNCITRAL's mandate. *Ibid.*, p. 923.
205. *See generally*, Frédéric Bachand, Court Intervention in International Arbitration: The Case for Compulsory Judicial Internationalism, 1 *Journal of Dispute Resolution* (2012). *See also*, Jeremy Waldron, *'Partly Laws Common to All Mankind': Foreign Law in American Courts* (Yale University Press, 2012); Thomas H. Bingham, *Widening Horizons: The Influence of Comparative Law and International Law on Domestic Law*, vol. 61 (Cambridge University Press, 2010).
206. *See* Slaughter, *A Global Community of Courts* (n. 127), pp. 192, 197, 200.
207. Bachand, *Judicial Internationalism* (n. 96), p. 240. This is the position taken in Singapore and increasingly in Germany; *See*, in general, Q. Loh, 'Judicial Internationalism and International Interpretation – The Singapore Experience', *ibid.*, pp. 185-215; M. Lorbacher, 'A German Judicial Perspective on International Interpretation', *ibid.*, pp. 217-227. Similarly, *see* Frédéric Bachand et al., 'Interpreting the Model Law: Methodology and the Singapore Experience', in

number of cases, the court should give the utmost consideration to that consensus. Although not formally binding, the court should generally treat such consensus as determinative.[208] This first step will resonate familiar amongst practitioners from civil law traditions, for it reflects the doctrine of *jurisprudence constante*, which compares to the stare decisis of common law traditions.

Bachand's proposed approach entails a subsidiary step. If there is not a single internationally acceptable answer to the question at issue, the court's analysis should seek to identify whether there is an agreement on one preferred solution.[209] If there is no significant internationally acceptable answer, courts should avoid following interpretative methods usually suitable in purely domestic cases. They should, instead, engage in an interpretative exercise following the rules that are better suited to achieve the purpose of the Model Law.[210]

As described above in this chapter, this work takes a different position. It proposes that the interpreter of national arbitration laws based on the Model Law should always engage in a special interpretative exercise, not leave it as a last resort step. Advancing better legal reasoning requires that each interpreter weighs in the persuasiveness of foreign cases rather than borrow them and their outcome.[211] This approach is followed in the next Chapter of this book, which analyses court decisions from Model Law jurisdictions.

[F] CONCLUSION

This chapter has presented and justified applying a nuanced international approach to interpreting the Model Law and national arbitration law based on it. That approach focuses on the text, context, and purpose of the legal instrument. Chapters 5 to 7 of this book follow this approach to interpret Article 8(1) of the Model Law.

Singapore International Arbitration: Law & Practice, ed. David Joseph QC and David Foxton QC (Singapore: LexisNexis, 2014), pp. 540-552.

208. Bachand, *Judicial Internationalism* (n. 96), pp. 240-241. Also, Bachand et al., *Interpreting the Model Law*, *ibid.*, p. 546. *See also*, Slaughter, *A Global Community of Courts*, p. 200, who emphasises that the important point when considering foreign case law is the proper use of 'persuasive, as opposed to precedential, authority'.
209. Bachand, *Judicial Internationalism*, p. 242.
210. *Ibid.*, p. 242.
211. Munroe Smith, *A General View of European Legal History and Other Papers* (Columbia University Press, 1927), p. 345 ('The rules and principles of case-law have never been treated as final truths but as working hypotheses, continually retested in those great laboratories of the law, the courts of justice.').

CHAPTER 4

Court Interpretation and Application of the Model Law

[A] INTRODUCTION

This chapter presents and analyses case law, which in this book is considered a necessary and influential means to assist legal interpretation (Chapter 3 above).[212]

As discussed in Chapter 3, predictability is one of the aims that drive uniformity of laws. Given its uniformity goal, the interpretative end result in Model Law jurisdictions is expected to be highly similar. A repeated judicial interpretative result across jurisdictions could reflect a consensus on the meaning of its provisions. This is especially the case where new decisions inquire and consider how courts in other Model Law jurisdictions have answered the same interpretative question. However, despite the similar outcomes in some jurisdictions, the discussions below reveal no *global* consensus regarding the interpretation of Article 8(1).

[B] SAMPLING AND ANALYSIS OF CASE LAW

This chapter involves qualitative elements and considerations rather than quantitative ones. For the purpose of analysis, this chapter considers a sample of court decisions that illustrate diverse views of the court's role when dealing with Article 8(1) actions. It proceeds upon the footing that the text of the local arbitration law is textually uniform with the Model Law. And that adopting the *prima facie* or the full merits standard of

212. In other contexts, and for some authors, case law might have a more significant value and role. The precedent that case law might create would constitute the law itself and not only become a component of legal interpretation. For Holmes, for example, '[t]he prophecies of what the courts will do in fact, and nothing more pretentious, are what I mean by the law'. Oliver Wendell Holmes, The Path of the Law, 110 *Harvard Law Review*, no. 5 (1997), p. 994 DOI: 10.1515/9780691186429-003.

review at the threshold of arbitration is a matter of statutory interpretation. It ultimately seeks to identify the judicial reasoning that most closely fits the language of the law in its context and according to the purpose that UNCITRAL aimed to achieve when adopting the Model Law.

[1] The Case Law Sampling

A total of eighty-eight States in 121 jurisdictions have adopted the Model Law.[213] It would not be realistic to thoroughly examine the implementation and interpretation of the Model Law in each of them and the case law produced by their courts. With this in mind, this work examines case law that illustrates the reasoning behind the *prima facie* and the full review approaches. It does not conduct a comparative analysis of practices between specific countries.

The divide between approaches does not arise from one jurisdiction to another or is based on different legal texts. The text is that of the Model Law,[214] embodied in national laws, and courts within the same State or jurisdiction have, at times, adopted opposing views when interpreting and applying their national arbitration legislation (and the Model Law).

The text of the legal instrument that this study synthesises (the Model Law) is not concerned with sovereignty and political boundaries. It transcends them. The court decisions considered here represent UNCITRAL and its Model Law's reach. The judgments commented on in this chapter are from several Model Law jurisdictions across Asia, Africa, North, Central and South America, Europe and Oceania. The judgments were rendered by Supreme Courts, Courts of Appeals and lower courts of both civil and common law traditions.

Some decisions from England are also commented on. Despite not being a Model Law jurisdiction, England enjoys a highly influential role in international arbitration.[215] This study shows that English case law influences even the interpretation of national legislation that has adopted the Model Law.

Notably, despite their textual dissimilarities, the UNCITRAL Model Law heavily influenced the drafting of the English Arbitration Act 1996. In the *Report on the Arbitration Bill*, Lord Justice Saville stated 'that at every stage in preparing a new draft Bill, very close regard was paid to the Model Law, and it will be seen that both the structure and the content (...) owe much to this model'.[216]

---

213. *Source*: UNCITRAL, Texts and Status: https://uncitral.un.org/en/texts/arbitration/modellaw/commercial_arbitration/status (Last accessed 4 October 2023).
214. Article 8(1) of the Model Law, which, in turn, mirrors Article II(3) of the New York Convention.
215. According to the Queen Mary University of London and White & Case annual survey, London is one of the most regularly chosen seats for international arbitrations. Three frequently mentioned reasons for its reputation are: its arbitration law, track record in enforcing agreements to arbitrate and arbitral awards, and the local courts and judiciary's support for arbitration (*see, e.g.*, the results of the surveys for the years 2021, 2020, 2019, 2018, 2016). Available at www.arbitration.qmul.ac.uk/research.
216. Lord Justice Saville, Departmental Advisory Committee on Arbitration Law 1996 Report on the Arbitration Bill 13, *Arbitration International*, no. 3 (1997), p. 275 DOI: 10.1093/arbitration/13.3.275.

The English Court of Appeal has also confirmed the value and influence of the Model Law in the local arbitration law. In *Patel v. Patel*, Lord Woolf M.R. observed that 'the terms of the UNCITRAL Model Law on International Commercial Arbitration (1985) should be considered because it is clear that those who are responsible for drafting the [1996 English Arbitration] Act had the provisions of the Model Law in mind when doing so'.[217]

For these reasons, this study examines some English decisions on the approach to the standard of review at the referral to arbitration stage.

[2] The Analysis of Case Law

The analysis of court decisions is qualitative rather than quantitative. Most of the national laws in Model Law jurisdictions do not significantly deviate from the language of its Article 8, which would validate the adoption of one review test to the total exclusion of the other. This work proceeds upon the assumption that the local arbitration and the Model Law share a sufficient degree of textual uniformity to allow a uniform outcome. Therefore, unless otherwise indicated, it should be assumed that there is textual uniformity between Article 8 of the Model Law and the local arbitration law under which the court decides the jurisdictional threshold question.

The analysis seeks to identify a pattern of interpretation and implementation of the Model Law and its impact on the adoption of the *prima facie* or full review of jurisdictional issues at the outset of an arbitration. In particular, whether the court read the text of Article 8(1) in its context, considered its drafting history, foreign case law, leading international commentators, and the hierarchical weight given to those sources.

Lastly, the analysis considers whether the court weighed the Model Law's international origin, its uniformity goal (Article 2A Model Law), and the policy the court intended to protect or prioritise. These concerns are closely connected and are central to the interpretative approach discussed in Chapter 3, section [E] above.

[C] THE PRIMA FACIE APPROACH

Some national courts have concluded that Article 8(1) of the Model Law (and corresponding Article II(3) New York Convention[218]) imposes or requires a limited examination of jurisdictional objections. The reasons vary and usually appear in a combination or a cumulative form.

One of the reasons is that the *prima facie* approach appears to be truthful to the competence-competence principle. Others are: respect for the parties' will, the role of arbitrators, the court's obligation of minimal intervention, the operation of the

217. Specifically, '[t]he new wording in section 9 of the Arbitration Act 1996 obviously originates from the UNCITRAL Model Law.'; *Patel (Jitendra) v. Patel (Dilesh)*, [1999] 3 W.L.R. 322, [2000] Q.B. 551, England and Wales Cour of Appeals, 24 March 1999.

218. *See* comments on the relationship between the Model Law and the New York Convention in Chapter 2, section [B][3].

presumptive validity of the arbitration agreement's principle and, more generally, the Model Law's pro-arbitration policy. These grounds are discussed in the following subsections.

[1] The Arbitrators Competence-Competence

Courts have held that applying the competence-competence principle requires, as a matter of course, a limited review of the jurisdictional challenge. The inquiry under Article 8(1) should aim to determine whether it appears, on a *prima facie* basis, that an obligation to arbitrate exists and that it covers the dispute.[219] Even 'where it is unclear if the arbitrator has jurisdiction, it is preferable to leave the issue to the arbitrator pursuant to the competence-competence principle'.[220] The court might subsequently review and decide the issue if a party requests it.

An opportunity to clarify the court's standard of review also arose in the High Court of Singapore in *Malini Ventura v. Knight Capital*. Judge Judith Prakash compared the dichotomy of the *prima facie* or full merits review with the brain teaser in the question: Which came first, the chicken or the egg?[221] She concluded that the competence-competence principle enshrined in the Model Law and the Singapore International Arbitration Act gives precedence to the arbitral tribunal. Consequently, arbitral tribunals should determine whether they enjoy jurisdiction over a particular dispute before national courts determine that question.[222] But, the judge did not explain where the rule of precedence stems from, especially because the text of the law is silent about it. It appears to assume a conflict of norms between the provisions that grant competence to courts and arbitrators and relies on the instrument's purpose (facilitating arbitration) to resolve it. However, it is doubtful whether the identification and consideration of the law's purpose are comprehensive or partial.

In recognising the negative effect of competence-competence,[223] the Supreme Court of Venezuela acknowledged that the term *prima facie* is vague. In clarifying its extent, it concluded that the court's review should be limited to the formal validity of the arbitration agreement (the in-writing requirement). Whether the parties have

219. *See, e.g., Sim Chay Koon and others v. NTUC Income Insurance Co-operative Limited,* [2015] SGCA 46, Singapore Court of Appeal, 20 August 2015, paras 4-5 ('The existence and applicability of the [competence-competence] doctrine means that as a general rule, where a party seeks to avoid its obligation to arbitrate its dispute, the court should undertake a restrained review of the facts and circumstances before it in order to determine whether it appears on a prima facie basis that there is an arbitration clause and that the dispute is caught by that clause.'). Similarly, *see* the dissenting opinion of Justice Thakker, C.K. in *S.B.P. & Co v. Patel Engineering Ltd. & Anr,* (2005) 8 SCC 618, Supreme Court of India, 26 October 2005, especially from para. 22.

220. *Ciano Trading & Services C.T. v. Skylink Aviation Inc.*, 2015 ONCA 89 (CanLII), Court of Appeal for Ontario, Canada, 9 February 2015, para. 7.

221. *Malini Ventura v. Knight Capital Pte Ltd and others,* [2015] SGHC 225, Singapore High Court, 27 August 2015, paras 1, 19.

222. *Ibid.*, paras 28, 36-37. The High Court of Singapore reviewed with approval this approach in *Maniach Pte Ltd v. L Capital Jones Ltd and another,* [2016] SGHC 65, High Court of Singapore, 22 April 2016, para. 60.

223. *See* comments in Chapter 1, section [C][1].

validly consented to arbitrate should be left for the arbitrators to decide first.[224] Again, the pro-arbitration policy transpires through judicial outcome, reached without a clear or explicit interpretative methodology.

Similarly, courts have found that the *prima facie* approach aligns with the obligation to respect party autonomy. If the parties to a contract have agreed to arbitrate their disputes, that agreement should be recognised and enforced. For example, a court reasoned that a mere allegation of contractual defect could not displace the authority of arbitrators to judge the arbitration agreement's validity. Accepting that 'would easily prevent the arbitration of disputes, thus departing from the original intention of the parties'.[225] Given the *bilateral* character of the bargain and agreement to arbitrate, a party should not be permitted to revoke it *unilaterally* by commencing a court action.[226]

That is precisely the recurrent issue in jurisdictional disputes. Jurisdictional challenges question the existence of the parties' consent to arbitration or its validity and enforceability. If it is clear and undisputed that the parties have agreed to arbitration, the law imposes on courts the obligation to discontinue the proceedings and refer the parties to arbitration. It is in situations where that agreement is disputed that the demarcation between the role of arbitrators and judges rises to the forefront.

[2] The Role of the Arbitrators and National Courts

Courts have explained that the *prima facie* standard of review is mindful and respectful of the role of arbitrators. It balances out judicial involvement in arbitration; Examining the jurisdictional matter further would be stepping over the arbitrator's function.[227] Therefore, a court engaging in a full review of the jurisdictional issue 'would constitute an "assault" to the jurisdiction of the arbitral tribunal',[228] or risk 'usurping' the role of the arbitrator. In the words of the Hong Kong Court of Appeal in *Triple V v. Star*:

224. *Astivenca Astilleros de Venezuela, C.A. v. Oceanlink Offshore*, Exp. No. 1067/2010, Venezuela, Tribunal Supremo de Justicia (Supreme Court of Justice), 3 November 2010.
225. *Camuzzi Argentina SA v. Sodigas Sur SA*, ED 185-125, National Court of Appeals (Comm), Argentina, 27 August 1999.
226. *Otto, Franke y Cía. c/ Provincia de Buenos Aires*, Fallos: 128:402, Argentina Supreme Court, 19 December 1918. This court decision adopting a *prima facie* approach was delivered almost seventy years ahead of the competence-competence principle finding normative reception in the UNCITRAL Model Law (Article 16(1)), and one hundred years prior to its statutory recognition in the court's country – Article 35(1) Argentina International Commercial Arbitration Law.
227. *Private Company 'Triple V' Inc v. Star (Universal) Co Ltd*, [1995] HKCA 617, Hong Kong Court of Appeal, 7 July 1995, para. 13. *See also*, *PCCW Global Ltd v. Interactive Communication Service Ltd* [2006] HKCA 434, Hong Kong Court of Appeal, 16 November 2006, para. 60. ('It is important for the court not to usurp the function of the arbitrators, and unless the point is clear, the matter should be stayed for arbitration.')
228. *Corporacion Cementera Argentina S.A. c Cia. Argentina de Motores Deutz Otto Legitimo S.A.*, La Ley 1948, 52, National Court of Appeals (Comm), Argentina, 31 July 1948. The same court reiterated this conclusion and adhered to the prima facie approach in *Peruzzotti Arturo v. Asociacion Argentina de Criadores de Aves, Conejos y Abejas*, La Ley, 76-324, National Court of Appeals (Comm), Chamber A (Argentina), 28 July 1954.

> If the judge were to go into the matter more deeply, he would, in effect be *usurping the function of the arbitrator*. Whilst, clearly, the judge had to make a judgment as to whether there existed an underlying agreement to arbitrate, he could do no more than to form a *prima facie* view.[229]

In *PCCW Global v. Interactive Communication*, the same Court of Appeal reiterated its position in the *Triple V* case. It held that to avoid *usurping the role of arbitrators*, courts should, as a matter of course, refuse to stay the proceedings only where the arbitration agreement is *clearly* unenforceable.[230]

As anticipated, along with discouraging dilatory strategies and facilitating arbitration, the *prima facie* approach has been found to be coherent with the general judicial non-intervention obligation that the Model Law imposes in Article 5.[231] For example, recalling a decision from Singapore, an Australian court clarified that the principle of 'minimal court intervention' equally applies to setting aside or enforcing arbitral awards and to stay proceedings under Article 8(1) Model Law.[232]

But, again, these court decisions did not engage in a rigorous statutory interpretation quest. Instead, they appear to have decided that the *prima facie* test is appropriate or justified as a policy matter for the advancement of arbitration.

Some decisions display such a strong policy direction that commencing a court action in breach of an (even putative) arbitration agreement faces an onerous cost sanction. For example, in addition to a limited jurisdictional review and decision (*prima facie* approach), some judges have found that imposing costs on an indemnity basis reaffirms party autonomy, facilitates arbitration, and is in line with the court's obligation to avoid interfering in arbitral proceedings. In this sense, the words of Judge Mimmie Chan in *Grandom v. Henry Wai* are illustrative:

> A party who takes an exceptional and high-risk strategy to challenge the validity of either an arbitral award or an arbitration agreement will have to take the risk and accept the higher costs consequences of its action, namely, costs on an indemnity basis.[233]

As noted elsewhere, combining a *prima facie* approach and indemnity costs may create a robust disincentive to breaching an arbitration agreement. However, it may also risk imposing an improperly high burden on a party that starts litigation relying on

229. *Triple V v. Star (Universal)*, [1995] HKCA 617, para. 13 (emphasis added).
230. *PCCW v. Interactive Communication*, [2006] HKCA 434, paras 49, 60 (emphasis added).
231. *See* analysis and discussion of Article 5 Model Law in Chapter 7, section 7.2.
232. *See Robotunits Pty Ltd v. Mennel*, [2015] VSC 268, Supreme Court of Victoria, Australia, 22 Jun 2015, para. 14. *See also Tomolugen Holdings Ltd and another v. Silica Investors Ltd and other*, [2015] SGCA 57, Singapore Court of Appeal, 26 October 2015, para. 67; *WDR Delaware Corporation v. Hydrox Holdings Pty Ltd; In the Matter of Hydrox Holdings Pty Ltd*, [2016] FCA 1164, Federal Court of Australia, 27 September 2016, para. 101.
233. *Grandom Asia Holding Ltd v. Henry Wai & Co (A Firm)*, [2018] HKCFI 31, Hong Kong Court of First Instance, 10 January 2018, para. 57. Similarly, *Chimbusco International Petroleum (Singapore) Pte Ltd v. Fully Best Trading Ltd*, [2016] 1 HKC 149, Hong Kong Court of First Instance, 3 December 2015, para. 14: 'Parties to an arbitration agreement should expect that the Court will recognize and enforce the arbitration agreement, and if they take the risk of instituting court proceedings in breach of such an agreement, they should expect to pay costs on a higher scale if they fail in their attempt to impeach the agreement'.

a legitimate legal impediment to arbitrate the dispute or reasonably arguable grounds.[234] Especially if the arbitral tribunal, exercising its competence-competence, subsequently finds it lacks jurisdiction.[235] This raises policy goal issues, like the presumption in favour of the validity of agreements to arbitrate disputes.

[3] Presumptive Validity of Arbitration Agreements

Some authorities have advanced the proposition that a cursory examination of the jurisdictional challenge is mandated by the pro-arbitration policy encapsulated in the presumptive validity of arbitration agreements.[236] The presumption is that arbitration agreements are valid and, therefore, readily enforceable.[237] Under that view, the presumptive validity principle does not simply produce a shift in the burden of proof; It also establishes a rule of chronological priority in favour of arbitrators. Applying the rule would mean that once the court finds that the parties consented to arbitrate their disputes, it is for an arbitral tribunal to be the first to hear and decide any jurisdictional challenge.

This logic has found support in case law. Even without naming and discussing the operation of the presumptive validity principle, some courts have given way to arbitrators based on putative arbitration agreements. Thus, once a party proves (even ostensibly) the existence of consent to arbitrate, courts have stayed litigation and referred to arbitrators the questions related to the effectiveness of the arbitration agreement. For example, in the *FirstLink* case, a Singaporean court reasoned that the word *unless* in the law strongly suggested the *presumptive validity* of an arbitration agreement.[238] Therefore, 'it would ... be sufficient for the purposes of a stay application that the court be satisfied of the agreement's validity on a *prima facie* basis without having to descend to a full review.'[239]

234. *See generally*, Fabricio Fortese, 'Breach of Arbitration Agreements: Should Parties Be Disciplined with Indemnity Costs?', in *Finances in International Arbitration: Liber Amicorum Patricia Shaughnessy*, ed. Sherlin Tung, Fabricio Fortese, et al. (Kluwer Law International, 2019), pp 189-204.
235. Or where a court – even the same one – reviewing the matter after an arbitral positive decision on jurisdiction concludes that the arbitration agreement was, in effect, 'null and void, inoperative or incapable of being performed'.
236. Gaillard et al., *Negative Effect of Competence-Competence* (n. 8), p. 258.
237. *See* Chapter 5, section [D][4] for an analysis on the source and extent of the presumptive validity of arbitration agreements.
238. The law provides that the court shall refer the parties to arbitration '*unless*' it finds that the agreement is null and void, inoperative or incapable of being performed.
239. *FirstLink Investments Corp Ltd v. GTPayment Pte Ltd et al.*, [2014] SGHCR 12, High Court of Singapore, 19 June 2014, para. 7. In *Triple V v. Star (Universal)*, the Hong Kong Court of Appeal agreed with the First Instance judge, who had stayed litigation in favour of arbitration. The lower court judge had concluded that, because there was '*prima facie* evidence of a dispute' between the parties, it was 'for the arbitrator to decide the effect, if any, of the alleged subsequent agreement cancelling the contract'; *Triple V v. Star (Universal)*, [1995] HKCA 617, para. 12, citing the First Instance decision (emphasis added). Similarly, also, *Paladin Agricultural Ltd. & Others v. Excelsior Hotel (Hong Kong) Ltd.*, [2001] HKCFI 1271, Hong Kong Court of First Instance, 6 March 2001, para. 16 ('Once a prima facie case has been made out, it is for the arbitrator to determine the issue of his own jurisdiction.'). Similarly, *Camuzzi v. Sodigas*,

It is worth emphasising that these decisions focus their attention on the *existence* of an arbitration agreement to trigger the staying of the litigation, not on its *invalidity* or *unenforceability*. In broad terms, the former questions the very existence of the parties' consent to arbitrate their disputes and, therefore, the formation of the arbitration contract. The latter, instead, focuses on legal defects in the parties' consent at the time of the conclusion of the arbitration agreement or at a later stage.

A different understanding of the operation of the presumptive validity principle is discussed in greater detail in Chapter 6, section [D][4] below. According to this understanding, the principle affords a shift in the burden of proof, not an automatic referral of the parties to arbitration. The decision in the *Townmore Construction* case is illustrative of that understanding. The Irish court explained that once the existence of the arbitration is proven, 'the onus shifts to the plaintiff to establish that the arbitration agreement is "inoperative" under Article 8(1)'[240] or 'to show that the arbitration agreement was null and void …'.[241] Similarly, a Kenyan bench ruled that once the party applying for the stay of the court proceedings proves that the matters in dispute fall within the agreement to arbitrate, 'the burden shifts to the opposing party to show the cause why effect should not be given to the arbitration clause'.[242]

Other decisions have sought to establish the minimum standard of proof required to trigger the stay and referral of the parties to arbitration rather than focusing on the objection against the enforceability of the agreement. The Hong Kong decision in *Pacific Crown v. Hyundai* focused on the onus that the party requesting the stay in favour of arbitration must meet. Namely, a '*good prima facie case*' or a '*plainly arguable case*' that an arbitration agreement *exists* and *binds* the parties.[243] In paragraph 16, Judge Burrel held that: 'When applying the [*prima facie*] test, the court should look at the evidence in support of the contention first. If, cumulatively, that evidence *is cogent and arguable, and not dubious or fanciful*, then the test has been satisfied.'[244]

ED 185-125; and, *Representaciones y Distribuciones Prodeco SRL v. Fratelli Branca Destilerias SA*, Court of First Instance 7 (Civ. & Comm) Salta, 13 February 2006.

240. *K & J Townmore Construction ltd. v. Kildare and Wicklow Education and Training Board*, [2019] IEHC 666, High Court of Ireland, 11 October 2019, para. 46.

241. *Sterimed Technologies International & Anor v. Schivo Precision Ltd & Ors* [2017] IEHC 35, High Court of Ireland, 27 January 2017, para. 12.

242. *East African Cables Ltd v. Mt. Kenya Cables Ltd*, Civil Case 97 of 2011, [2012] eKLR, High Court of Kenya, para. 4. This view was reiterated in *Jatin Shantilal Malde et al. v. Transmara Investment Limited*, High Court of Kenya (Nairobi), 20 July 2018, paras 13-14.

243. *Pacific Crown Engineering Ltd v. Hyundai Engineering and Construction Co Ltd*, [2003] HKCFI 924, Hong Kong Court of First Instance, 23 April 2003, paras 6, 12, [emphasis added]. Other cases reviewed this approach, with approval. For example, *T v. TS*, [2014] HKCFI 1426, Hong Kong Court of First Instance, 28 July 2014, para. 16; *Ling Yan Temple Ltd v. Ng Yook Man*, [2010] HKCFI 441, Hong Kong Court of First Instance, 14 May 2010, paras 18-19; *Leung Kwok Hung trading as Kaiser (M&E) Decoration Engineering Company v. Johnson Controls Hong Kong Limited*, [2018] HKCFI 1500, Hong Kong Court of First Instance, 28 June 2018.

244. *See also*, *Neo Intelligence Holdings Ltd v. Giant Crown Industries Ltd*, [2017] HKCFI 2088, Hong Kong Court of First Instance, 27 November 2017, para. 9 ('The onus is on the applicants for a stay to show that there is a *prima facie*, or plainly arguable case, that the parties are bound by an arbitration clause.').

To the same effect, another court decision held that: '[t]he applicant for stay has only to demonstrate that there is a *prima facie* case that the parties are bound by an arbitration clause, and unless the point is clear, the Court should not attempt to resolve the issue but should stay the matter in favour of arbitration'.[245] But even where it is not disputed that the parties are bound to arbitrate, courts have declined to stay litigation where the scope of the arbitration clause clearly does not cover the dispute between the parties.[246]

In adopting a limited review of jurisdictional objections at the threshold stage, judges have pondered on the pro-arbitration purpose of the relevant law.

[4] The Pro-arbitration Purpose of the Law

Other court decisions have engaged in the hermeneutics of arbitration law at a more general level to guide the interpretation and application of specific local versions of Article 8(1) of the Model Law.

By way of example, the Federal Court of Malaysia underlined that to appreciate the standard of review under section 10(1) of the Arbitration Act 2005 (which incorporates Article 8(1) Model Law), judges had to consider their statutory obligation of minimal court intervention,[247] and the competence-competence principle (section 18). The court not only read the language of those provisions but also recalled the 'intention of Parliament' when adopting the arbitration law and its amendments. These were: (i) to limit court involvement and discourage the use of inherent court power, and (ii) to recognise and respect the authority of arbitrators to decide on their jurisdiction without interference.[248] This contextual construction led the Court to conclude that to comply with section 10(1), it should 'restrict its enquiry only to the issue of whether there is in existence a binding arbitration agreement.'[249] Still, the decision appears to be purpose- and policy-driven, with lower regard for the particularities of the facts and defences argued.

A purposive interpretative approach directed an Australian court to adopt a *prima facie* standard of review in the *Hancock Prospecting v. Rinehart* case.[250] The claimants had lodged a court action against Mrs Rinehart, Hancock Prospecting and others, alleging that the respondents' misconduct had diminished the value of the assets in the trusts they were beneficiaries of. In response, Mrs Rinehart sought an

245. *Lim Choon Hock v. Hung Ka Hai Clement,* [2016] HKCFI 1439, Hong Kong Court of First Instance, 24 August 2016, para. 10.
246. That was the case in, for example, *Liu Man Wai and Another v. Chevalier (Hong Kong) Ltd.*, [2002] HKCA 280, Hong Kong Court of Appeal, 26 June 2002, paras 6-9. Also in *New Sound Industries Ltd. v. Meliga (HK) Ltd.*, [2005] HKCA 7, Hong Kong Court of Appeal, 11 January 2005, para. 21.
247. *Arbitration Act* (Malaysia) Act 646 (15 March 2006), section 8: 'No court shall intervene in matters governed by this Act, except where so provided in this Act.'
248. *Press Metal Sarawak Sdn Bhd v. Etiqa Takaful Bhd,* [2016] 5 MLJ 417, Malaysia Federal Court, 15 August 2016, paras 39-43.
249. *Ibid.*, para. 44.
250. *Hancock Prospecting Pty Ltd v. Rinehart,* [2017] FCAFC 170, Federal Court of Australia, 27 October 2017.

order to stay the court proceedings and the parties' referral to arbitration (according to section 8(1) of the New South Wales Arbitration Act 2010). In opposing that request, the claimant argued that the underlying contracts and the arbitration agreements they contained were void. Allegedly, their assent to those contracts had been procured due to Mrs Rinehart's misrepresentations.

When discussing the extent of review and finality of its jurisdictional decision, the Full Federal Court of Australia sought to balance out: (i) the operation of Article 8(1) with other provisions of the law, including its interpretative guidelines, (ii) the proper interpretative attitude when assessing the parties' evidence, (iii) the purpose of the law, and (iv) other means of interpretation (case law and scholars' opinions).

The text of the New South Wales Arbitration Act guided the Court's interpretative exercise. Similarly to Article 2A(1) of the Model Law, the Act calls to consider the need to promote uniformity in its application and the observance of good faith. A deviation from the language of the Model Law is the reference in the local arbitration act to its preparatory works to assist the interpretative exercise. Section 2A(3) of the New South Wales law provides that:

> [i]n interpreting this Act, reference may be made to the documents relating to the Model Law of:
>
> (a) the United Nations Commission on International Trade Law, and
> (b) its working groups for the preparation of the Model Law.[251]

Notably, the Arbitration Act spells out a pro-arbitration guiding policy and goal that steers its purposive interpretation and bolsters the arbitrators' authority and function. Section 1C[252] provides that:

> (1) The paramount object of this Act is to facilitate the fair and final resolution of commercial disputes by impartial arbitral tribunals without unnecessary delay or expense.
> (3) This Act must be interpreted, and the functions of an arbitral tribunal must be exercised, so that (as far as practicable) the paramount object of this Act is achieved.[253]

From that text, the Federal Court inferred that a preliminary full determination of the jurisdictional challenge would undermine the *legitimacy and authority of the arbitral tribunal*. It would also contradict the effective operation of section 8, the paramount object of which is to facilitate, not impede, the arbitral process.[254] The court highlighted the purpose of facilitating arbitration as a dispute resolution system rather than focusing on resolving the instant dispute 'without unnecessary delay or expense'. It did not pass a judgment of what delays or expenses might be necessary, nor what would be more efficient considering the particularities of the case in front of the court.

251. *Commercial Arbitration Act 2010 (New South Wales, Australia)* (Australia, New South Wales), section 2A.
252. An identical provision is found in Australia International Arbitration Act, section 2D.
253. *Commercial Arbitration Act 2010 (NSW)*, section 1C.
254. *Hancock v. Rinehart*, [2017] FCAFC 170, paras 146-147, 378.

The Federal Court, then, declared that the word 'finds' in section 8 of the Arbitration Act (... 'unless the court *finds* that the agreement is null ...') did not require a thorough judicial determination of a jurisdictional challenge at the threshold of the arbitration.[255] Instead, priority should be given to the arbitral tribunal to make a first determination of the jurisdictional dispute, subject to subsequent court review.[256]

Further, the Federal Court justified its preference for the *prima facie* approach by drone-viewing the arbitration law and not its provisions discretely. It sought to ensure the coherence of section 8 with other provisions of the Arbitration Act. It noted that section 16 of the law, which conforms to Article 16 of the Model Law, empowers arbitral tribunals to rule on their own jurisdiction (positive effect of competence-competence).[257] Therefore, when sections 8 and 16 are read together, the construction of the word 'finds' in section 8 should not be as mandating a full merits finding. According to the court, doing so would be a practical mistake. It would also be inconsistent with the competence principle that section 16 embodies, which should be read to include disputes directed to attack the very existence of the arbitration agreement.[258]

Although the court referred to the UNCITRAL Analytical Draft Text of the Model Law[259] to assess whether the dispute was 'commercial', it did not explicitly examine the preparatory works when interpreting sections 8 and 16. Instead, the court considered domestic and international case law and some scholarly works.

The court started its analysis of the standard of review under section 8 of the Arbitration Act by referring to case law from Singapore, Canada, Hong Kong, New Zealand, Ireland, England, and Wales. These cases were noted to exemplify jurisdictions that use either a *prima facie* or full merit standard of review.[260] However, in adopting a deferential approach to arbitration, the court was influenced by decisions from a non-Model Law jurisdiction (England and Wales), which had decisive weight.

In deciding the timing of full judicial determination of jurisdictional issues, the court heavily relied on the decision of the English High Court in *A v. B*. In that decision, Colman J favoured arbitral tribunals (under certain circumstances) to decide jurisdictional issues before a court does, 'provided that the arbitrators had

255. *Ibid.*, paras 146-147, 378, 394.
256. *Ibid.*, paras 147-148, 367, 370, 378.
257. Some scholars have advanced this position. For example, Bachand (n. 7), p. 473; Fortier, Delimiting the Spheres of Judicial and Arbitral Power (n. 7), pp. 148-149.
258. *Hancock v. Rinehart*, [2017] FCAFC 170, paras 372-376. In Singapore, *The Titan Unity* case, the Assistant Registrar also adopted that standard of review to determine the existence of an arbitration agreement in a stay proceedings. AR Leong noted that, although a court should not lightly accept a jurisdictional objection, 'there is no need for the court to descend into a protracted examination of the evidence to make a finding on the merits that an arbitration agreement exists on a balance of probabilities at the stay stage.'; *The 'Titan Unity'*, [2013] SGHCR 28, High Court of Singapore 19 December 2013, p. 34. To the same effect, *see Wilson Taylor Asia Pacific Pte Ltd v. Dyna-Jet Pte Ltd*, [2017] 2 SLR 362, Singapore Court of Appeal, where the Court said at para. 15, that applying a *prima facie* standard of review does not mean that the court turns a 'blind eye to obvious drawbacks in [an applicant's] case'.
259. UN, Analytical Commentary on Draft text of a Model Law on International Commercial Arbitration: Report of the Secretary-General, 18th session A/CN.9/264 (25 March 1985).
260. *Hancock v. Rinehart*, [2017] FCAFC 170, paras 140-142, 145.

kompetence-kompetence'.[261] The Australian court also relied on the discussions of Lord Collings about the competence-competence principle in the *Dallah* case[262] and of Devlin J in *Christopher Brown*.[263] It also referred to the discussions and opinions of several scholars on the topic.[264]

The Australian Full Federal Court did not indicate why these English decisions had such an influential weight or how they supported the harmonious application and development of the Model Law. Especially because, even where courts in England *permit* the *prima facie* approach,[265] they typically propose a full merits judicial review to determine the arbitration agreement's *existence* and *scope*.[266]

Paradoxically, although the Full Federal Court adopted a *prima facie* approach, it nevertheless discussed at length and settled the jurisdictional dispute related to the scope of the arbitration agreement (instead of leaving the issue to the arbitrators' preliminary determination). That is, the arbitration legislation's extended meaning of 'party'. In particular, it decided whether some third-party companies could claim 'through or under' the contracts, including the arbitration agreement.[267] In the end, the Court stayed the proceedings for all the parties in the court proceedings. For the parties bound by the arbitration agreement, the stay was ordered under section 8(1) of the Arbitration Act. For the litigants outside the scope of the arbitration agreement, the stay was justified in the interest of justice because the substantive claims were 'fundamentally adjectival' to those involving the parties to the arbitration.[268]

In weighing the purpose of international arbitration legislation, other court decisions have justified adopting the *prima facie* approach with a general view to discouraging dilatory tactics[269] and strengthening the efficacy of arbitration.[270] This was, for example, the reasoning of the Supreme Court of Canada in *Dell Computer v.*

261. *A v. B*, [2006] EWHC 2006 (Comm), England and Wales High Court (Commercial Court), 28 July 2006, para. 137. The English court also explained that arbitration would most likely be the appropriate forum to determine heavily intertwined jurisdiction and substantive issues.
262. *Dallah Real Estate and Tourism Holding Company v. The Ministry of Religious Affairs, Government of Pakistan*, [2010] UKSC 46, United Kingdom Supreme Court, 3 November 2010.
263. *Brown (Christopher) Ltd. v. Genossenschaft Oesterreichischer*, [1954] 1 Q.B. 8, Queen's Bench Division, 7 October 1953.
264. *Hancock v. Rinehart*, [2017] FCAFC 170, paras 148, 368-370, 373-376, 390.
265. *Fiona Trust & Holding Corporation & Ors v. Yuri Privalov & Ors*, [2007] EWCA Civ 20, England and Wales Court of Appeal (Civ Division), 24 January 2007, para. 34: '[I]t will, in general, be right for the arbitrators to be the first tribunal to consider whether they have jurisdiction to determine the dispute.'
266. *See, e.g., Joint Stock Company 'Aeroflot-Russian Airlines' v. Berezovsky & Ors*, [2013] EWCA Civ 784, England and Wales Court of Appeal (Civil Division), 2 July 2013, paras 77-79.
267. A further appeal of this case to the High Court of Australia did not take heed at this apparent contradiction, as it also discussed and decided the same issue.
268. *Hancock v. Rinehart*, [2017] FCAFC 170, para. 415.
269. *Tomolugen v. Silica*, [2015] SGCA 57, paras 57-66. *Shin-Etsu Chemical Co. Ltd v. M/S. Aksh Optifibre Ltd. & Anr*, (2005) 7 SCC 234, Supreme Court of India, 12 August 2005 ('... the object [of Article 8] is to avoid delay and accelerate reference to arbitration leaving the parties to raise objection, if any, to the validity of the arbitration agreement before the arbitral forum and/or post award under Section 34 of the Act.').
270. *Hancock v. Rinehart*, [2017] FCAFC 170, para. 378 ('Section 8 should, (...) be construed to facilitate, not impede, the process of arbitration.').

Union des Consommateurs.[271] In this case, the threshold question was analysed and answered under the arbitration legislation of Quebec. Quebec's Code of Civil Procedure (QCCP) incorporates the Model Law and the New York Convention.[272]

The court regarded the New York Convention as a formal source for interpreting Quebec law.[273] It noted that although the Convention (and Quebec legislation) empowers national courts to rule on the validity and applicability of arbitration agreements, this does not mean they are required to do so *before* the arbitrators.[274] The Supreme Court interpreted the Quebec version of Article 8(1) Model Law and Article II(3) New York Convention from a contextual perspective, explicitly rejecting its literal interpretation. In reading Article 940.1 QCCP, the court took note of its language, context, and the legal values of the arbitral system.

The Supreme Court sought to establish a uniform approach applicable to objections that attack the validity, effectiveness and scope of arbitration agreements, without distinction.[275] Yet, in establishing its version of the *prima facie* test, the court framed a division based on the nature of the question in dispute.

In doing so, the Court articulated a general rule: the arbitral tribunal must be the first to resolve a challenge to its own jurisdiction.[276] The Court also carved out two exceptions: courts may depart from the rule of systematic referral to arbitration if the jurisdictional challenge is based exclusively on a question of law. In this situation, courts should resolve the objection immediately and conclusively (exemption 1).[277]

271. *Dell Computer Corp. v. Union des consommateurs*, 2007 SCC 34, Supreme Court of Canada, 13 July 2007. The *prima facie* approach had in fact already been adopted in Canada, for example, in the leading case *Gulf Canada Resources Ltd. v. Arochem International Ltd.*, 1992 CanLII 4033 (BC CA), Court of Appeal for British Columbia, Canada, 10 March 1992. Also in *Dalimpex Ltd. v. Janicki*, 2003 CanLII 34234 (ON CA), Court of Appeal for Ontario, Canada, 30 May 2003, when dealing with questions related scope of the arbitration agreement. These two cases were cited with approval by the majority of the Supreme Court of Canada *Dell Computer* (para. 82). Even a few years earlier the Supreme Court of Ontario had held that '[q]uestions as to the ambiguity and scope of an arbitration agreement are to be determined by the proper arbitrator in the first instance.' *OEMSDF Inc. v. Europe Israel Ltd.*, [1999] O.J. No. 3594 (as discussed in H. Alvarez, N. Kaplan and D. Rivkin, *Model Law Decisions* (Kluwer Law International, 2003), pp. 68-69), Supreme Court of Ontario, Canada. *See also*, *Cecrop Co. Ltd. v. Kinetic Sciences Inc. and Inmega*, 2001 BCSC 532, British Columbia Supreme Court, Canada 9 April 2001; *Turnbridge v. Cansel Survey Equipment (Canada) Ltd.*, 2000 BCSC 287 (CanLII), Supreme Court of British Columbia, Australia, 17 February 2000.
272. Article 940.1 QCCP provides: 'Where an action is brought regarding a dispute in a matter on which the parties have an arbitration agreement, the court shall refer them to arbitration on the application of either of them *unless* (...) *it finds the agreement null* [emphasis added]. Book I of the Code of Civil Procedure (Bill 91, 1986), which contained Article 940, was replaced by the Code of Civil Procedure, CQLR c C-25.01.
273. The court had established this position in a case it decided in 2005, *GreCon Dimter inc. v. J.R. Normand inc.*, [2005] 2 SCR 401, Supreme Court of Canada, 22 July 2005, para. 41: '... The New York Convention is (...) a formal source for interpreting the domestic law provisions governing the enforcement of arbitration agreements.'
274. *Dell Computer*, 2007 SCC 34, para. 73.
275. *Ibid*., para. 82.
276. *Ibid*., para. 84. The court recently affirmed this approach in *Uber Technologies Inc. v. Heller*, 2020 SCC 16, Supreme Court of Canada, 26 June 2020, paras 34-35.
277. *Dell Computer*, 2007 SCC 34, para. 84. The court reasoned that this would permit resolving jurisdictional issues one and for all, to avoid duplication of a strictly legal debate (para. 84), and discourage dilatory tactics (para. 86). Justice D.M. Dharmadhikari of the Supreme Court of

Second, where the challenge raises questions of mixed law and fact, the case should be referred to arbitration unless the question requires only a superficial examination of the documentary evidence in the record (exemption 2).[278] In this scenario, the court should decide the jurisdictional dispute.

Deschamps J, delivering the vote for the majority, made clear that these two exemptions should be applied with caution. Courts retain and should exercise discretion when examining the circumstances surrounding the jurisdictional challenge. The point to highlight here is the Court's broad view of the law's purpose: to facilitate arbitration but always be mindful of fairness and efficiency in resolving the dispute.

With the explicit aim of discouraging dilatory tactics and strengthening the efficacy of the arbitration proceedings, the Supreme Court held that 'even when considering one of the exceptions, the court might decide that to allow the arbitrator to rule first on his or her competence would be best for the arbitration process'.[279]

Although there was a dissenting opinion, the full bench agreed that, as a general rule, arbitrators should take chronological priority to rule on the jurisdictional dispute.[280] The vote of the minority also concurred with the policy that a discretionary approach favouring arbitration would better serve the legislator's intention to promote arbitration and its efficiency while preserving the judiciary's supervisory role.[281]

The arbitrators' power to determine their own jurisdiction also contributed to the Canadian Supreme Court's adoption of a *prima facie* juridical standard of review.[282] In her analysis, Deschamps J acknowledged the existence of the competence-competence principle in the international context. She briefly analysed the Model Law, foreign non-Model Law legislation, national and foreign case law, and scholarly writings.[283] This international background assisted the Court in construing Quebec law in a way that is 'truthful' to the competence-competence principle, and to the *prima facie* approach that 'is increasingly gaining acceptance around the world'.[284]

India also indicated that legal questions of 'sufficient complexity' should be decided by the court, not by arbitrators *Shin-Etsu Chemical Co. Ltd v. M/S. Aksh Optifibre Ltd. & Anr,* (2005) 7 SCC 234, para. 112.

278. *Dell Computer,* 2007 SCC 34, paras 84-85, For a recent application of the same standard in Canada, *see Kore Meals LLC v. Freshii Development LLC,* 2021 ONSC 2896, Supreme Court of Ontario, Canada 19 April 2021, para. 14: ('Questions of mixed fact and law are to be referred to the arbitrator. ... This is in keeping with the inherent authority of an arbitrator as set out in art. 16 of the Model Law', i.e., the competence-competence principle). The Federal Court of Malaysia found persuasive the *Dell Computer* approach, and adopted it in *Press Metal v. Etiqa Takaful,* [2016] 5 MLJ 417, paras 48, 108-109.
279. *Dell Computer,* 2007 SCC 34, paras 86, 176.
280. The dissenting judges thought it appropriate to make a distinction between challenges to the validity of the arbitration agreement and those directed at its scope. In their opinion, issues of validity should not be referred to arbitration, unless in circumstances which 'truly merit the label of "international commercial arbitration"'. In those cases, it may be more efficient if the arbitrators heard first the jurisdictional question. *Ibid.,* paras 176-178.
281. *Ibid.,* para. 176.
282. Like Article 16 Model Law, Article 943 QCCP explicitly recognises the arbitrators' power to decide challenges to their jurisdiction: 'The arbitrators may decide the matter of their own competence.'
283. *Dell Computer,* 2007 SCC 34, paras 69-75.
284. *Ibid.,* para. 83.

The Supreme Court of Canada has essentially repeated its *Dell Computer* formulation in other cases.[285] It extends it to any Canadian legislation with its genesis in or is influenced by the Model Law and the New York Convention, regardless of textual dissimilarities. This is plain from the Supreme Court's decision in *Seidel v. Telus,* where it held that:

> Quebec's arbitration legislation is not unique to the civil law traditions but was based on two international texts relating to arbitration: the Model Law and the New York Convention. The general test adopted in Dell for dealing with challenges to an arbitrator's jurisdiction in this context was based on the interpretation of these documents.[286]

Other Canadian courts have followed the *Dell Computer* test in subsequent cases[287] in British Columbia,[288] Ontario[289] and New Brunswick,[290] although not consistently.[291]

The Supreme Court of India also found the purpose of the law to play a crucial role when deciding whether to follow a 'plainly arguable' or *prima facie* standard of review. In *Shin-Etsu v. M/S Aksh,*[292] the court declined to thoroughly examine the jurisdictional objection in the understanding that doing so would defeat 'the credo and

285. *See, e.g., Rogers Wireless Inc. v. Muroff,* 2007 SCC 35, Supreme Court of Canada, 13 July 2007, paras 11-13; *Seidel v. TELUS Communications Inc.,* [2011] 1 SCR 531, Supreme Court of Canada, 18 March 2011 para. 29; *Uber v. Heller,* 2020 SCC 16, paras 34-35.
286. *Seidel v. TELUS,* [2011] 1 SCR 531, paras 28-29, 69. This had also been the position adopted by other Canadian courts. *See, e.g., MacKinnon v. National Money Mart Company,* 2009 BCCA 103, Court of Appeal for British Columbia, Canada, 13 March 2009, para. 66.
287. *See, e.g., Jean Estate v. Wires Jolley LLP,* [2009] ONCA 339, Court of Appeal for Ontario, Canada, 29 April 2009, para. 40: '[T]he purpose of Article 8(1) ... is to grant parties limited access to the courts to resolve jurisdictional disputes of a legal nature due to the court's expertise compared with that of the arbitrator, the desire to avoid multiple legal disputes over the jurisdiction of the arbitral tribunal, and the interest of finality.' Similarly, *see Bombardier Transportation v. SMC Pneumatics (UK) Ltd.,* [2009] QCCA 861, Court of Appeal of Quebec, Canada, 4 May 2009; *Ontario v. Imperial Tobacco Canada Limited,* 2011 ONCA 525 (CanLII), Court of Appeal for Ontario, 20 July 2011.
288. *McMillan v. McMillan,* 2016 BCCA 441 (CanLII), Court of Appeal for British Columbia, Canada, 9 September 2016.
289. *See, e.g., Dancap Productions Inc. v. Key Brand Entertainment Inc.,* [2009] ONCA 135, Ontario Court of Appeal, Canada, 13 February 2009; *Patel v. Kanbay International Inc.,* [2008] ONCA 867, Ontario Court of Appeal, Canada, 23 December 2008; *EDF (Services) Limited v. Appleton & Associates,* [2007] CanLII 36078 (ON SC), Ontario Superior Court of Justice, Canada, 4 September 2007.
290. *UBS Holding Canada Ltd. v. Harrison et al.,* 2014 NBCA 26, Court of Appeal of New Brunswick, Canada, 24 April 2014.
291. *See, e.g., PS Here, L.L.C. v. Fortalis Anstalt,* [2009] QCCA 538, Court of Appeal of Quebec, Canada, 19 March 2009, where the Court found that it likely did not have jurisdiction due the parties' arbitration agreement, but, in any case, I declined jurisdiction on the grounds of *forum non conveniens*. And, *H & H Marine Engine Service Ltd. v. Volvo Penta of the Americas, Inc.,* 2009 BCSC 1389 (CanLII), Supreme Court of British Columbia, Canada, 9 October 2009, paras 52-57, where the court concluded that the *Dell Computers* test applied where the competence-competence principle formed part of the governing legal framework, which was not the case in the instant dispute.
292. *Shin-Etsu Chemical Co. Ltd v. M/S. Aksh Optifibre Ltd. & Anr,* (2005) 7 SCC 234.

ethos of the [Arbitration] Act',[293] i.e., to enable expeditious arbitration without avoidable intervention by the judicial authorities.[294]

In its interpretative exercise, the Supreme Court examined international case law,[295] considered the Arbitration Act's legislative purpose, and was mindful of the context and interplay of section 45 – which corresponds to Article 8(1) Model Law[296] – with other provisions of the statute. It found that performing a full review of the jurisdictional objection at the threshold of the arbitration could make other provisions of the Act redundant, an outcome which the legislator 'could surely not have intended'.[297] It held that:

> If the finding made under Section 45 as to the validity of the arbitral agreement were to be treated as final, then the competent court, while entertaining an application for enforcement of a foreign award ... might decline to go into the same question. The court before which enforcement is sought may not re-examine whether the agreement was valid. ... The principles analogous to res judicata ... might preclude the party from raising the defence.[298]

It also held that the court should summarily decide the jurisdictional objection based on the material and evidence on the record. But if the court was inclined to reject the referral to arbitration, it should afford the parties a full (or reasonable) opportunity to produce documentary or oral evidence. That way, the court can decide the issue as a preliminary matter in a regular civil suit and pass a reasoned judgment.[299]

Other leading Model Law jurisdictions have addressed the thorny matter of the court's role at the arbitration threshold. For example, in *Tomolugen v. Silica*,[300] the Singapore Court of Appeal dealt with the threshold question when deciding a dispute involving arbitrability issues, the scope of the arbitration agreement and the extent of a stay order beyond the disputes (or parties) covered by the arbitration agreement.

In delivering the court's judgment, Justice Menon analysed the UNCITRAL Working Group II's discussions on Articles 8 and 16 and draft Article 17 of the Model Law. Although he was persuaded that the preparatory works were inconclusive or equivocal as to the appropriate approach, the judge observed that the discussions at UNCITRAL offered a little more support for the *prima facie* approach.[301]

The Court of Appeal also noted a textual dissimilarity between Singapore's International Arbitration Act and the Model Law. Section 6(1) of the Arbitration Act

293. *Ibid.*, para. 72.
294. Especially because in the Supreme Court's view, 'the arbitral proceedings would have to be in limbo' while the court makes its final determination. *Ibid.*
295. The court considered and relied on decisions from Hong Kong and Canada.
296. Section 8 of India Arbitration and Conciliation Act 1996 refers to stay proceedings in favour of arbitrations seated in India, and section 45 where the seat of the arbitration is abroad. The amendments to the arbitration law in 2015 introduced the words 'prima facie' to section 8 of the Act, and to section 45 with the 2019 Amendment Act.
297. *Shin-Etsu Chemical Co. Ltd v. M/S. Aksh Optifibre Ltd. & Anr,* (2005) 7 SCC 234, para. 85.
298. *Ibid.*, para. 76.
299. *Ibid.*, para. 111. This is because a court decision refusing the referral to arbitration is subject to appeal (section 50 India Arbitration & Conciliation Act 1996).
300. *Tomolugen v. Silica,* [2015] SGCA 57. *See also FirstLink Investments v. GTPayment,* [2014] SGHCR 12.
301. *Tomolugen v. Silica,* [2015] SGCA 57, paras 32-41, 65.

uses the word 'satisfied' instead of the term 'find' adopted in the Model Law (and the New York Convention). Notably, the language of the stay provision in the English Arbitration Act 1996 also uses the word 'satisfied', whereas Articles 8 of the Model Law and II of the New York Convention use the word 'finds'.[302] However, it is a settled opinion both in Singapore and England that such semantic distinction conveys no different meaning for the level of court examination of the preliminary jurisdictional dispute.[303] However, the Singaporean and English courts part ways in how those terms apply *in practice*. For the Singapore Court of Appeal, the words 'satisfied' and 'finds' do not require a full merits approach,[304] whereas they do for the English Court of Appeal.[305]

The synergy of relevant provisions and principles also supported the Singapore Court of Appeal's opinion against the full merit review. It held that, in practical terms, deciding the threshold issue with final effects: (i) would significantly hollow the arbitral tribunal's authority to determine its own jurisdiction, (ii) would be in tension with the principle of judicial non-intervention, and (iii) would facilitate dilatory strategies.[306] However, a contextual reading of the Singapore Arbitration Act encumbers those conclusions. The law does not afford exclusive or priority powers to arbitrators to determine their jurisdiction. If anything, the text of the law permits parallel proceedings and provides that judges cannot order arbitrators to suspend an arbitral process.

Further, the law does not restrict the extent of court intervention, where permitted (further discussed in Chapter 6 section [B]). Also, this court decision assumes that dilatory tactics are one-sided (by claimants that initiate the court action) without assessing the probability or even plausibility that the initiation of the court action and defences the claimant advances are dilatory manoeuvres.

In preferring the *prima facie* approach, the same court reiterated its position in the *Tjong Very Sumito v. Antig Investment* case. In that decision, the Court had concluded that it should settle jurisdictional issues (instead of referring parties to arbitration) only in the *clearest* cases.[307] After examining the position in other jurisdictions (England, Hong Kong, and Canada), the Singapore Court of Appeal held

302. *Arbitration Act* (UK Public General Acts 1996 c. 23), section 9(4): ... 'the court shall grant a stay unless *satisfied* that the arbitration agreement is null and void, inoperative, or incapable of being performed' [emphasis added].
303. For example, according to the English Court of Appeal, the study of the words 'satisfied' and 'finds' leads to the application of the same standard of review for threshold questions; *Aeroflot v. Berezovsky,* [2013] EWCA Civ 784, para. 77.
304. *Tomolugen v. Silica,* [2015] SGCA 57, paras 69-70.
305. The High Court held that 'the use of the word "satisfied" ... is an indication that the court must come to a clear conclusion that the agreement is null and void, inoperative or incapable of performance'. *Joint Stock Company 'Aeroflot Russian Airlines' v. Berezovsky & Ors,* [2012] EWHC 1610 (Ch), England and Wales High Court (Chancery Division), 18 June 2012, para. 73. On appeal, the court confirmed that '[t]he words "satisfied" and "find" suggest that, ... the standard of proof which must be attained in order that the court should refuse a stay is one of the balance of probabilities'; *Aeroflot v. Berezovsky,* [2013] EWCA Civ 784, para. 77.
306. *Tomolugen v. Silica,* [2015] SGCA 57, paras 66-69.
307. *Tjong Very Sumito and Others v. Antig Investments Pte Ltd,* [2009] SGCA 41, Singapore Court of Appeal, 26 August 2009, para. 24.

(and echoed in the *Dyna-Jet* case[308]) that to grant a stay order under section 6(1) of the International Arbitration Act (IAA), the court needs only be satisfied on a *prima facie* basis that:

(a) there is a valid arbitration agreement between the parties to the court proceedings;
(b) the dispute in the court proceedings (or any part thereof) falls within the scope of the arbitration agreement;
(c) the agreement is not null and void, inoperative or incapable of being performed.[309]

Nevertheless, the Court fell short of applying that approach when addressing the arbitrability of the substantive dispute.[310] It started its analysis by observing that non-arbitrability was not a distinct ground for refusing to stay court proceedings. It accepted that the issue would fall within either the 'inoperative' or the 'incapable of being performed' exceptions to the referral of the parties to arbitration (*see* Chapter 5, section [D][9]).[311]

After recalling, as the Court did, that there is a legal presumption of arbitrability, it would have been possible (and perhaps expected under the Court's preferred *prima facie* approach) for the Court to stay the proceedings and refer the parties to arbitration. However, the Court examined the arbitrability issue in detail (paragraphs 71 to 106 of its judgment). It concluded its analysis by making a final determination of the issue, holding that the subject matter in dispute was arbitrable.

As mentioned earlier, the Malaysia Federal Court has also preferred an interpretation favouring the *prima facie* approach. Yet, it too reached a final determination of arbitrability issues, even after recognising that the effect of non-arbitrability falls within the 'null and void' exception for not granting a stay request.[312]

It is unclear what determining factors in these two cases justified the courts departing from a *prima facie* standard of review and, instead, taking upon themselves the resolution of the arbitrability disputes. Ultimately, an arbitration agreement will be 'null and void', 'inoperative', or 'incapable of being performed', whether based on non-arbitrability issues or other grounds (fraud, misrepresentation, lack of capacity,

308. *Dyna-Jet,* [2017] 2 SLR 362, para. 11. *See also Nippon Catalyst Pte Ltd v. PT Trans-Pacific Petrochemical Indotama,* [2018] SGHC 126, High Court of Singapore, para. 14.
309. *Tomolugen v. Silica,* [2015] SGCA 57, paras 63, 70. *See also, Heartronics Corporation v. EPI Life Pte. Ltd.,* [2017] SGHCR 17, High Court of Singapore, 17 October 2017.
310. The question was whether disputes over oppression or unfairly prejudicial conduct towards minority shareholders under the Companies Act were capable of being resolved in arbitration.
311. The Court of Appeal had established this in an earlier case; *Larsen Oil and Gas Pte Ltd v. Petroprod Ltd (in official liquidation in the Cayman Islands and in compulsory liquidation in Singapore),* [2011] SGCA 21, Singapore Court of Appeal, 11 May 2011, para. 26 ('[E]ven though s 6(2) of the AA does not make arbitrability of the dispute a pre-condition for the grant of a stay of proceedings, it cannot be seriously argued that a non-arbitrable claim should be allowed to proceed to arbitration.').
312. *Arch Reinsurance Ltd v. Akay Holdings Sdn Bhd,* [2019] 1 CLJ 305, Federal Court of Malaysia, 29 January 2018. Similarly, in *Comandate Marine Corp. v. Pan Australia Shipping Pty. Ltd,* [2006] FCAFC 192, Federal Court of Australia, 20 December 2006, paras 242-243.

duress, etc.).[313] Further, although the subject matter of the dispute may not be arbitrable in the jurisdiction where the judge sits, it may well be under the law governing the arbitration agreement or at the seat of the arbitration if it is different to the jurisdiction where the court action was lodged.[314]

The case law analysis in this section suggests that adopting the *prima facie* approach responds to pro-arbitration policy considerations and associated pragmatic solutions. Although these are legitimate reasons and commendable solutions, they fail to support claims that the Model Law *imposes* that approach following a distinct, nuanced and uniform method of legal interpretation.

The following section examines case law that adopts the opposite approach, i.e., a full standard of review and determination of jurisdictional challenges at the threshold of an arbitration.

[D] THE FULL REVIEW APPROACH

Court decisions have also interpreted Article 8(1) of the Model Law to require a full review of the jurisdictional objection before referring parties to arbitration. Some judgments highlight that the Model Law mandates the recognition of agreements to arbitrate so long as some defined conditions are met. A court's duty to refer parties to arbitration would only be triggered where all the conditions set out in Article 8(1) are fulfilled and its exceptions dispelled.[315] In this sense, the existence of an agreement to arbitrate is the first and most basic condition precedent to the granting of a stay and referral to arbitration request.[316]

---

313. For example, the Supreme Court of India held that where there are serious allegations of fraud (or any criminal wrongdoing), 'it would be more appropriate for the Court to deal with the subject matter rather than relegating the parties to arbitration, then alone such an application under Section 8 should be rejected.'; *A. Ayyasamy v. A. Paramasivam & Ors,* (2016) 10 SCC 386, Supreme Court of India, 4 October 2016.
314. *See, e.g., Anupam Mittal v. Westbridge Ventures II Investment Holdings*, [2023] SGCA 1, Singapore Court of Appeal, 6 January 2023, para. 55: '... the arbitrability of a dispute is, in the first instance, determined by the law that governs the arbitration agreement'.
315. A court put this in plain language when it ruled that the defendant in the substantive action 'bears the initial burden of establishing that the various requirements for the application of Article 8(1) are satisfied'. *K & J Townmore Construction ltd. v. Kildare and Wicklow Education and Training Board,* [2019] IEHC 666, para. 46. Further, the court found that, '[i]n particular, it bears the burden of establishing that the proceedings concern a matter or matters which is or are the subject of an arbitration agreement.'
316. A court held that '[i]t is of course crucial in any application for a stay (whether under section 6 of the Ordinance or Article 8 of the Model Law) that there exists an arbitration agreement.'; *Tommy CP Sze & Co v. Li & Fung (Trading) Ltd,* [2002] HKCFI 682, Hong Kong Court of First Instance, 28 October 2002, para. 18. *See also, Sterimed Technologies v. Schivo,* [2017] IEHC 35, para. 12: '[t]he onus is on the defendant to establish the existence of the arbitration agreement.'; *Joint Stock Company 'Aeroflot Russian Airlines' v. Berezovsky & Ors,* [2012] EWHC 1610 (Ch), para. 75: 'a pre-condition of the jurisdiction to grant the statutory stay, [is] a conclusion that an arbitration agreement has been made.' In the US, although based on the Federal Arbitration Act (not the Model Law), the Supreme Court held that 'the first task of a court asked to compel arbitration of a dispute is to determine whether the parties agreed to arbitrate ...'; *Mitsubishi Motors Corp. v. Soler Chrysler-Plymouth, Inc,* 105 S.Ct. 3346, Supreme Court of the United States of America, 2 July 1985, paras 2-3.

[1] Judicial Competence-Competence

The Supreme Court of Austria interpreted section 584 of the local arbitration law[317] (and Article II(3) of the New York Convention) to require a full merits approach when enforcing arbitration agreements. In doing so, the Court referred and relied on its competence-competence, not the arbitrators. It concluded that the court seized of the action bears the duty of clarifying whether the arbitration agreement is null and void, inoperative or incapable of being performed, or whether the dispute is covered by it. To fulfil that duty, the court 'has to check the content of the alleged arbitration agreement and not just *prima facie* its existence'.[318]

Somewhat similarly, the decision in another Model Law jurisdiction was that the arbitral competence-competence principle did not negate the court's jurisdiction to determine whether the parties had indeed validly agreed to arbitrate their disputes. In *Barnmore v. Alandale*, the High Court of Ireland held that:

> [W]hilst the doctrine of 'Kompetenz-Kompetenz', which is given effect in Article 16, provides that the arbitral tribunal has the jurisdiction to determine whether or not the arbitration agreement ever existed, that power does not mean that the Court does not have the power to consider and decide whether or not an arbitration agreement exists.[319]

Another decision concluded that a referral-to-arbitration request entailed a decision on the court's own jurisdiction (whether or not it has been ousted[320]). Similarly, a different judgment concluded that national courts can ascertain their jurisdiction because, '[a]fter all, it is for the court finally to decide the issue of whether or not to refuse a stay because the arbitration agreement is "null and void" or "inoperative"'.[321]

Other decisions have relied on the general supervisory role that courts exercise over arbitration to justify a full and final determination of the validity of an arbitration agreement at the referral stage. In this understanding, the Supreme Court of Mexico concluded that it could not limit its role to a *prima facie* standard of review. It reasoned that 'the competence of the arbitrators comes from party autonomy. So, if there is a

317. This section of the act incorporated Article 8 of the Model Law; *Arbitration Act* (Austria) BGBl. I Nr. 118/2013 (2013).
318. *T GesmbH v. O, Inc., USA*, OGH 5 Ob 72/16y, Supreme Court of Austria, 1 March 2017, p. 14, paras 12.12.-12.13.
319. *Barnmore Demolition and Civil Engineering Ltd v. Alandale Logistics Ltd & Ors*, [2010] IEHC 544, High Court of Ireland, 11 November 2010, para. 5. For a similar outcome, but in Canada, *see*, *Methanex New Zealand Ltd. v. Fontaine Navigation S.A., Tokyo Marine Co. Ltd, The Owners and all Others Interested in the Ship Kinugaw*, [1998] 2 FC 583,1998 CanLII 9039 (FC), Federal Court of Canada, Trial Division, 9 January 1998.
320. *A. Ayyasamy v. A. Paramasivam & Ors*, (2016) 10 SCC 386 ('While dealing with (...) an application under Section 8 of the Act, the focus of the Court has to be on the question as to whether jurisdiction of the Court has been ousted instead of focusing on the issue as to whether the Court has jurisdiction or not.').
321. *Aeroflot v. Berezovsky*, [2013] EWCA Civ 784, para. 78.

"defect on the parties" will in the act that grants authority to the arbitrator, then the issue must be resolved by the court'.[322]

One court linked the possibility of recognising the negative effects of competence-competence to the explicit reception of its positive aspect in the local legislation. Consequently, the *prima facie* approach operates only where the competence-competence principle expressly forms part of the governing legal framework, regardless of the seat of the arbitration. In the case before that court,[323] the governing legal framework was the rules of the Arbitration Institute of the Stockholm Chamber of Commerce. The (then in force) rules did not expressly provide for the arbitrators' power to rule on their jurisdiction, and the court thought it impermissible to assume they did.[324]

This supports the understanding that competence-competence is neither an 'inherent' power of the arbitrators nor a legal effect of an arbitration agreement. It was viewed, instead, as a prerogative of statutory origin. In some (non-Model Law) jurisdictions (e.g., the United States of America), it is considered a contractual matter that requires 'clear and unmistakable' evidence that the parties have agreed to delegate to the arbitrators the decision of the jurisdictional issue.[325]

[2] Party Autonomy (a Two-Way Street)

As illustrated earlier, the concept of party autonomy has played a role in justifying the adoption of a *prima facie* approach. But it also does for the full merits approach. In *Cockwell v. Gordon Flatt*, the Supreme Court of Bermuda dealt with a stay action that required a determination on several aspects of Article 8(1) of the Model Law. The case involved a decision on: (i) the meaning of 'party' with legitimacy to request the stay and referral to arbitration, (ii) the time limit to raise the jurisdictional challenge, and (iii) the scope of the arbitration agreement.

The significant observation here is that the Court linked the contractual nature of arbitration to the standard of review when enforcing an obligation to arbitrate. It held that it would be inconsistent with party autonomy to compel parties to arbitrate when they have not contracted to do so. If the Court were 'to attempt to coerce [the parties]

322. *LDC, S.A. de C.V. v. Cámara Nacional de Comercio de la Ciudad de México and ADT Security Services, S.A. de C.V.*, Contradicción de Tesis 51/2005-PS, Supreme Court of Mexico, Chamber I, 01 September 2016, p. 16.

323. *H & H v. Volvo*, 2009 BCSC 1389 (CanLII), para. 55: 'In the absence of an evidentiary or statutory basis for application of the competence/competence principle, however, I conclude that the Court should determine whether an arbitration agreement exists before Section 8 of the International Commercial Arbitration Act can be invoked.'

324. *Ibid.*, paras 52-54. In this case, the court was not satisfied that an arbitration agreement existed (even superficially). Therefore, whether the prima facie test was applicable or not, the requested stay was not granted (para. 56).

325. *See, e.g., First Options of Chicago, Inc. v. Kaplan*, 514 US 938, US Supreme Court, 22 May 1995, para. 944. *See also, generally*, George A. Bermann, The 'Gateway' Problem (n. 13).

to [arbitration] by refusing to hear their dispute [it] would be acting unlawfully and in breach of their constitutional right (...) to a fair hearing within a reasonable time'.[326]

In addition to relying on the UNCITRAL Secretariat's 2012 Digest, the Court considered case law from Model Law and other jurisdictions. It found support in paragraph 12 of the Digest, which suggests that '[r]eferral to arbitration may be denied on the ground that the respondent to the referral application never undertook, or never validly undertook, to resort to arbitration'.[327] And, it was persuaded by the English Court of Appeals in *Al-Naimi v. Islamic Press*, which held that:

> [O]n a proper construction of section 9, it can be said with force that a court should be satisfied (a) that there is an arbitration clause and (b) that the subject of the action is within that clause, before the court can grant a stay under that section.[328]

The question for the Supreme Court of New South Wales in the *WesTrac v. Eastcoast* case was similar. It required the Court to determine whether a cross-claim had to be stayed and referred to arbitration. Although the existence of an arbitration agreement was not in dispute, its scope was. It is worth noting that the Supreme Court undertook the fact-finding task (rather than refer it to the arbitrators) of determining whether the cross-claim had arisen 'out of or in connection with' the contract. It held that in answering that question:

> [I]t is necessary, first, to identify each matter to be determined in the proceeding and, second, to construe the agreement so as to identify each matter that, in pursuance of it, is capable of settlement by arbitration. To the extent that there is correspondence between the results of the two inquiries, the matters concerned will be matters in respect of which the Act will require that the proceeding be stayed.[329]

Ensuring that the action before the court was 'a matter which is the subject of an arbitration agreement' was a prerequisite to ordering the stay also for the Federal Court of Canada in *Simmonds v. Eurocom*.[330] In doing so, the court recalled the House of Lords decision in *Heyman v. Darwins*. In it, Lord McMillan held that in enforcing an arbitration agreement by way of a stay order, the court must first establish the nature of the dispute. It must then determine whether the dispute falls within the scope of the

326. *Ian Cockwell v. Gordon Flatt*, [2014] Bda LR 89, Supreme Court of Bermuda, 23 September 2014, para. 33. According to section 23 of the Bermuda International Conciliation and Arbitration Act 1993, the Model Law has the force of law in Bermuda.
327. UNCITRAL, Digest of Case Law on the Model Law on International Commercial Arbitration.
328. *Ahmad Al-Naimi (t/a Buildmaster Construction Services) v. Islamic Press Agency Incorporated*, [2000] EWCA Civ 17, England and Wales Court of Appeal (Civ.), 28 January 2000.
329. *WesTrac Pty. Ltd. v. Eastcoast OTR Tyres Pty. Ltd*, [2008] NSWSC 894, Supreme Court of New South Wales, Australia, 29 August 2008, para. 18.
330. *Simmonds Capital Limited v. Eurocom International Limited*, 1998 CanLII 7229 (FC), Canada Federal Court, 15 January 1998, para. 10. Similarly, *see Shell Hong Kong Ltd v. Esa Consulting Engineers Ltd and Another*, [1998] HKEC 971, Hong Kong Court of First Instance, 25 November 1998, para. 10: 'Before I am able to exercise the power contained in Article 8, the ... defendant must satisfy me that the pre-condition for the exercise of that power exists.'

parties' agreement. Lastly, the court must determine whether the arbitration clause is still effective or whether something has happened to render it no longer operative.[331]

The German Federal Court of Justice, too, sought certainty beyond a *prima facie* basis to establish the existence and validity of the parties' obligation to arbitrate. It referred the parties to arbitration only after being satisfied that the agreement met the German law's formal and substantive requirements.[332] Nonetheless, it is fair to acknowledge that the German legislation justified adopting a comprehensive standard of review. Although the law does not explicitly impose a standard of review, its operation results from a contextual reading of other statutory provisions.[333]

[3] The Law's Purpose

In the *Comandate Marine* case, the Full Federal Court of Australia relied on the context, purpose and policies behind the Model Law and the New York Convention to guide the interpretation of the Australian legislation. It held that '[t]he proper construction and interpretation of the International Arbitration Act, (...) requires an understanding of the context of those international instruments and an understanding of the subjects of concern and debate in the Working Groups, meetings and other discussion leading up to their formation'.[334]

The Federal Court expressed its conviction that the 'finding' required in the Model Law and the New York Convention relates to a duty that the judge must discharge, not the arbitrators.[335] Interestingly, the Court appeared to propose a somewhat flexible approach, depending upon the circumstances of the case. If the party resisting the referral advances a credible case, 'the Court should not grant a stay and should allow that issue to be heard by the Court before any arbitration'.[336] Further, the Court doubted the prospect of always deciding a stay application on a *prima facie* basis. In particular, the Court noted that it is not generally feasible to dispose of certain invalidity claims (e.g., misrepresentation) in an interlocutory motion for a stay.[337] The case's factual and legal complexities might affect the degrees of court involvement.

331. *Heyman v. Darwins Ltd,* [1942] A.C. 356, House of Lords, 20 February 1942, p. 370. *See also, Ahmad Al-Naimi v. Islamic Press Agency,* [2000] EWCA Civ 17.
332. *Z v. AG,* III ZR 265/03, BGH (Federal Court of Justice, Germany), 13 January 2013 p. 6, para. 2.
333. *See* the discussion in Chapter 6 below.
334. *Comandate Marine v. Pan Australia Shipping,* [2006] FCAFC 192, para. 191.
335. *Ibid.*, para. 215. ('Certainly, the notion of the court 'finding' the state of affairs, (...), assumes a responsibility of the court.').
336. *Ibid.*, para. 217. Years later the full bench of the same Federal Court reiterated 'any rigid taxonomy of approach is unhelpful, as are the labels "*prima facie*" and "merits" approach'. How a judge deals with an application under section 8 of the C[ommercial] A[rbitration] A[ct] will depend significantly upon the issues and the context.' *Hancock v Rinehart,* [2017] FCAFC 170, p. 145.
337. *Comandate Marine v. Pan Australia Shipping,* [2006] FCAFC 192, para. 216 ('[I]f the claim for nullity or voidness is properly directed to the arbitration clause itself, the need for the court to deal with the issue can be readily appreciated.').

In the end, after hearing the parties' submissions on the different jurisdictional objections, the Court granted the stay of the proceedings in favour of arbitration.[338]

Despite the uncertainties in the law and the conflicting approaches to the timing and extent of judicial review of arbitral jurisdictions, not all court decisions have embarked on an explicit statutory interpretative exercise.

[4] No Explicit Statutory Interpretation

In several instances, national courts have directly heard and determined jurisdictional disputes without debating the extent of their review power at the threshold stage. This was the case in *Paquito v. Rainbow* before the Hong Kong Court of Final Appeal. The Court concluded that an arbitration agreement did not exist when the dispute arose. Therefore, the Court found no ground for staying the court action.[339]

A few years earlier, Judge Kaplan had ordered the stay of the litigation between *Lucky-Goldstar v. Ng Moo Kee Engineering*[340] after deciding the jurisdictional dispute. The judge reviewed the language of the poorly drafted arbitration clause, considered case law and the writings of Professor van de Berg on Article II(3) of the New York Convention. This was sufficient for Kaplan J to conclude (not merely at a *prima facie* level) that the arbitration agreement was not 'null and void inoperative or incapable of being performed'.[341]

In *Thorn Security v. Cheung Fee,*[342] the Hong Kong Court of Appeal reversed the decision of the lower court that had granted a stay of the proceedings in favour of arbitration. The Court did not discuss the standard of review either or whether an arbitral tribunal should first hear the dispute regarding the existence of an arbitration agreement. Instead, the Court assessed the evidence, heard the parties' arguments, and settled the jurisdictional dispute. It found that the dispute resolution agreements that the parties had concluded did not amount to an arbitration agreement.[343] In the Court's

338. Although the Court took upon itself to determine a disputed issue of arbitrability. It concluded that the dispute between the parties was indeed a matter capable of settlement by arbitration; *ibid.*, paras 242-243.
339. *Paquito Lima Buton v. Rainbow Joy Shipping Ltd. Inc.*, [2008] HKCFA 30, Hong Kong Court of Final Appeal, 28 April 2008, para. 40.
340. *Lucky-Goldstar International (H.K.) Limited v. Ng Moo Kee Engineering Limited,* [1993] HKCFI 14, High Court of Hong Kong, 5 May 1993.
341. The arbitration clause provided that: 'Any dispute or difference arising out of or relating to this contract, or the breach thereof which cannot be settled amicably without under delay by the interested parties shall be arbitrated in the 3RD COUNTRY, under the rule of the 3RD COUNTRY and in accordance with the rules of procedure of the International Commercial Arbitration Association. The award shall be final and binding upon both parties.'
342. *Thorn Security (H.K.) Ltd v. Cheung Kee Fung Cheung Construction Co. Ltd,* [2004] HKCA 217, Hong Kong Court of Appeal, 20 July 2004.
343. In a similar fashion, the Federal Court of Australia engaged in a full-merit examination of the parties' e-mail negotiations to determine whether or not they amounted to an agreement to arbitrate. The court concluded that '[t]here was no agreement to arbitrate reached between any of the parties to [the] proceedings and therefore nothing to enforce.' *APC Logistics Pty. Ltd. v. C.J. Nutracon Pty. Ltd,* [2007] FCA 136, Federal Court of Australia, 16 February 2007, para. 27.

view, the parties' bargains had merely conferred on the parties an option to resort to arbitration or litigation before national courts.[344]

The same Court of Appeal (but with a different bench) had the opportunity to examine the same contractual provisions in another dispute involving the same defendant under the same construction project (*Grandeur Electrical v. Cheung Kee*). Contrary to the earlier decision, the Court did stay the proceedings after making a thorough and final determination regarding the existence and application of the arbitration agreement.[345] It concluded that the agreement did not contain an option to choose between arbitration and litigation. In reality, it referred to 'an option as to whether or not to take the matter further - in other words, an option between (a) accepting the decision of the contract manager as final and binding (...), or (b) not accepting that decision (...) and referring it to an arbitrator'.[346] Despite the outcome of the judgment, what is worth noting here is that the Court engaged in a full determination of the issue instead of letting the arbitrators have the first word.

In *Tommy CP v. Li & Fung*, Judge Ma examined the existence, validity and scope of an arbitration agreement before ordering the stay of the proceedings and the parties' referral to arbitration. In the analysis, Ma J noted that all applications for stay must follow an essential four-question checklist.[347]

First, judges should inquire whether the clause in dispute is an arbitration agreement.[348] If the court concludes that an arbitration agreement exists, the second question is whether such an agreement is valid, operative, and capable of being performed.[349] Although the judge did not discuss the appropriateness of the *prima facie* or full examination of the arbitration agreement, the decision categorically held the following: '[b]efore any dispute or difference is referred to arbitration, the court *must be sure* that this is viable; i.e., that arbitration can take place ... Where, for instance, the alleged agreement is void (...), frustrated or simply incapable of being performed, it cannot and will not be enforced'.[350]

The third inquiry is for the court to decide whether there is, in fact, a dispute between the parties.[351] Lastly, before remitting the parties to arbitration, the court should be satisfied that the dispute (if it exists) falls within the ambit of the arbitration clause.[352]

Other courts have developed similar building-up inquiries to stay (or not stay) a court action in favour of arbitration. For example, in Canada, Justice Lauwers suggested that courts take the following five-inquiry analytical framework: Is there an arbitration agreement? What is the subject matter of the dispute? What is the scope of the arbitration agreement? Does the dispute arguably fall within the scope of the

344. *Thorn Sec. v. Cheung Fee* [2004] HKCA 217, paras 16-17.
345. *Grandeur Electrical Co. Ltd v. Cheung Kee Fund Cheung Construction Co. Ltd,* [2006] HKCA 305, Hong Kong Court of Appeal, 25 July 2006, paras 9-12, 31-34.
346. *Ibid.*, para. 32.
347. *Tommy CP v. Li & Fung,* [2002] HKCFI 682, paras 19-22.
348. *Ibid.*, para. 19.
349. *Ibid.*, para. 20.
350. *Ibid.*, paras 38-39.
351. *Ibid.*, para. 21.
352. *Ibid.*, para. 22.

arbitration agreement? Are there grounds on which the court should refuse to stay the action?[353]

Further, court decisions have found engaging in a detailed statutory interpretation exercise unnecessary. In their view, the language 'unless the agreement is null and void, inoperative or incapable of being performed' is clear. That language allows advancing factual and legal arguments and evidence, and not on a preliminary basis only.[354] This extends to the very existence of a dispute[355] and the scope of the arbitration agreement.[356]

Without discussing the approach to the interpretation of the Model Law, the High Court of Ireland in *Sterimed Technologies v. Schivo* accepted the full judicial standard of review on a dispute over the scope of the arbitration agreement (i.e., the identity of the parties bound by the agreement).[357] In an earlier decision, the same Court had concluded that given the language of Article 8(1), there was 'a particularly strong case for the argument that any review as to the very existence of the arbitration agreement should be on the basis of full judicial consideration'.[358]

At first blush, these decisions insinuate a distinction between disputes related to the existence of the obligation to arbitrate and disputes about the scope of the agreement. However, a few months later, Justice McGovern held in *Kellys of Fantane v. Bowen Construction* that a full judicial consideration was also required to determine whether the matter sought to be referred to arbitration was within the scope of the arbitration agreement.[359]

353. *Haas v. Gunasekaram,* 2016 ONCA 744 (CanLII), Court of Appeal for Ontario, Canada, 13 October 2016, para. 17. Further, as reiterated in *Kore Meals v. Freshii,* 2021 ONSC 2896, para. 18: '[U]nless the fifth question is answered in the affirmative (...) a stay of proceedings is called for.'
354. *Yusuf Abdalla Ibrahim Abdi v. Ibrahim Noor Hillowly,* Civil Case 39 of 2017, [2017] eKLR, High Court of Kenya (Nairobi), 24 March 2017 paras 13-14. *See also Zaid Iqubal Dean v Samuel Gakiria Kingori & another,* Civil Case 116 of 2013, [2014] eKLR, High Court of Kenya (Mombasa), 3 April 2014.
355. *UAP Provincial Insurance Company Ltd v. Michael John Beckett,* Civil Appeal 26 of 2007, [2013] eKLR, Court of Appeal at Nairobi, 4 October 2013 where the court held that it was essential 'to consider whether there is in fact a genuine dispute when considering an application for stay proceedings'. Because the action before the court was for the enforcement of the parties' settlement agreement 'there was no dispute between parties capable of being referred to arbitration' (paras 24-25).
356. *East African Cables Ltd v. Mt. Kenya Cables Ltd,* Civil Case 97 of 2011, [2012] eKLR, para. 4 ('The onus of proving the matters in dispute fell within a valid and subsisting arbitration clause referred to by the applicant is on the party applying to the court for stay of proceedings.').
357. *Sterimed Technologies v. Schivo,* [2017] IEHC 35, para. 17. Similarly, Judge Osiemo in Nairobi explained that: 'I think ... it is incumbent upon the Judge seized of the matter to deal with it as a whole, to discover whether any of the legal impediments set out in the section exist as to disentitle the applicant of a stay.' *Virginia E. Wanbuy Otieno-Mbugua v. Africa Air Rescue Health Services (K) Ltd,* Civil Case 563 of 2006, [2006] eKLR, High Court at Nairobi (Milimani Law Courts), 12 September 2006.
358. *Barnmore v. Alandale,* [2010] IEHC 544, para. 8. The court found it unnecessary to take a conclusive stance on these conflicting approaches, as the respondent had not met the requirements even under the *prima facie* test.
359. *Kellys of Fantane Ltd v. Bowen Construction Ltd & another,* [2017] IEHC 357, High Court of Ireland, 1 June 2017, para. 18.

[5] A Contextual View Reading of the Law

Other decisions have considered the relationship (and tension) between the courts' role at the front-end of a dispute and the competence-competence power of arbitrators. As already explained in this work, that is the interplay between Articles 8(1) and 16(1) of the Model Law.

For example, a Court of Appeal in Paraguay concluded that the competence-competence principle does not have a negative effect, as it does not fully exclude the court's authority to determine jurisdictional questions at the outset of a dispute. In reaching this decision, the Court noted the high degree of textual similarity between Article 11 of the local arbitration act, Article 8(1) of the Model Law, and Article II(3) of the New York Convention. Guided by the New York Convention, the Court held that:

> [T]here are no doubts that the judge has the competence to analyse the existence of an arbitration agreement without violating the competence-competence principle, since this principle is limited to give the arbitral tribunal the competence to decide on its own competence [...] when the parties have decided to take such matter to the arbitral tribunal, but this without prejudice to the fact that if such matter is taken first to the judiciary, then the judge can also decide about the existence and validity of the arbitration agreement in order to refer, or not, the parties to arbitration.[360]

A close reading of the law has also guided judicial decisions based not only on the terms used but also on their silences or omissions. For example, for the Spanish Supreme Court, a specific legislative silence spoke loudly in favour of adopting a full merit standard of review. The Court noted that where the arbitration law aimed to limit court intervention, it did so expressly.[361] This was not the case where the arbitration legislation concerning the negative effect of competence-competence.[362] Given that the law did not explicitly displace the court's jurisdiction, the Supreme Court followed the general standard of review of jurisdictional challenges in scenarios other than arbitration. According to that standard, when determining disputes over their jurisdiction ('declinatoria' – a declinatory procedure), Spanish courts are not limited to a *prima facie* examination of the issue.[363]

360. *Edupca v. Rosario del Pilar López,* A/CN.9/SER.C/ABSTRACTS/186, p. 6, Civil Court of Appeals of Asunción, Paraguay, 7 April 2014. After concluding that it had competence to decide on the validity of the arbitration clause, the Court decided that the arbitration clause was clearly ambiguous, therefore rendering the clause inoperative because it could not be established with certainty the parties' intention to arbitrate their eventual disputes.
361. *Agrumexport S.A. v. Banco Popular Español S.A.*, Case No. 409/2017, Supreme Court of Spain, 27 June 2017, para. 3.
362. Spain adopted the Model Law in 2003 (Law 60/2003).
363. Articles 39 and 63(1) of the Spanish Law on Civil Procedure. *Agrumexport v. Banco Popular*, Case No. 409/2017, p. 3. Some authors have criticised this point, highlighting that in 'declinatoria' procedures a full-merit approach is permitted but is not mandatory. The discretionary powers of the court allow the court to adopt a prima facie approach depending on the circumstances of the case at hand. *See*, Manuel Penadés Fons et al., 'The New York Convention and the Enforcement of Arbitration Agreements by National Courts: What Level of Review?', in *60 Years of the New York Convention: Key Issues and Future Challenges*, ed. Katia Fach Gomez and Ana M. Lopez-Rodriguez (Kluwer Law International, 2019), pp. 7-8.

In the Supreme Court's view, the language of Article II(3) of the New York Convention and Article 8(1) of the Model Law also foresee a (full) court determination of the validity, effectiveness and application of the arbitration agreement to the dispute, before referring the parties to arbitration.[364]

Notably, the Supreme Court analysed the legislative history of the 2011 amendments to the Arbitration Act. During the Spanish parliamentary discussions, the drafters considered a proposal to specify that courts should refer the parties to arbitration unless they found the agreement was manifestly null or ineffective. However, that proposal was rejected. The Supreme Court inferred from that rejection that the legislator preferred not to limit the court review to a *prima facie* test.[365]

That reasoning is not new. It resembles one of the debates that took place twenty-seven years earlier at UNCITRAL when drafting Article 8(1) of the Model Law. As Chapter 5 will show in greater detail, the UNCITRAL Working Group discussed and dismissed a proposal to add language to Article 8(1) so that courts would have to deny a referral to arbitration request when the agreement was *manifestly* null and void.[366] Had it been adopted, such language would have a limited judicial review to *prima facie* findings.[367] In their 1989 authoritative commentary on the Model Law, Holtzman and Neuhaus stated that by rejecting that proposal, the Working Group made it clear that courts should 'settle' disputes relating to the existence and validity of the agreement to arbitrate before triggering the referral of the parties to arbitration.[368]

In a similar light, for the Supreme Court of India, legislative silence meant authorisation to conduct a full-fledged review. Although in the context of court appointment of arbitrators (rather than Article 8(1)), the Supreme Court of India preferred the full merits instead of the *prima facie* standard of review. The Supreme Court held that the Arbitration and Conciliation Act authorises the Chief Justice to appoint an arbitrator after being satisfied, on the merits, that the conditions for the appointment were present in the case. That is, there existed: (i) a valid arbitration agreement, (ii) a dispute capable of being arbitrated, and (iii) whether the arbitration agreement binds the parties.[369] The Supreme Court reasoned that:

> [I]n the absence of any restriction in the Act, [the judicial authority] has necessarily to decide whether, in fact, there is in existence a valid arbitration agreement and whether the dispute that is sought to be raised before it, is covered by the

364. *Agrumexport v. Banco Popular*, Case No. 409/2017, para. 4. The Supreme Court recalled that even the Brussels I Regulation 1215/2012 (Recast) confirms the idea that State courts can assess the validity of arbitration agreements (although arbitration is outside the scope of the Regulation – Article 1.2.d. Recital 12, Preamble).
365. *Ibid.*, paras 5-6.
366. *See* Chapter 6, section [F][3](viii). *See also*, UNCITRAL, Report of the Working Group on International Contract Practices, on its fifth session (22 February-4 March 1983) A/CN.9/233, para. 77.
367. Howard M. Holtzmann et al., *A Guide to the Model Law* (n. 83), p. 303. *See also* Peter Binder, *International Commercial Arbitration* (n. 96), para. 2-089, and the commentary of Julian D.M. Lew et al., *Comparative International Commercial Arbitration* (Kluwer Law International, 2003), para. 14-61.
368. Holtzmann et al., *A Guide to the Model Law* (n. 83), p. 303.
369. *S.B.P. v. Patel* (2005) 8 SCC 618, paras 10-11, 38. The Supreme Court explicitly excluded issues related to the scope of the arbitration agreement. It indicated that whether a claim comes within the purview of the arbitration clause should be decided by the arbitral tribunal first (para. 38).

> arbitration clause. It is difficult to contemplate that the judicial authority has also to act mechanically or has merely to see the original arbitration agreement produced before it, and mechanically refer the parties to an arbitration.[370]

The Supreme Court was aware of the competence-competence principle but limited it to its positive effects. When jurisdictional issues arise before the arbitral tribunal, arbitrators 'can and possibly, ought to decide them. ... But where the jurisdictional issues are decided (...) before a reference is made, Section 16 cannot be held to empower the arbitral tribunal to ignore the decision given by the judicial authority or the Chief Justice before the reference to it was made. The competence to decide does not enable the arbitral tribunal to get over the finality conferred on an order passed prior to its entering upon the reference by the very statute that creates it'.[371]

Interestingly, the Supreme Court was also mindful of party autonomy considerations and rightfully noted that these had two aspects. One is that a party should not be allowed unilaterally to disregard its contractual obligation to arbitrate. The other is that a party should not be forced to arbitrate if it has not agreed to do so. In the words of the Court, to do otherwise 'can certainly affect the right of that party and, even on monetary terms, impose on him a liability for meeting the expenses of the arbitration, even if it be preliminary expenses, if his objection is upheld by the arbitral tribunal.'[372]

The Court was also wary of respecting the minimal curial intervention principle and balancing it with efficiency considerations. Deferring court involvement until after the award is rendered and challenged 'does mean considerable expenditure and time spent by the party before the arbitral tribunal.'[373]

[6] Efficiency Considerations

An initial full review of jurisdictional objections in Article 8(1) actions has also found ground on procedural economy concerns: a balance of finality of decisions and the need to avoid multiplicity of proceedings.

For example, in *The Lisheen Mine v. Mullock,* the High Court of Ireland concluded that in the interest of proper case management and cost efficiency, courts should fully consider issues related to the existence of an arbitration agreement.[374] In its decision, Cregan J viewed the *prima facie* test to be wasteful of costs, as the parties might have to fight the same issue repeatedly: before the court (Article 8(1) Model Law), then before the arbitrators (Article 16(1) Model Law) and then again before the court (Article 34(2)(a)(1) Model Law).[375] The court explained its rationale in three points.

370. *Ibid.*, para. 18.
371. *Ibid.*, para. 19.
372. *Ibid.*, para. 24. In this vein, the Court also indicted that '[i]t is fundamental to our procedural jurisprudence, that the right of no person shall be affected without he being heard' (at para. 36).
373. *Ibid.*, para. 31.
374. *The Lisheen Mine v. Mullock & Sons (Shipbrokers) Ltd & ors,* [2015] IEHC 50, High Court of Ireland, 12 January 2015, para. 135. Like the stance the Supreme Court of Canada took in the Dell Computer case, the court held that, given that the question of whether there is an arbitration agreement is a question of law, courts are best positioned to make such determinations.
375. *Ibid.*

First, it would be unsatisfactory and a total waste of costs if a court should only decide on a *prima facie* basis whether an arbitration agreement exists after having heard the matter argued before it. Second, if the court only conducts its analysis at a *prima facie* review level, the parties might have to fight the issue on no less than three separate occasions. This cannot be in the interests of proper case management. Third, issues related to the existence of an arbitration agreement are usually questions of law, which are best decided by a court. Courts are well used to considering whether, based on the evidence, there is a valid contract between parties. Even if there are disputed facts on the evidence in the record, the court can hear oral evidence to resolve such conflicts of facts.[376]

Similarly, the Supreme Court of India held that the full-merit approach would prevent 're-agitating of same issues over and over again' and, thus, further the cause of justice.[377] For the Court, determining the validity and enforceability of the arbitration agreement are fundamental issues. Further, the legislator intended for courts to settle them in a final manner before referring the parties to arbitration.[378] In reaching its conclusion, the Court indicated that the proper interpretation and application of its arbitration law required its reading in the context of the New York Convention.

After noting the relationship between the Convention and the national statute, the Court found guidance in a soft-law instrument: the International Council for Commercial Arbitration (ICCA) Guide on the Interpretation of the New York Convention, which contains a roadmap to Article II.[379] Based on that Guide, the Court concluded that litigants must be referred to arbitration if there is an affirmative answer to these questions:

(1) Does the arbitration agreement fall under the scope of the Convention?
(2) Is the arbitration agreement evidenced in writing?
(3) Does the arbitration agreement exist, and is it substantively valid?
(4) Is there a dispute? Does it arise out of a defined legal relationship, whether contractual or not, and did the parties intend to have this particular dispute settled by arbitration?
(5) Is the arbitration agreement binding on the parties to the dispute that is before the Court?
(6) Is this dispute arbitrable?[380]

376. *Ibid.*
377. *Chloro Controls India Pvt. Ltd. v. Severn Trent Water Purification Inc. & Ors.*, (2013) 1 SCC 641, Supreme Court of India, 28 September 2012, para. 130. The Court also recalled from previous case law that such a decision produces *res judicata* effects, so the question of existence and validity of the arbitration agreement could be reopened before the arbitral tribunal (at paras 123-125).
378. *Ibid.*, para. 132.
379. Throughout the interpretative process of its arbitration act, the Supreme Court sought guidance also from national and international case law, and scholarly works. It did not, however, refer to the Model Law or the New York Convention's preparatory works.
380. *Chloro Controls v. Severn*, (2013) 1 SCC 641, paras 57-58.

In what is usually identified as a pro-arbitration stance, the Court explained that the expressions 'null and void, inoperative or incapable of being performed' have to be construed restrictively. The aim is to ensure that the decision provides certainty and is correct in law and fact. Especially because the decision 'has the effect of depriving the party of its *right of reference to arbitration*'.[381]

A few years after that Supreme Court decision, the High Court of India took a different approach. In *GMR Energy v. Doosan*,[382] the Delhi court made a *prima facie* determination on the validity of the arbitration agreement. However, the court made an important distinction depending on the type of action sought and its timing. According to the judgment, where the arbitration has already been initiated, it would be the domain of the arbitral tribunal to determine the jurisdictional question first. Also, because the court action and its referral to arbitration request were not provided in section 45 of the Act,[383] the court needed to decide 'without going into a full-fledged trial.'[384] If the action and referral request were under section 45 of the law, the court would have to examine the validity issue thoroughly and render a final decision.[385]

Conversely, other court decisions from jurisdictions that typically adopt a full review approach have taken a flexible stance to permit a stay under the *prima facie* approach where the circumstances of the case call for it or depending on the ground for the jurisdictional challenge.

For example, English courts adopt a full merit approach when determining stay applications under section 9 of the 1996 Arbitration Act.[386] However, where a court cannot determine whether the arbitration agreement is either null and void, inoperative or incapable of being performed by reviewing the evidence in the record, the court may consider whether or not to order a full trial under its inherent jurisdiction.[387] In this sense, the High Court held that, in that situation, it would have to be an exceptional case for the court to give way to the arbitrators to determine the jurisdictional issue.[388]

381. *Ibid.*, para. 76.
382. *Gmr Energy Limited v. Doosan Power Systems India,* CS(COMM) 447/2017, High Court of Delhi, New Delhi, India, 14 November 2017.
383. Section 45 of India Arbitration and Conciliation Act is the equivalent of Article 8 Model Law, and it applies to arbitrations seating outside of India. Instead, the jurisdictional question before the Court was within an action for the appointment of arbitrators.
384. *Gmr Energy Limited v. Doosan Power Systems India,* CS(COMM) 447/2017, paras 25.26-25.27.
385. This was the stand of the Supreme Court of India in *S.B.P. v. Patel,* (2005) 8 SCC 618.
386. *See, e.g., Dallah* [2010] UKSC 46, para. 96 ('The consistent practice of the courts in England has been that they will examine or re-examine for themselves the jurisdiction of arbitrators.'). Also, *Aeroflot v. Berezovsky,* [2013] EWCA Civ 784, para. 77 ('The words "satisfied" and "find" suggest that, in the context of civil proceedings in the English court, the standard of proof which must be attained so that the court should refuse a stay is one of the balance of probabilities.').
387. *See, e.g., Golden Ocean Group Ltd v. Humpuss Intermoda Transportasi Tbk Ltd & Anor,* [2013] EWHC 1240 (Comm), England and Wales High Court (Comm), 16 May 2013, para. 59. For a summary of the position in England and Wales, *see also,* Law Commission, *Review of the Arbitration Act 1996: Second Consultation Paper* (March 2023), paras 3.74-73.79. Available at: lawcom.gov.uk/project/review-of-the-arbitration-act-1996/.
388. *Nasharty & Ors v. J Sainsbury Plc,* [2003] EWHC 2195 (Comm), England and Wales High Court (Comm. Division), 30 September 2003, para. 29.

Another decision went further and explained that this would depend on the following:

- the extent to which the resolution of the issue will involve findings of fact which impact on substantive rights and obligations of the parties;
- whether the trial can be confined to a relatively circumscribed area of investigation or is likely to extend widely over the substantive matters in dispute between the parties.[389]

Although the words 'satisfied' and 'finds' in the legislation[390] require a full merits review, the appropriate course to take in those situations would be to grant a stay and let the arbitrators decide the jurisdictional point.[391]

More recently, the courts in a Model Law jurisdiction favoured a similar flexible, discretionary approach but to justify the opposite result. Efficiency considerations led the Federal Court of Australia in *Dialogue Consulting v. Instagram*[392] to conclusively dispose of jurisdictional challenges, instead of giving arbitrators an opportunity to preliminary decide the matter.

In dismissing the respondent's stay request in favour of arbitration, the Court found that the parties' agreement to arbitrate had become 'inoperative'.[393] The question before the court was whether the respondent's participation in the litigation amounted to a waiver of the right to arbitrate.[394] In the court's opinion (confirmed by the Full Federal Court), accepting Instagram's reliance on the arbitration agreement almost a year into the litigation would have prejudiced Dialogue. It would have caused unnecessary expense and inefficiency. Instagram's unreasonable delay in raising the court's lack of jurisdiction had 'misled Dialogue into thinking that the proceedings was the appropriate forum'.[395]

In appeal, the Full Federal Court further noted that this would have caused Dialogue 'to lose the benefits of arbitration, namely the expedient, efficient and cost-effective resolution of disputes'.[396] It would also have caused Dialogue 'to engage in time-consuming and costly litigation steps that might be wasted.'.[397]

And the Full Federal Court confirmed that the lower court properly exercised its discretion in determining the jurisdictional challenge rather than referring the question to arbitration.[398] The parties had accepted that the court *could* decide the issue, although the respondent had (unsuccessfully) contended that the court *should* prefer to

389. *A v. B*, [2006] EWHC 2006 (Comm), para. 137.
390. Section 9(4) English Arbitration Act and Article II(3) of the New York Convention.
391. *Aeroflot v. Berezovsky*, [2013] EWCA Civ 784, para. 79. This finding reflected the decision of Colman J in *A v. B*, [2006] EWHC 2006 (Comm), para. 137.
392. *Dialogue Consulting Pty Ltd v. Instagram, Inc*, [2020] FCA 1846, Federal Court of Australia, 22 December 2022.
393. *Ibid.*, para. 599.
394. *Instagram Inc v. Dialogue Consulting Pty Ltd*, [2022] FCAFC 7, Federal Court of Australia – Full Court, 4 February 2022, para. 91.
395. *Dialogue v. Instagram*, [2020] FCA 1846, para. 588.
396. *Instagram v. Dialogue*, [2022] FCAFC 7, para. 95.
397. *Ibid.*
398. *Ibid.*, para. 56.

allow the arbitrators to have the first say. This contrasts with the views is most jurisdictions, which appear to interpret the Model Law in binary terms rather than as a matter of judicial discretion.

[E] CONCLUSIONS

The case-law analysis in this chapter shows that courts have yet to embrace or grapple with a distinct, nuanced, and uniform interpretative approach when addressing the synergic application of their local arbitration legislation, the Model Law, and the New York Convention. If they have, this was not done explicitly. Some points, however, seem to have been common ground, at least in the better-reasoned decisions.

A low degree of textual dissimilarity between the local arbitration law and the Model Law or the New York Convention has translated into a distinction without a difference. At least when testing the phrase 'unless the court is *satisfied*' (e.g., Singapore International Arbitration Act) and 'unless the court *finds*' (Model Law and New York Convention). The understanding is that the law requires the same standard of review to *find* and be *satisfied* that the arbitration agreement is not null and void, inoperative or incapable of being performed. It is in the extent of the review itself that courts have reached opposing results.

The explicit uniformity goal of Article 2A of the Model Law is not commonly described or mentioned in the reasoning for adopting one or the other standard of review. Uniformity is addressed implicitly but directly through case law, in a kind of cross-judicial dialogue where judges consider decisions from other Model Law jurisdictions and, often, from England and Wales. Some court decisions discuss with approval the outcome and reasoning of other judges, but, at times, the discussions lead them to disagreement and adopt opposing views.

The judgments analysed show that the records of the discussions at UNCITRAL when drafting the Model Law play a role in the interpretative exercise, even in jurisdictions where preparatory works do not usually carry a pivotal interpretative weight. Some decisions do not draw much guidance from the Model Law's drafting history – they find it 'inconclusive'. But others take the drafter's discussions and decision not to include the terms '*prima facie*' or 'manifest'[399] to carry significant interpretative value. They find it clear, conclusive, and convincing evidence that the full merits approach is required – especially where similar discussions took place at the national parliamentary level. They infer meaning from the statutory silence. If the legislator considered and rejected limiting the court review, the intention must have been that the full review was preferred. Though, the Model Law's preparatory works do not explicitly state this conclusion (*see* further discussion in Chapter 5, section [E][1]).

399. In the phrase 'the court shall refer the parties to arbitration, unless it *prima facie (or manifestly)* finds that the arbitration agreement is null and void, inoperative and incapable of being performed.'.

Some decisions observe that where the drafters wanted to limit the national courts' powers, they did so. What court decisions appear to struggle with is the extent of their involvement where the law does provide for it.

Those discussions have been linked to the general principle of minimal court intervention (Article 5 Model Law). No decision disagrees with the view that court intervention should be limited and that courts should not assault or usurp the role of arbitrators. However, it is not an assault when the law allows or requires court involvement. As discussed in Chapters 5 and 6 below, the Model Law explicitly provides for such court involvement at the pre-award stage regarding jurisdiction disputes. Article 8(1) provides that a court should *make a finding* concerning the validity and operativity of arbitration agreements. But even if a court retains a case for a full review of the jurisdictional challenge, the arbitrators can hear and determine the issue (Article 8(2) Model Law[400]).

The competence-competence principle consistently appears as a factor for balancing court involvement (Article 16(1) Model Law). No court decision denies the positive effects of competence-competence, whether rooted in the parties' (putative) agreement or the law. However, some decisions reflect the view that arbitral competence-competence does not dictate the extent of the courts' powers to determine theirs. Courts, too, enjoy the competence to decide on their own competence, including whether it has been displaced by an agreement to arbitrate.

Facilitating, promoting, and encouraging arbitration as a means of dispute resolution are guiding policies typically relied upon to prefer the *prima facie* standard of review. Discouraging dilatory tactics and avoiding unnecessary delays too, though there seems to be only a partial view of dilatory tactics. Courts focus on the claimant's potential ill-intended manoeuvres. However, they seem less inclined to initially suspect a delaying tactic from the defendant that, in the court action, requests the referral to arbitration.

Several court decisions channel pro-arbitration policies and goals through the *prima facie* approach. The principle of 'presumptive validity' of arbitration agreements encapsulated in Article 8(1) serves as a theoretical avenue for this. The argument is that where there is *prima facie* evidence of an arbitration agreement, it is for the arbitrators to decide its validity and extent. On a fuller analysis, that conclusion does not clarify the appropriate standard of review under Article 8(1). As discussed in the next chapter (section [D[4]), the validity presumption shifts the burden of proof to the party resisting the discontinuation of the substantive court action. It does not establish whether it must be discharged before a judge or arbitrators in the first place.

Courts also link the validation presumption to the concept of party autonomy because there is predictability in holding parties to their bargains. Case law shows that the obligation to respect party autonomy has a flip side. On the one hand, courts must recognise and enforce the parties' agreement to arbitrate their disputes. On the other, it requires that courts respect the parties' will not to enter into an arbitration agreement – that is, not to compel parties to arbitrate when they have not contracted to do so.

400. *See* further the discussion in Chapter 5, section [F].

Other court decisions find procedural economy in deciding the jurisdictional issue at once. That way, the parties avoid re-agitating the same jurisdictional dispute. The most elaborate decisions focus on the facts of the case to adopt either (*prima facie*/full review) approach. In their view, the test is specific and flexible. Courts find efficiency in letting arbitrators decide first, even when the courts have the authority to make a final (conclusive) determination.

In short, the analysis of case law that proposes the *prima facie* or the full merits approaches is illustrative and significant. It underscores the lack of a uniform and distinct approach to legal interpretation. It tests the normativity of the Model Law and unveils the implications of the critical question analysed here in judicial practice and potential legislative action.

It also evidences that, in general, courts interpret Article 8 in binary and exclusionary terms, concluding that the law permits *only* either a *prima facie* or a full merit review standards of review. Even where some court decisions adopt intermediate or middle-ground solutions, the starting point does not differ – their interpretative exercise appears to result in the law imposing one approach or the other.

The following chapters address whether Article 8 of the Model Law *imposes* such a conclusion, or if policy preferences and outcomes have overthrown its contextual reading, and the instrument's legislative purpose.[401] As it will become evident from the remainder of this book, the text of Article 8 (Chapter 5 below), read in its context (Chapter 6), does not impose one approach and exclude the other. On the contrary, the purpose of the Model Law affords the opposite interpretative outcome. No approach is imposed; both are permitted. Applying one or the other in specific cases is a matter of judgment (rather than opinion) to achieve a fair and efficient resolution of the dispute at hand (Chapter 7).

401. Some scholars argue that the most important obstacle to legal interpretation is cognitive. A critical fallacy is in the tendency of policy preferences to influence the reading of a text without the reader's awareness of it. *See*, Ward Farnsworth et al., Policy Preferences and Legal Interpretation, 1 *Journal of Law and Courts*, no. 1 (2013) DOI: 10.1086/668603.

CHAPTER 5
The Language of Article 8 of the Model Law

[A] INTRODUCTION

This chapter examines the text of Article 8 of the Model Law and its scope of application. Given that the interpretative approach proposed in Chapter 3[402] recognises a primary value of the Model Law's preparatory works, this chapter examines the extensive and well-documented deliberations at UNCITRAL leading to the text of Article 8 (Model Law). It seeks to uncover the meaning the epistemic community of international arbitration gave to the terms used in its final draft. This will contribute to the debate when the interpretative outcome diverges from what UNCITRAL intended with the words selected for achieving the instrument's purpose.

This chapter starts with general remarks on the significance of the law(s) governing several aspects of agreements to arbitrate (section [B]). It continues with an introduction of the language of Article 8 and its relationship to Article II(3) of the New York Convention (section [C]). The remainder of the chapter is divided into two main sections, in line with the two paragraphs that compose Article 8. The first analyses Article 8(1). It relates to a national court's obligations and powers when confronted with an action covered by an arbitration agreement (section [D]). It also considers the impact of substantive arbitrability on the timing of the court's (conclusive) settlement of jurisdictional challenges (section [E][2](2)).

The second section [F] analyses Article 8(2), which relates to the parties' and arbitrators' discretionary powers to commence or continue arbitral proceedings in parallel with the court action described in the preceding section. The chapter ends with a conclusion (section [G]).

Before moving on to those discussions, it is important to note that no territorial limits bind the operation of Article 8. It applies regardless of the jurisdiction where the

402. *See* Chapter 3, section [E].

arbitration proceedings are to take place. Article 1(2) of the Model Law explicitly provides that '[t]he provisions of this Law, except articles 8(...) apply only if the place of arbitration is in the territory of this State'.[403]

That the Model Law extends the application of Article 8 beyond the potential seat of an arbitration is a (out of many) clear example of the instrument's driving aims: facilitating international arbitration. As the records of the Working Group discussions show, its drafters understood that 'an arbitration agreement can only be effective if it prevents the parties from bringing an action before a court in *any* State' [emphasis added].[404]

[B] THE APPLICABLE LAWS

Judges see arbitration agreements through legal lenses. Therefore, determining the law applicable to the arbitration agreement is a threshold concern, antecedent to the court's finding on the existence, validity, and enforceability of such an agreement.

Law is the pervasive thread that pulls together and legitimises the arbitration agreements' existence, interpretation, validity, and enforceability. As contracts, agreements to arbitrate are subjected (largely, but not only) to contract law challenges and defences. Other general or specific laws may apply to impose formal requirements or restrict or exclude the substantive arbitrability of certain disputes. Law is also the avenue to determine the identity of the parties to an agreement and their legal capacity. Consequently, the laws that govern the several dimensions of arbitration agreements are an essential, instructive tool for judges to make the *finding* that Article 8(1) imposes.

It follows then that deciding on an arbitration agreement's enforceability requires the court to identify the law(s) applicable to the given jurisdictional dispute. Identifying the governing law is only the first (challenging) step to judging an agreement's existence, validity, and enforceability. Ascertaining its content is the second challenge, and applying it to the facts of the case is the third.

An important consequence of the separability presumption relates to the law applicable to an arbitration agreement.

Briefly put, separability is the presumption according to which arbitration clauses are separable from the underlying contract. The second and third sentences of Article 16(1) of the Model Law provide that, in determining whether the arbitral tribunal has jurisdiction:

> [A]n arbitration clause which forms part of a contract shall be treated as an agreement independent of the other terms of the contract. A decision by the arbitral tribunal that the contract is null and void shall not entail *ipso jure* the invalidity of the arbitration clause.

403. Article 1(2) Model Law: 'The provisions of this Law, except articles 8, 9, 17 H, 17 I, 17 J, 35 and 36, apply only if the place of arbitration is in the territory of this State.'
404. Working Paper Submitted to the Working Group on its Seventh Session, A/CN.9/WG.II/WP.49 (21 December 1983), para. 19.

Given its presumed autonomy from the contract that contains it, an arbitration clause may be governed by a different law. Article 8 of the Model Law is not explicit as to the law to test the court's referral obligation. Article II(3) of the New York Convention is not of assistance either. And this silence has motivated much doctrinal debate and jurisprudential disagreements.

Arguably, a contextual reading of the Model Law answers applicable law questions related to the validity of the arbitration agreement. Its Article 34 establishes a hierarchy of sources for award-annulment proceedings, where the point of departure is party autonomy (the parties' choice of law). Where the parties have failed to agree on the law to govern their arbitration agreement, Article 34(2)(a)(i) looks to the law of the place where the award was made as the default choice-of-law rule.[405] Article 36(1)(a)(i) of the Model Law[406] and Article V(1)(a) of the New York Convention offer the same solution for the recognition and enforcement of arbitral awards.[407] Given that annulment, recognition and enforcement proceedings are the ultimate court controls over the arbitration agreement, it would be coherent to rely on these default rules and on the same law(s) to determine the validity of the arbitration agreement at the referral stage (Article 8(1) Model Law and Article II(3) New York Convention).[408]

The Model Law and the New York Convention provide similar guidance for non-arbitrable matters and public policy issues.[409] The law of the forum governs those issues in the award recognition and enforcement context. But, again, the Model Law and the New York Convention are silent on the applicable law at an earlier stage, where the recognition and enforcement of arbitration agreements are controverted. Technically, the court seized in an Article 8(1) action could run the arbitrability and public policy tests according to its own laws, even if the parties have chosen a foreign law to govern the arbitration agreement or where the arbitration will take place, and the award will be made elsewhere. However, there is case law that has (correctly) linked

405. The Model Law's Analytical Commentary confirms this understanding. According to it, the relevant law for arbitration agreements is the one that the court would apply at the post-award stage in setting aside proceedings against the arbitrators' award. This is because those proceedings 'constitute the ultimate court control over the tribunal's decision'. Analytical Commentary on the Draft Text of a Model Law on International Commercial Arbitration: Report of the Secretary-General, 18th session, A/CN.9/264 (25 March 1985), Article 16, para. 13 (p. 38).
406. *See, ibid.*, p. 38, para. 33.
407. *See*, e.g., ICCA, *Guide to the Interpretation of the 1958 New York Convention: A Handbook for Judges*, Pieter Sanders (International Council for Commercial Arbitration, 2011), p. 60. Although this conclusion is not without opposing views; *see, e.g.*, Piero Bernardini, 'Arbitration Clauses: Achieving Effectiveness in the Law Applicable to the Arbitration Clause', in *Improving the Efficiency of Arbitration Agreements and Awards*, ed. AJ van den Berg, no. 9 (Kluwer Law International, 1999) ('[T]he law to be applied by a court ... as contemplated by Article II(3) of the New York Convention, has nothing to do with the law to be applied by a court, in case of a request for enforcement, under Art. V(1)(*a*) of the Convention.').
408. That is, under Article 8(1) Model Law and Article II(3) New York Convention.
409. Articles 34(2)(b)(i) and 36(1)(b)(i) of the Model Law and Article V(2)(a) of the New York Convention provide: 'Recognition and enforcement of an arbitral award may also be refused if the competent authority in the country where recognition and enforcement is sought finds that: (a) The subject matter of the difference is not capable of settlement by arbitration under the law of that country.'

and answered questions of substantive matter arbitrability according to the law applicable to the arbitration agreement.[410]

In turn, the text of the New York Convention and the Model Law appear to have different approaches in the law applicable to the capacity of the parties. In the context of enforcement proceedings of foreign arbitral awards, the New York Convention explicitly points to 'the law applicable to them' (i.e., the parties) to answer questions on their legal capacity (Article V(1)(a)). But, the Model Law did not replicate this in Articles 34 and 36, as its drafters were unpersuaded by the vagueness of the phrase that the Convention uses.[411]

In broad terms, the capacity of legal entities is commonly governed by the laws of the place of their incorporation. Where, instead, the parties to the arbitration agreement are human beings, legal capacity issues are usually ruled by the laws of their domicile. Conversely, the laws of a different legal system may govern the formal or substantive validity of an arbitration agreement, distinct from those applicable to the parties' capacity. The same may happen where parties other than those initially bound by the arbitration agreement are entitled to rely on it.

The solution that these default rules appear to offer for the post-award stage has not been unanimously accepted for the pre-award or referral stage. In practice, courts have advanced different criteria to determine the proper law for the arbitration agreement. For example, some courts rely on their local choice-of-law rules in the absence of the parties' express choice of law. Others apply the laws of the place where the parties concluded the agreement. Yet, other courts seek to determine whether the parties made an implied choice. That is the case where the parties designated a law to govern the contract that contains the arbitration clause. In those cases, the same law would apply to the substantive contractual relationship and the arbitration agreement. This approach finds support in commercial reasonableness. The parties likely intended the chosen law to govern their entire contract without distinction for the arbitration clause.[412]

Where none of those laws could be identified, some court decisions have relied on the system of law with which the arbitration agreement has the 'closest and most real connection' with the arbitration.[413] Usually, that is the seat of the arbitration.

410. *See, e.g.*, *Anupam Mittal v. Westbridge Ventures II Investment Holdings*, [2023] SGCA 1, Singapore Court of Appeal, 6 January 2023.

411. *See*, Report of the United Nations Commission on International Trade Law on the Work of its Eighteenth Session, A/40/17 (21 August 1985), paras 280-282.

412. Unless commercial parties are versed in arbitration law, it is likely that they are not aware that the arbitration clause in their contract is considered a separate agreement, independent of the rest of the contract. However, this conclusion is at odds with the separability presumption codified in Article 16(1) of the Model Law. However, the separability presumption was not developed for choice-of-law purposes but to avoid *automatically* carrying the invalidity of the underlying contract over to the arbitration clause. The law applicable to both contracts *may* be the same.

413. *See, e.g.*, the Singapore decision in *BNA v. BNB and BNC*, [2019] SGCA 84, Singapore Court of Appeal, 27 December 2019, and English decisions in the *Sulamerica v. Enesa* case and more recently in *Enka v. Chubb*. These decisions have sparkled extensive debate and commentary worldwide; *Sulamerica CIA Nacional De Seguros SA & Ors v. Enesa Engenharia SA & Ors*, [2012]

However, additional uncertainty unravels where the parties have not chosen the law applicable to their substantive contract or have not selected the seat of the arbitration.

These comments aim to illustrate the possibility of a myriad of laws applicable to different questions related to the enforceability of arbitration agreements and to highlight the intricacies of the matter.[414] Although the issue is essential in practice, its interesting and complex study exceeds the scope of this work. The point in all of this is obvious for any legal scholar, lawyer or law student: contracts (including arbitration contracts) are valid in accordance with their governing law. While elemental, this premise carries a critical weight for the extent of a court's involvement when finding whether an arbitration agreement is invalid or unenforceable at the referral stage.[415]

This calls for a reconsideration of the complexities in laying out a correct, coherent and consistent standard of court review of jurisdictional challenges under Article 8(1) of the Model Law. And to underline the depth of the difficulties that a judge may need to wrestle with when deciding a (threshold) jurisdictional dispute. It gives perspective to the court's task of *finding* whether the arbitration agreement is null and void, inoperative or incapable of being performed. Specifically, whether it is: (i) required, (ii) desirable or (iii) even possible, at the referral stage, for a court to determine those enforceability issues on a *prima facie* basis. Could a court *find* that an arbitration agreement is invalid without running a significant number of legal (and factual) inquiries? Does the *prima facie* review really involve a 'finding' or a 'prediction'?

[C] ARTICLE 8(1) MEETS ARTICLE II(3)

Article 8(1) of the Model Law is closely modelled on Article II(3) of the New York Convention. In the presence of an arbitration agreement, Article 8 prevents national courts from exercising their jurisdiction to consider and decide substantive disputes. It directs them to refer the parties to arbitration.[416]

Structurally, the courts' obligation to discontinue the proceedings and refer the parties to arbitration consists of two components:

- Preconditions: (i) the court action is the subject of an arbitration agreement; (ii) the agreement binds the parties; (iii) a party requests the referral.
- Exceptions: the arbitration agreement is null and void, inoperative or incapable of being performed.

EWCA Civ 638, England and Wales Court of Appeal, 16 May 2012; *Enka Insaat Ve Sanayi AS v. OOO 'Insurance Company Chubb' & Ors*, [2020] UKSC 38, United Kingdom Supreme Court, 9 October 2020.

414. This is why the drafters of the Model Law did not list the grounds that would render the parties' agreement 'null and void, inoperative or incapable of being performed'. It was too complex an issue to clearly address uniformly in a model law. *See*, Report of the Working Group on International Contract Practices, on the Work of its Third Session, A/CN.9/216 (23 March 1982), para. 25.
415. *See* the analysis in section [E][2].
416. Analytical Commentary (A/CN.9/264), p. 24, para. 23.

The first and second preconditions are of a *substantive* character. They are met if an arbitration agreement exists (at least ostensibly), the court action falls within its scope, and the agreement binds the disputing parties. The third precondition is of a *procedural* nature: without a party request, courts cannot refer the parties to arbitration.

The exceptions are not specific to arbitration. Given that arbitration agreements are a type of contract, the exceptions reflect the general (contract law) idea that courts should not enforce 'inexistent' or 'invalid' contracts, particularly if it would deprive the parties of the fundamental right to court access.

As already described, Article 8(1) of the Model Law provides that:

> A court before which an action is brought in a matter which is the subject of an arbitration agreement shall, if a party so requests not later than when submitting his first statement on the substance of the dispute, refer the parties to arbitration unless it finds that the agreement is null and void, inoperative or incapable of being performed.

This is the language of Article II(3) of the New York Convention:

> The court of a Contracting State, when seized of an action in a matter in respect of which the parties have made an agreement within the meaning of this article, shall, at the request of one of the parties, refer the parties to arbitration, unless it finds that the said agreement is null and void, inoperative or incapable of being performed.

Like the Model Law, the New York Convention does not shed any light on the extent of the judicial review of the grounds that a party may raise for non-enforcement of the arbitration contract.

As noted earlier, in interpreting and applying Article II(3) of the New York Convention and Article 8(1) of the Model Law, national courts have generally adopted one of the two main approaches at the referral stage: a full or a *prima facie* review.[417]

Because Article 8(1) Model Law and Article II(3) New York Convention are intended to produce the same legal effects, some discussions on the New York Convention inform and affect the interpretation and application of Article 8 Model Law. And vice-versa. Therefore, some cross-references are made in this chapter, where the Convention has explicitly influenced the drafting of Article 8 of the Model Law.

[D] ARTICLE 8(1): THE POWERS OF THE COURT

This section focuses on paragraph 1 of Article 8, which is directed at national courts and the parties involved in the litigation. Its text guides its addresses' conduct and

417. *See* Marike R.P. Paulsson, *The NYC in Action* (n. 134), pp. 66-67; Dorothée Schramm et al., 'Article II', in *Recognition and Enforcement of Foreign Arbitral Awards: A Global Commentary on the New York Convention*, ed. Patricia Nacimiento et al. (Kluwer Law International, 2010), pp. 109-114; UNCITRAL Secretariat Guide on the Convention on the Recognition and Enforcement of Foreign Arbitral Awards (2016), pp. 62-68.

imposes the conditions under which the court may or should exercise its authority to refer the parties to arbitration.

The following subsections dissect its text and describe and analyse the debates during its drafting history. The first subsection refers to Article 8(1)'s scope of application.

[1] A Substantive Claim Is Needed

The first part of Article 8(1) sets the scope of its application: 'A court before which an *action* is brought *in a matter* which is the subject of an arbitration agreement (…)'.[418]

The 'action' brought to the court's decision must be a substantive claim. A party's objection to the court's jurisdiction acts as a *defence* to resist litigation of the substantive dispute. The 'action' refers to a substantive dispute that the parties have (purportedly) agreed to submit to arbitrators for determination. If the court is not seized of a (substantive) action, Article 8 is not triggered, and no referral to arbitration may be requested.

In broad terms, that would be the situation where, for example, a party to an arbitration agreement requests an interim measure from a court.[419] Such a request cannot be understood as a waiver or repudiation of the arbitration agreement, as interim measures do not aim to settle the substantive disputes between the parties.[420] They usually seek to preserve evidence, maintain, restore the *status quo* pending the determination of the dispute, preserve assets out of which a subsequent award may be satisfied, or assist in the production of evidence (e.g., hearing testimony from a witness domiciled in the territory of the court).[421]

These situations do not create a conflict of authority (jurisdiction) between courts and arbitral tribunals. On the contrary, recognising the national courts and arbitrators' concurrent powers to grant interim measures supports the arbitral process.

Similarly, Article 8(1) cannot be relied upon in declaratory actions. That is, with the sole purpose of requesting a national court to declare whether a valid and enforceable arbitration agreement exists.[422] However, national legislators can deviate from the Model Law when adopting it and include the possibility of declaratory actions. That is the case, for example, in Germany. When adopting the Model Law, the German legislator deviated from Article 8(1) by providing that '[p]rior to the constitution of the

418. Emphasis added.
419. Or to assist in the constitution of the arbitral tribunal, Article 11 of the Model Law.
420. In this respect, Article 9 of the Model Law provides that '[i]t is not incompatible with an arbitration agreement for a party to request, before or during arbitral proceedings, from a court an interim measure of protection and for a court to grant such measure.'
421. *See, e.g.*, Article 17 of the Model Law.
422. Some court decisions have exceptionally allowed actions with the sole purpose of determining the valid existence of an arbitration agreement. *See, e.g.*, the decision of the Ontario Court of Appeals in *Jean Estate v. Wires Jolley LLP*, [2009] ONCA 339, Court of Appeal for Ontario, Canada, 29 April 2009.

arbitral tribunal an application may be made to the court to determine whether or not arbitration is admissible'.[423]

A study of the Model Law's drafting history reveals that there was some support for adopting a similar provision under what was then draft Article 17.[424] Yet, the drafters of the Model Law understood that allowing declaratory actions could risk inviting dilatory tactics, and it would conflict with the competence-competence principle set out in Article 16.[425]

It is worth noting that the Model Law recognises party autonomy in delimiting the substantive scope of Article 8's application. It refers not to every possible substantive dispute between the parties but only those they have agreed to arbitrate.

Arbitration agreements can be narrow or broad in scope. Usually, they are worded in the broadest possible terms to cover all the disputes 'arising out of', 'related to' or 'connected with' the parties' legal relationship. But nothing prevents the parties from limiting their obligation to arbitrate. Parties may, inadvertently (by poor drafting) or intentionally (by sound drafting), exclude the resolution of certain disputes to a different forum or the remedies available to the arbitrators.[426]

Controversies arise when it is unclear whether a given dispute falls within the scope of the arbitration agreement. For example, this might happen where a contractual matrix governs the parties' legal relationship, containing conflicting arbitration clauses or some no dispute resolution clauses at all. It could also happen if a dispute arises once the parties' contract that contained an arbitration clause is terminated, out of the other party's post-termination conduct, or after the novation of the contracts. These and similar situations require a construction of the language of the agreement and the parties' intention to determine whether the dispute is the subject of the agreement to arbitrate. Thus, they are mainly fact-based inquiries guided by canons of contract interpretation and the relevant law.[427]

All this may take a toll on the court's decision under Article 8(1); it is a precondition to granting the referral to arbitration that the arbitration agreement covers the action before the judge. Consequently, the court shall not refer the parties to arbitration if the substantive claim falls outside the agreement's scope. The essential

423. *Arbitration Law 1998 (Book 10 Code of Civil Procedure)* (Germany), § 1032. *See* Chapter 6, section [D] for further comments and examples of national arbitration laws in Model Law jurisdiction that have deviated from the text of Article 8(1).

424. Draft Article 17(1), '[Notwithstanding the provisions of article 16,] a party may [at any time] request the Court specified in article 6 to decide whether a valid arbitration agreement exists and [if arbitral proceedings have commenced,] whether the arbitral tribunal has jurisdiction [with regard to the dispute referred to it].'

425. *See* further comments on concurrent proceedings under draft Article 17 and its conflict with competence-competence in Chapter 6, section [2]. Report of the Working Group on International Contract Practices, on its Seventh Session, A/CN.9/246 (6 March 1984), paras 54-55.

426. Statutes may also impose limitations on the breadth of the arbitration agreement. Certain subject matters are not capable of being resolved in arbitration, even if they fall within the scope of the arbitration agreement. They are characterised as *arbitrability* issues, and are discussed in section [E][2](2) below.

427. For example, arbitration agreements are presumed valid, their terms and scope interpreted broadly, against ineffectiveness, and with a view to resolving ambiguities and vagueness in favour of arbitration. *See* section [D] above.

question is to what extent the court should hear and determine if the action falls within or outside the agreement's scope. Should it do so on a *prima facie* basis, or should the court determine the matter thoroughly and conclusively before any arbitral decision? This issue is at the heart of Article 8(1) of the Model Law[428] and this publication.

Even where a court is seized of a substantive action covered by a valid arbitration agreement, the court would refrain from entertaining the dispute only if the other Article 8(1) conditions are also met. Crucially, a *party request* must exist because the court cannot refer them to arbitration 'sua sponte'.

[2] No Referral 'Sua Sponte'

Courts cannot discontinue the action before them and refer the parties to arbitration on their own motion. Although the Model Law does not spell this out explicitly, its drafting history makes it clear. When discussing this point, the drafters considered and declined a proposal to delete from Article 8(1) the phrase 'at the request of a party'.[429]

One concern arose in the scenario where the respondent in the litigation did not appear before the court. Its non-appearance might be an informed and calculated decision, but it could be because appearing is not feasible. The claimant may have initiated the court action in a foreign country as a dilatory tactic to burden and exhaust the opposing party.

The drafters debated whether courts should have the power to, sua sponte, declare their lack of competence to hear and determine the substantive disputes. With this and similar situations in mind, the drafters preferred to approve the text of Article 8(1), according to which the referral to arbitration can happen only at a party's request.[430]

This is in line with the language and interpretation of Article II(3) of the New York Convention. During its drafting conference, the delegates discussed and decided to exclude the proposed phrase 'on its own motion' in the text of Article II(3).[431] The UNCITRAL drafters followed the same approach for the Model Law, in the understanding that this position acknowledges and strengthens party autonomy.[432] If the parties to an arbitration agreement wish to waive their right to arbitrate their disputes, they should be allowed to do so. This is a corollary of the consensual character of

428. And Article II(3) of the New York Convention.
429. Report of the Working Group on International Contract Practices, on the Work of its Fifth Session, A/CN.9/233 (28 March 1983), para. 76. *See also*, Summary Records of the 312th Meeting, A/CN.9/246, annex; A/CN.9/263 Add.1-2, A/CN.9/264 (6 June 1985), UNCITRAL Yearbook, para. 3.
430. Analytical Compilation of Comments by Governments and International Organizations on the Draft Text of a Model Law on International Commercial Arbitration. Report of the Secretary-General, 18th Session, A/CN.9/263 (19 March 1985), p. 21, para. 24.
431. United Nations Conference on International Commercial Arbitration, Summary Records of the Twenty-fourth Meeting, E/CONF.26/SR.24 (10 June 1958), p. 9.
432. UNCITRAL, Digest of Case Law on the Model Law on International Commercial Arbitration, para. 6: 'Courts have emphasized the importance, while applying the Model Law, of taking into consideration that party autonomy is one of its philosophical cornerstones.'

arbitration; i.e., it only exists where the contracting parties have agreed to arbitrate their disputes.[433]

As discussed in the following subsection, the referral request to the proper dispute resolution forum must meet a minimum threshold.

[3] The Referral Request

Article 8 presupposes that (and applies only where) there is an agreement to submit to arbitration (all or certain) disputes regarding the parties' defined legal relationship. That relationship may be contractual or not – as long as it is the basis for one party to seek a legal remedy from the other and the cause for agreeing to arbitrate the dispute.[434]

The 'request' to discontinue the litigation based on that agreement touches upon three critical concerns. One is the obvious need for a party to actively file a referral request. Additionally, the issue involves *who* and *what* questions: *Who* enjoys legitimacy to make the request, and *what* would the requesting party need to prove?

(a) The 'What Needs to Be Proved' Question

The Model Law does not explicitly address what the requesting party needs to prove for a court to grant a referral to arbitration. It is also unclear which party bears the burden of proof or the standard of proof to trigger the discontinuance of the court action in favour of arbitration.

Despite that silence, it is uncontroversial that the party resisting the court action should prove the existence of the parties' *consent* to arbitrate disputes. This conclusion is based on the fact that the enforcement of the arbitration agreement is dependent on a party's request. This responds to the generally accepted procedural-law rule that the burden of proof rests on the party that raises the argument. At a policy level, requiring (some) evidence that such an agreement exists precludes parties from making groundless allegations that would merely delay the resolution of the substantive dispute.

Consent to arbitrate may take different forms. To effectively substantiate a referral request, the question boils down to a matter of evidence. To that end, a written agreement may evidence consent, even if it is poorly drafted.[435] It may also capture the

433. For a rare example of the opposite view, *see* the decision in *2T" Sh.p.k. v. 'Iren Acqua e Gas' (IAG), Albanian Branch,* Decision No. 181, Supreme Court of Albania, 1 June 2016, where at para. 1 the court held that: '... The court may review [the jurisdictional objection] even ex officio, as jurisdiction is closely related to the administration of the judicial process and to due process as protected in Art. 6 of the [European Convention for the Protection of Human Rights and Fundamental Freedoms].'

434. Article 7 Model Law (Option I and II). *See, e.g., Tommy CP Sze & Co v. Li & Fung (Trading) Ltd,* [2002] HKCFI 682, Hong Kong Court of First Instance, 28 October 2002, para. 18: 'It is, of course, crucial in any application for a stay (whether under section 6 of the Ordinance or Article 8 of the Model Law) that there exists an arbitration agreement. By this is meant an agreement between the parties by which present or future disputes or differences between them are required to be resolved by the arbitral process.'

435. For example, in the *Lucky-Golden* case, the High Court of Hong Kong enforced an arbitration agreement that provided for arbitration in a '3rd country, under the rules of a 3rd country and

parties' implied consent. Parties may impliedly agree to arbitrate their disputes through, for example, the exchange of communications recorded in any form (signed or not)[436] or their conduct.[437] Courts have found consent to arbitration where the parties performed a contract that included an arbitration clause.[438] Courts have consented to arbitrate disputes by participating in the negotiation and performance of contracts.[439] Some courts have even found that consent could be inferred from trade usages where the parties are active players in the field.[440]

Proof of the existence of consent to arbitrate does not 'necessarily' require proof that a *formally* and *substantially* valid arbitration agreement exists. Questions related to the formal and substantive validity of the arbitration agreement are usually reserved for a subsequent step or inquiry. Because arbitration agreements are presumed valid, those issues are discussed only if a party resists the enforcement of the agreement to arbitrate. This pro-enforcement approach to arbitration law is embedded in the New York Convention and the Model Law's philosophy, and it enjoys doctrinal and jurisprudential acceptance. This is known as the principle of 'presumptive validity' of arbitration agreements and is addressed in section [D][4] ('A Burden-Shifting Presumption').

in accordance with the rules of procedure of the [non-existent] International Commercial Arbitration Association'. In enforcing this agreement, Kaplan J. concluded that he was satisfied that the arbitration agreement was valid in terms of consent since 'the parties clearly expressed the intention to arbitrate any dispute which may arise under this contract'; *Lucky-Goldstar International (H.K.) Limited v. Ng Moo Kee Engineering Limited,* [1993] HKCFI 14, High Court of Hong Kong, 5 May 1993.

436. Referring to the New York Convention, a court held that 'Article II does not say that the only agreement to which it refers is one which was formed or concluded by the act of signing or by the dispatch or receipt of a letter or telegram. What is required is that there be more than a unilateral statement in writing of the arbitration clause or arbitration agreement.' *Comandate Marine Corp. v. Pan Australia Shipping Pty. Ltd,* [2006] FCAFC 192, Federal Court of Australia, 20 December 2006, para. 149 (Further, *see* paras 147-156.).
437. *Barnmore Demolition and Civil Engineering Ltd v. Alandale Logistics Ltd & Ors,* [2010] IEHC 544, High Court of Ireland, 11 November 2010, para. 4: 'It is possible for the agreement to arbitrate to be concluded orally or by the conduct of the parties or by other means provided the content of the arbitration agreement is recorded in any form.'
438. *Smita Conductors Ltd. v. Euro Alloys Ltd,* Civil Appeal 12930 of 1996, Supreme Court of India, 31 August 2001, p. 5, *Consmaremma – Consorzio tra produttori agricoli Società Cooperativa a responsabilità limitata v. Hermanos Escot Madrid, SA,* Spain No. 32/E15, Yearbook Commercial Arbitration 2001 – Volume XXVI, pp. 858-862, Supreme Court of Spain, 20 February 2001, p. 860, para. 810: 'The contract of 30 August, together with the later contract of 30 October, the contents of both and especially Escot's position as to the latter, as well as the means of evidence available, show that the parties intended to submit disputes under their contract to arbitrators.'
439. *Bridas SAPIC v. Government of Turkmenistan,* 447 F.3d 411, United States Court of Appeals, 5th Circuit, 21 April 2006. For an opposite view, *see* the decision of the UK Supreme Court in *Dallah Real Estate and Tourism Holding Company v. The Ministry of Religious Affairs, Government of Pakistan,* [2010] UKSC 46, United Kingdom Supreme Court, 3 November 2010.
440. *Buyer v. Seller,* III ZR 30/9142, Federal Supreme Court of Germany (Bundesgerichtshof), 3 December 1992 p. 668, para. 665: 'Trade usages can lead to the tacit conclusion of an arbitration agreement, as far as typical contracts of that trade are concerned and the parties involved are regularly active in that particular trade.'; *Leadertex, Inc. v. Morganton Dyeing & Finishing Corp,* 67 F.3d 20, United States Court of Appeals, Second Circuit, 28 September 1995, where the court held that 'New York law allows arbitration agreement to rest on evidence of trade usage or of prior course of dealings'.

Proving the existence of consent also closely relates to the formal requirements of arbitration agreements *if* the applicable law imposes, for example, the written form.[441] In these cases, producing a written arbitration agreement would serve two purposes: crystallisation of the parties' commitment to arbitrate their disputes and compliance with the formalities required by the law applicable to the arbitration agreement. As long as the content of the agreement is recorded, the arbitration agreement would be formally valid.

Modern international commercial transactions most commonly generate documented evidence in e-mail communications, formally executed contracts in paper or electronic formats, with or without signatures. The traceable record they produce is widely recognised to meet the in-writing form requirement.[442]

Naturally, evidence of the existence of consent is also closely linked to the *who* question: who can request the discontinuance of the litigation and the referral to arbitration? This matter is addressed next.

(b) The 'Who Can Request the Referral' Question

It is crucial to make the following clear: the parties to the court action must be the parties to the arbitration agreement. Otherwise, the requesting party would have no legitimacy to make a request, and the court would have no authority to refer the parties that are not before it. As the Supreme Court of Bermuda wittily put it, granting the referral requested even though there is no arbitration agreement between the litigants would be '*arbitration heresy*.'[443]

Three distinct problems could arise regarding the *who* question. One relates to the past and present identity of the parties to the arbitration agreement. Another relates to the situation where not all the litigants in the court action are parties to the arbitration contract. The third relates to the legal capacity of the relevant parties.

There are complex contractual matrices where the identity of the original parties to the arbitration agreement is changed or replaced. Several legal theories serve as the basis for becoming a party to an arbitration agreement (e.g., the group of companies doctrine, agency, third-party beneficiary). Some of those legal or contractual bases may

441. For instance, Article 7 Option II of the Model Law does not impose formal conditions. However, Article 7(2) of Option I imposes the in-writing requirement for its valid formation. It provides that '[t]he arbitration agreement *shall* be in writing'. Some jurisdictions have followed this approach. For example, when adopting the Model Law, Egypt made explicit that '[t]he arbitration agreement must be *in writing, on penalty of nullity*' [emphasis added]. *Law Concerning Arbitration in Civil and Commercial Matters* (Egypt) Law No. 27/1994, (21 April 1994), Article 12.

442. *See, e.g.*, the UNCITRAL Recommendations on the interpretation of Articles II(2) and VII(1) of the New York Convention, which concluded that, according to the business realities of modern times, the 'signature' requirement or the exchange of 'letters or telegrams' where not exclusive means of concluding arbitration agreements 'in writing'. Also, parties are allowed to avail themselves of rights they may have under the law or treaties of the country where an arbitration agreement is sought to be relied upon; Report of the Commission on the Work of its Thirty-Ninth Session, General Assembly A/61/17 (SUPP) (14 July 2006), para. 181.

443. *Ian Cockwell v. Gordon Flatt*, [2014] Bda LR 89, Supreme Court of Bermuda, 23 September 2014, para. 31.

be recognised in one country but not in others.[444] Parties may also be or become bound to arbitrate by their conduct,[445] subrogation,[446] novation,[447] or assignment[448] of the substantive contract that contains an agreement to arbitrate. Non-signatories of an arbitration agreement have been bound to arbitrate when involved in inter-connected agreements related to a single commercial project.[449] Also, where a non-signatory sought to enforce a contractual right under an agreement that included an obligation to arbitrate disputes.[450]

The matters might also get complicated where only some - not all - the parties in the court action are bound by the obligation to arbitrate. One of the early concerns amongst the UNCITRAL Working Group II members was whether the Model Law should deal with this situation.[451] According to the records of those discussions, there was general agreement that the Model Law should not. Instead, it should leave the issue to the parties' discretion to, for example, consolidate arbitral proceedings, join, or extend the agreement to the non-parties.[452]

The jurisdictional issue here would be whether the arbitration agreement extends over those disputing parties. This may be characterised as a matter of the scope of the arbitration agreement.

As anticipated, a question of legal capacity may arise when assessing a party's referral request. It is unquestioned that parties must enjoy legal capacity to (validly) enter into an arbitration agreement. Without it, an arbitration agreement cannot be recognised and enforced. An argument can even be made that no contract emanates from a party that lacks capacity (issue of the agreement's *existence*). Further, a contract

444. For example, this is the case with the 'group of companies' doctrine, which is recognised in France but not in England. In broad terms, the doctrine permits the binding to arbitration agreements of parties that were involved in the negotiations, performance and termination of the contract. The Court of Appeal of Paris recognised this when confirming the arbitral jurisdictional decision in the *Dow Chemical* case, ICC Award No. 4131. England rejected it in the *Petersen Farms* case [2004] EWHC 121.
445. *See, generally*, Stavros Brekoulakis, 'Parties in International Arbitration: Consent v. Commercial Reality', in *The Evolution and Future of International Arbitration*, ed. Stavros L. Brekoulakis et al. (Kluwer Law International, 2016); William W. Park, 'Non-signatories and International Contracts: An Arbitrator's Dilemma', in *Multiple Party Actions in International Arbitration*, ed. PCA (Oxford University Press, 2009).
446. *West Tankers Inc v. RAS Riunione Adriatica Sicurta Spa & Anor*, [2007] EWHC 2184 (Comm), England and Wales High Court (Commercial Court) Decisions, 2 October 2007.
447. Bernard Hanotiau, *Complex Arbitrations: Multi-party, Multi-contract and Multi-issue*, 2d ed. (Kluwer Law International, 2020), p. 199. *CMA CGM SA v. Hyundai Mipo Dockyard Co Ltd*, [2008] EWHC 2791 (Comm), England and Wales High Court (Commercial Court) 14 November 2008.
448. *See, e.g.*, *Rinehart & Anor v. Hancock Prospecting Pty Ltd & Ors*, [2019] HCA 13, High Court of Australia, 8 May 2019, para. 73.
449. *Chloro Controls India Pvt. Ltd. v. Severn Trent Water Purification Inc. & Ors.*, (2013) 1 SCC 641, Supreme Court of India, 28 September 2012, para. 168.
450. *Dickson Valora Group (Holdings) Co Ltd v. Fan Ji Qian*, [2019] HKCFI 482, Hong Kong Court of First Instance, 20 February 2019, paras 20-27.
451. Report of the Secretary-General: Study on the Application and Interpretation of the Convention on the Recognition and Enforcement of Foreign Arbitral Awards, A/CN.9/168 (20 April 1979), para. 27. Also, Working Paper on Possible Features of a Model law on International Commercial Arbitration, A/CN.9/WG.II/WP.35 (1 December 1981), UNCITRAL Yearbook, para. 22.
452. Working Group Report A/CN.9/216, para. 37.

is invalid when the party's limited capacity does not authorise it to enter that specific contract. In either case, the immediate effect is that the agreement is unenforceable. But, the distinction may become relevant when identifying *who* (the court or the arbitrator) should be the first to determine the jurisdictional issue.

The Model Law's drafters discussed this critical issue. Given its complexities and the disparities of opinions and approaches between jurisdictions, they decided that the question of capacity fell outside the scope of the Model Law. Therefore, no such provision was included.[453]

The critical observation here is that all these complexities might muddle the court's task when deciding whether the requesting party has standing to make the request and whether its content sufficiently meets the burden of proof.

Because parties can explicitly or implicitly manifest their consent to arbitrate disputes, the crux of the matter is the degree of clarity or certainty needed to establish its existence to trigger the parties' referral to arbitration or a jurisdictional challenge. To a great extent, this will depend on the different laws that may govern the (formal and substantive) validity of arbitration agreement and the capacity of the parties.

Regardless of the standard of proof for the existence of consent to arbitrate (e.g., 'balance of probability' or 'good arguable case'), once it is established, the court can *presume* that it is valid and enforceable. This presumption puts a significant legal effect in motion, which is addressed next.

[4] A Burden-Shifting Presumption

According to Article 8(1) of the Model Law,[454] arbitration agreements are presumed valid and enforceable. The Model Law does not explicitly state this. Still, it transpires from its mandatory language ('shall') and the shift of the burden of proof ('unless') to the party opposing the enforcement of such agreement:[455]

> A court (...) *shall* (...) refer the parties to arbitration *unless* it finds that the agreement is null and void, inoperative or incapable of being performed.[456]

The term 'unless' in Article 8(1) imposes an imperative condition of substantive law. The general rule is that arbitration agreements are readily enforceable. But this

453. *Ibid.*, para. 28. Like, for example, the one in the European Convention on International Commercial Arbitration (1961), Article VI(2): 'In taking a decision concerning the existence or the validity of an arbitration agreement, courts of Contracting States shall examine the validity of such agreement with reference to the capacity of the parties, under the law applicable to them ...'.
454. Article II(3) of the New York Convention bears the same effect. *See*, ICCA, *ICCA's Guide* (n. 407), p. 37 ('[T]he Convention sets forth a "pro-enforcement", "pro-arbitration" regime which rests on the presumptive validity – formal and substantive – of arbitration agreements.').
455. *See, e.g.*, Gary B. Born, *International Commercial Arbitration* (n. 15), p. 697 ('[C]ontemporary international and national legal regimes unequivocally embrace the principle that international arbitration agreements are presumptively valid, subject only to enumerated and narrowly-construed exceptions, based on generally-applicable rules of contract law.'). Also case law, *e.g.*, *GWJ Blackman and Co SA v. Oliver Davey Glass Co Pty Ltd and Noel Searle Pty Ltd*, [1966] VicRp 77, Full Court of the Supreme Court of Victoria, Australia, 10 June 1966, p. 5.
456. Article 8(1) Model Law [emphasis added].

presumption is rebuttable; The opposing party can produce evidence against the presumed fact. For that reason, a court is not required to enforce the agreement if it finds that it is null and void, inoperative or incapable of being performed. Put differently, courts shall refer the parties to arbitration if a valid agreement exists and covers the dispute between the parties.

This interpretation of the wording of Article 8(1) is consistent with the presumptive validity and enforceability of arbitral awards. It mirrors the allocation of the burden of proof where a party attacks the award's validity or resists its recognition and enforcement. The party that relies on the award does not bear a negative burden of proof. It is not burdened to prove the award's validity or enforceability. Instead, the burden of proving its invalidity or non-enforceability rests on the party that claims it. That party must prove the existence of one of the grounds listed in the Model Law (Article 34 – set aside – or Article 36 – resist its enforcement[457]) or the New York Convention (Article V),[458] as the case may be.

The legal presumption does not apply to the *existence* of consent to arbitrate. As discussed earlier, arbitration is a matter of contract and, therefore, requires the agreement of the disputing parties to displace the default mechanism of dispute resolution: litigation. The presumption is limited to the *validity* and *operation* of the arbitration agreement. It is triggered once a party proves (even ostensibly) the existence of consent to arbitrate.

There is some controversy regarding the effects of the presumption. Some authorities are of the view that it supports or is in line with the *prima facie* standard of review. Thus, the presumption would establish a rule of chronological priority favouring arbitrators.[459] The logic of that argument is as follows. Once a party has proved the existence of consent or an arbitration agreement, the law presumes its validity. Thus, faced with a (presumably) valid arbitration agreement, the court should stop the court action (if so requested) and refer the parties to arbitration. This way, the court gives priority to the arbitrators to decide the jurisdictional challenge against the enforceability of such an agreement.

However, that conclusion is at odds with the text of the law. The presumption appears only to shift the burden of proof from the party relying on the arbitration agreement to the party resisting its enforcement.[460] The presumption disappears if the resisting party meets its burden by proving that the arbitration agreement is invalid or unenforceable.

---

457. Article 36 of the Model Law mirrors the Convention's language (Article V), although its scope of application is broader. It applies to arbitral awards irrespective of the country in which it was made.
458. Paulsson, *The NYC in Action*, p. 67 '(The strong reasons that would persuade the court not to recognize the arbitration agreement must be proven by the respondent. Under that approach, Article II would allocate the burden of proof in much the same way as Article IV and V [of the New York Convention]).'
459. *See, e.g.*, Gaillard et al., *Negative Effect of Competence-Competence* (n. 8), p. 258.
460. This seems to be the position of the High Court of Ireland in *Sterimed v. Schivo*, where it held that '[t]he onus is on the defendants to establish the existence of the arbitration agreement. If it discharges that burden then the onus shifts to the plaintiffs to show that the arbitration agreement was null and void if the court proceedings are not to be stayed.'; *Sterimed Technologies International & Anor v. Schivo Precision Ltd & Ors* [2017] IEHC 35, High Court of Ireland, 27 January 2017, para. 12. Similar court decisions were discussed in Chapter 5 above.

The question of whether the resisting party has discharged that burden is for the court to answer. Otherwise, the immediate referral would pre-empt the presumption's burden-shifting effect. For the court action and the referral, the presumption would become irrefutable. That result would transform the 'presumption' into an 'assumption'. However, Article 8(1) does not assume that arbitration agreements are valid and that courts should, inevitably, refer parties to arbitration. Instead, the legal text presumes that they are, allows evidence to the contrary, and conditions the referral to the court finding that the disputed agreement is not null and void, inoperative or incapable of being performed.

The validity presumption does not stretch to impose a *prima facie* review of jurisdictional objections and its consequent obligation to refer the parties to arbitration immediately. At least, this is not the extent that the language of Article 8(1) of the Model Law and Article II(3) of the New York Convention seems to support.[461]

Despite the effect and extent of the validity presumption, it is undisputed that its operation strengthens party autonomy and the Model Law's pro-arbitration attitude. In addition, the language of Article 8(1) of the Model Law fosters procedural efficiency by imposing a *time limit* for the parties to request the referral to arbitration.

[5] The Time Limit

As noted earlier, Article 8(1) of the Model Law replicates the language of Article II(3) of the New York Convention. It copies it almost word for word. The Model Law adds a time-limit requirement absent in the New York Convention. The referral should be requested no later than when submitting the first statement on the substance of the dispute.[462]

The Model Law imposes a similar time frame to bringing jurisdictional challenges during the arbitral proceedings. According to Article 16(2), '[a] plea that the arbitral tribunal does not have jurisdiction shall be raised not later than the submission of the statement of defence'.

Failure to request the referral in time is generally considered a waiver of the right to rely on the arbitration agreement in the subsequent stages of the court proceedings.[463] This favours a focused and prompt dispute resolution process before the appropriate forum. Requesting the referral to arbitration within Article 8(1)'s peremptory time frame

461. *East African Cables Ltd v. Mt. Kenya Cables Ltd,* Civil Case 97 of 2011, [2012] eKLR, High Court of Kenya, para. 4, reiterated in *Jatin Shantilal Malde et al. v. Transmara Investment Limited,* High Court of Kenya (Nairobi), 20 July 2018, paras 13-14. *See also, Cooper v. Ateliers de la Motobecane, S.A.,* 57 N.Y.2d 408, Court of Appeals of New York, 18 November 1982, p. 412 (the New York Convention 'eased the difficulty in enforcing international arbitration agreements by minimising uncertainties and *shifting the burden of proof* to the party opposing enforcement'. [emphasis added]).

462. The Working Group added this time limit at the suggestion of the Secretariat. *See* Report of the Secretary-General: Possible Features of a Model Law on International Commercial Arbitration, A/CN.9/207 (14 May 1981), UNCITRAL Yearbook, para. 60. And, Report of the Working Group on International Contract Practices, on the Work of its Fourth Session, A/CN.9/232 (10 November 1982), p. 50.

463. *See, e.g., Dialogue Consulting Pty Ltd v. Instagram, Inc,* [2020] FCA 1846, Federal Court of Australia, 22 December 2022.

produces a negative effect on the court's general procedural powers. It removes its powers to retain jurisdiction over the substantive dispute covered by the arbitration agreement. It also restrains a party from raising a late request.

The time-bar addition in Article 8(1) was modelled on the 1961 European Convention.[464] Its Article VI(1) limits the period during which a party can object to the jurisdiction of a national court on the grounds of the existence of a valid arbitration agreement under penalty of estoppel.[465]

The Model Law does not foresee any exceptions to admitting a later referral request but does not explicitly prohibit it either. Thus, at least arguably, the court would not have to discontinue the litigation but *could* do so if all the other Article 8(1) requirements were met and appeared reasonable under the circumstances of the case.[466] Nevertheless, this issue may have been resolved by the drafters' concerns related to the effects produced by the failure to object to the jurisdiction of the court (Article 8(1)) or the arbitral tribunal (Article 16(2)). The doubts were whether the failure to raise a timely objection should preclude the party from relying on the arbitration agreement in the future, within the same dispute, or in any other arbitrations or subsequent court proceedings.[467]

In the end, the drafters discussed and declined to add language to the Model Law regulating the effects of such a failure due to the complexities of the issue. They did reiterate, though, their conviction that the failure to make a timely referral request is considered a waiver of the right to rely on the arbitration agreement in the subsequent phases of the court proceedings.[468] This solution is consistent with the Model Law's general provision on 'waiver of rights'. According to Article 4:

> A party who knows that any provision of this Law from which the parties may derogate or any requirement under the arbitration agreement has not been complied with and yet proceeds with the arbitration without stating his objection to such non-compliance without undue delay or, if a time-limit is provided therefor, within such period of time, shall be deemed to have waived his right to object.

Whether the referral is requested in good time does not directly affect the discussions on the extent of court review of the enforceability of a disputed arbitration agreement.

---

464. European Convention on International Arbitration.
465. *See* Working Group Report A/CN.9/232, para. 50.
466. In addressing the question '[w]hat if the request was made after the requesting party has submitted his statement ...', a court in Fiji concluded that '[t]he short answer is, in that case, the court is no longer mandated to refer the matter to arbitration. However, the court still has a discretion as to whether or not to refer the matter to arbitration.', *South Pacific Fertilizer Limited v. Allied Harvest International Pte Ltd,* HBC 142 of 2017, High Court of Fiji, 8 May 2019, para. 34.
467. A/CN.9/WG.II/WP.50, paras 15-16.
468. Working Group Report A/CN.9/246, para. 22, and the Analytical Commentary (A/CN.9/264), p. 24, para. 24. *See CLOUT Case 1174,* A/CN.9/SER.C/ABSTRACTS/121, p. 6, Supreme Court of Republic of Slovenia, 16 December 2009 ('[A]n objection to jurisdiction that has not been raised within the proper time limit may not be entered during subsequent court proceedings to enforce the award.'). To the same effect, *see,* amongst others, *Instagram Inc v. Dialogue Consulting Pty Ltd,* [2022] FCAFC 7, Federal Court of Australia – Full Court, 4 February 2022.

Faced with a timely request, the court is bound to discontinue the proceedings and refer the parties to arbitration, where all the substantive requirements are also met. The judge does not enjoy discretionary powers to order the referral (or not) where an arbitration agreement covers the dispute between the litigants.

[6] No Discretionary Powers

It appears superfluous to explain that mandatory words impose an obligation and permissive words grant discretion. However, stating the obvious here aims to invite the interpreter to read the language of Article 8(1) closely. The terms it uses impose on courts an *obligation* to refer the parties to arbitration, where an arbitration agreement between them covers the litigated dispute. The provision's use of the word 'shall' indicates that the court has no discretion to refuse a request to refer the case to arbitration when the appropriate conditions are met.[469] This is in line with the scheme of the Model Law, which removed the general or residual powers that national courts otherwise enjoy.[470] It also signals respect for the parties' bargain to arbitrate their disputes.[471]

This issue is not controversial, and case law confirms it. If the dispute falls within the scope of an arbitration agreement, the court *must* discontinue the litigation. As an illustration, in confirming that the referral to arbitration is not discretionary, a judge in Hong Kong noted that:

> If I had found that the matter was one for my discretion, I would probably have refused a stay at this stage and invited the parties to frame a preliminary issue for trial. But that is not the case; I have no discretion, and I must hold the parties to their agreement.[472]

Similarly, the Irish High Court held that:

> Article 8 of the Model Law does not create a discretion to refer or not to refer matters to arbitration. If there is an arbitration clause and the dispute is within the scope of the arbitration agreement (...), then a stay must be granted.[473]

---

469. *See, e.g., P. Anand Gajapathi Raju & Ors v. P.V.G. Raju (Died) & Ors,* Supreme Court of India, 28 March 2000, para. 4 ('The language of Section 8 is peremptory. It is, therefore, obligatory for the Court to refer the parties to arbitration in terms of their arbitration agreement.').
470. Article 5 of the Model Law. *See* further comments in Chapter 6, section [B] below.
471. *See, e.g., TELUS Communications Inc. v. Welman,* 2019 SCC 19 (CanLII), Supreme Court of Canada, 4 April 2019 p. 63 ('This general rule reaffirms the concept of party autonomy and upholds the policy underlying the Arbitration Act that parties to a valid arbitration agreement should abide by their agreement.').
472. *Westco Airconditioning Ltd v. Sui Chong Construction & Engineering Co. Ltd,* [1998] HKCFI 946, Hong Kong Court of First Instance, 3 February 1998, para. 16. In *Methanex v. Kinugawa,* the Federal Court of Canada held that, 'the motions Judge had no discretion in the circumstances but to refer the claim ... to arbitration ... *provided it was bound by the arbitration agreement*' [emphasis in the original judgment]; *Methanex New Zealand Ltd. v. Fontaine Navigation S.A., Tokyo Marine Co. Ltd, The Owners and all Others Interested in the Ship Kinugaw,* [1998] 2 FC 583, 1998 CanLII 9039 (FC), Federal Court of Canada, Trial Division, 9 January 1998.
473. *BAM Building Ltd v. UCD Property Development Company Ltd,* [2016] IEHC 582, High Court of Ireland, 20 October 2016, para. 6.

Nevertheless, it is clear by now that referral requests are denied in some circumstances. The circumstances under which the court's obligation to refer the parties to arbitration does not arise are where the court finds that the arbitration agreement is: *(i) 'null and void' or (ii) 'inoperative' or (iii) 'incapable of being performed'*. The same applies under Article II(3) of the New York Convention.

But there are some rare exceptions. For example, the Israel Supreme Court has denied referrals to arbitration even where cases fell within the scope of Article II(3) of the New York Convention. The Supreme Court found that it had discretion to retain jurisdiction where the case involved serious allegations of bribery and fraud, and a third party to the arbitration agreement was involved because these issues were of public interest.[474]

More generally, it could be argued that the court's discretion lies in determining whether those exceptional (invalidating) conditions are met in the case at hand. Indeed, it is undisputed that judges enjoy a margin of factual and legal appreciation as an inherent element of their adjudicatory function. Nonetheless, that margin of appreciation is not an exercise of unfettered discretion. It results from a judgment governed by the laws applicable to the arbitration agreement.[475]

In any case, once the judge has decided on the arbitration agreement's existence, validity, scope, and enforceability, the 'margin of appreciation' or discretion ends, and the obligation (to refer the parties to arbitration) starts.

[7] The Referral Decision

One related matter is the type of decision that courts can render when granting the referral request. While Article 8(1) of the Model Law directs national courts to 'refer the parties to arbitration', it is silent on the type of decision and its consequence. Unless the national legislation indicates a specific kind of decision, courts may *decline* jurisdiction in the understanding that they are incompetent to entertain the substantive dispute. Courts can also *stay* the action (not dismiss but suspend it) or adopt a flexible approach that will permit adjusting the type of decision and effects according to the language of the arbitration agreement or the characteristics of the case.[476]

The critical observation here is that, under the Model Law, courts do not 'force' or 'compel' a specific performance (i.e., the commencement of arbitration). Instead, they recognise the effect of the arbitration agreement and 'indirectly' enforce it by not

---

474. *Siemens AG v. Israeli Electric Cooperation Ltd*, Case No. 3331/14, Supreme Court of Israel, 13 August 2014; the same applied where the dispute involves issues of clinical tests in the pharmaceutical industry (*Teva Pharmaceuticals Ltd. v. Pronauron Biotechnologies Inc*, 2009), as reported in Daphna Kapeliuk-Klinger, 'National Report for Israel', in *ICCA International Handbook on Commercial Arbitration*, ed. Bosman (Kluwer Law International, 2019), pp. 12-13.
475. *See* Tom Bingham, *The Rule of Law* (Penguin UK, 2011), pp. 48-54, where the author explains that legal issues are resolved by application of the law and not the exercise of discretion. Even where judges are required to exercise a discretion, such discretion is closely constrained by the law.
476. For example, some disputes (or parties) in a court action are not covered by an arbitration agreement and, thus, may still be litigated.

deciding the substantive dispute. This works as a jurisdictional bar, and the only avenue available for the claimant to adjudicate the dispute is arbitration (or desist from seeking adjudication).[477]

The drafting history of Article 8(1) reveals that its corresponding provision in the New York Convention offered little guidance. Article II(3) of the Convention is also not explicit on the type of decision that the court should render when discontinuing the litigation in favour of arbitration.

The drafters of the Model Law did consider the need and possibility of clarifying this issue. They discussed whether a *stay* order would be appropriate rather than a *dismissal* of the court action[478] or whether the court should *decline jurisdiction* or decide it *had no jurisdiction*. This was controversial because, in some legal systems, the court would not lose its jurisdiction but would decline to exercise it when faced with an arbitration agreement.[479] The records of the Working Group's deliberations show that it may even be possible for the court case to remain open (but suspended) pending a further potential application.[480] The drafters also considered whether the referral should include an order to compel the parties to arbitrate their dispute.[481]

None of these discussions led to the adoption of a uniform approach. For conformity purposes between the Model Law and the New York Convention, the matter was left to be determined at the national level, according to local procedural law.[482]

Before proceeding, an important caveat must be made clear. The terms 'stay' and 'decline' do not have a narrow and technical meaning in this book. Instead, they are used broadly to represent the *discontinuance* of the court action to recognise and (indirectly) enforce the parties' agreement to arbitrate. It aims to reflect Article 8(1)'s silence on the matter and embrace the different possible approaches that national laws and courts may adopt in practice.

In any case, a more relevant matter for the purpose and focus of this work is the one discussed next. It relates to the extent of court review when deciding to grant or reject the referral to arbitration request. This happens when a party asks the court *to find* that the arbitration agreement does not exist or is unenforceable.

---

477. This type of decision (stay) is widely accepted and traces back to England and Wales, in the *Common Law Procedure Act 1854*, Part XI – 'If Action commenced by One Party after all have agreed to Arbitration, Court or Judge may stay Proceedings'). Some authority even state that it precedes that act. *See*, Mustill, *The History of International Commercial Arbitration* (n. 34), pp. 5-12.
478. The representative of Sweden, for example, observed that under its law a court would not refer the parties to arbitration, but would merely dismiss the case. *See*, the Secretariat Report (A/CN.9/263), p. 21, para. 25.
479. *See* Working Group Report A/CN.9/233, paras 76, 78. And, Report of the Working Group on International Contract Practices, on the Work of its Sixth Session, A/CN.9/245 (22 September 1983), p. 186.
480. Summary Records 312th Meeting, paras 7, 12-13.
481. *See, e.g.*, the Secretariat Report A/CN.9/207 para. 60. This is currently the approach in some jurisdictions, where courts are empowered to discontinue a court action *and* compel the parties to arbitrate according to their agreement (USA) or order anti-suit injunctions (England).
482. Working Group Report A/CN.9/216, para. 36; Working Papers of the Working Group on International Contract Practices at its Sixth Session, A/CN.9/WG.II/WP.45 (13 June 1983), para. 186.

[E] THE COURT'S FINDING

As already mentioned, the exception to the referral to arbitration is triggered by a court finding. There is value in repeating here the wording of Article 8(1):

> A court before which an action is brought in a matter which is the subject of an arbitration agreement shall, (…), refer the parties to arbitration *unless it finds* that the agreement is null and void, inoperative or incapable of being performed. [emphasis added]

The language of this provision could be more explicit or less vague. The problem is not in the term 'unless', which connotes a subordination of the referral to the existence of an arbitration agreement that is valid, operative, and capable of being performed. The qualifier 'unless' introduces a negative implication and establishes a rule of priority. It modifies the referral obligation, making it dependent on or subject to an event. In this case, it is to a 'finding', or, more precisely, the lack of one. In case of conflict, the subordinating clause ('unless it finds …') prevails over the subordinated one ('the court shall refer the parties …').

It is also undisputed that the subject of the verb 'finds' (represented by the term 'it') refers to the seized court, not to an arbitral tribunal. The contrary would require a significant textual change in Article 8(1) along these lines: 'A court … shall (…) refer the parties to arbitration *unless an arbitral tribunal finds* that the agreement is null and void, inoperative or incapable of being performed.'

Instead, the quarrel rests on the breadth of the meaning of the verb 'to find'. Some scholars have emphasised that it is possible to read the verb 'find' in Article 8(1) with the view that the court's finding should be on a *prima facie* basis.[483] However, a fair reading of the term (finds) seems to suggest the opposite.[484] Its use appears to imply that the court should review and judge, determine or establish that the agreement is valid and operative before discontinuing the court action.

In a legal context, a court's 'finding' (of fact or law) results from a judicial inquiry, investigation or examination. It is related to attaining or arriving at, as a conclusion. To find, a court must search or be presented with the results of a search. This involves a determination supported by evidence (usually presented at a trial or hearing).

Therefore, the verb *to find* in Article 8(1) refers to making a judgment. An evaluative judgment rather than a predictive or mechanical one. One that begs for an application of the syllogism of identifying, interpreting, and applying the proper law to

483. Bachand supports this reading, arguing that it is in line with the positive effect of the competence-competence principle. Bachand (n. 7). For the opposite view, *see* Born, *International Commercial Arbitration* (n. 15), pp. 1174-1175.

484. 'Fair reading' is meant here as the interpretation that a reasonable reader, competent in the English language, would give to the term 'find' in the context of Article 8(1). A reasonable reader may not necessarily be legally trained. It is identified with commercially minded persons that read the law to understand what her or his legal options are. This definition is based on the one that Scalia & Garner endorsed in Antonin Scalia et al., *Reading Law* (n. 91), p. 33.

the facts of the case to assign a value (e.g., legal validity or not) to the disputed agreement.[485]

A decision on the face value of a putative arbitration agreement does not require a search but rather an observation or impression, as if the court finding were a matter of opinion rather than judgment. Then, it may not be a stretch for the verb 'to hold', to replace or be used as a synonym of 'to find'. For example: 'The court shall refer the parties to arbitration, unless it *holds* [or, "unless it is of the opinion"] that said agreement is null and void, inoperative or incapable of being performed.'

Further, it would be implausible for a party to argue that a court needs explicit and specific permission from the arbitration law to refuse enforcement of a *manifestly* invalid contract. This argument would risk ignoring the judiciary's adjudicatory function and powers. Notably, it would risk erasing the meaning and consequence of the last sentence of Article 8(1) instead of giving effect to each word of the legal text. The same interpretative result would be reached if the Article's language were reduced to:

> A court before which an action is brought in a matter which is the subject of an arbitration agreement shall (...) refer the parties to arbitration, (unless it finds that the agreement is null and void, inoperative or incapable of being performed.)[486]

Under such shortened wording, a court would decline to enforce the arbitration agreement anyway if it was *obviously/manifestly* invalid, inoperative or incapable of being performed.

Likewise, focusing on the first part of the Article undermines the value and operation of the 'presumptive validity' principle. As already discussed, the law shifts the burden of proving the invalidity and inefficacy of the arbitration agreement to the party that resists its enforcement. To do that, the party that alleges the invalidity or inefficacy of the putative agreement should be heard and allowed to present its case. At least a reasonable opportunity to do so, given the circumstances of the case. Therefore, proving, even superficially, that an arbitration agreement covers the dispute between the parties is only halfway through the text of Article 8(1) and the triggering point of a shift in the burden of proof.

Because the interpretation of the term 'finds' cannot be exhausted by studying its semantics, the other components of the interpretative technique proposed above (Chapter 3, section [E]) will be examined in the following chapters to give the term

485. For a distinction of judgments and predictions or opinions, *see* Daniel Kahneman et al., *Noise: A Flaw in Human Judgment* (Little, Brown, 2021), pp. 39, 48-50.

486. The Egyptian and Colombian legislation are examples using that drafting approach. They do not include the phrase 'unless it finds that the agreement is null and void, inoperative or incapable of being performed'. *Egyptian Arbitration Law 27/1994*, Article 13(1): 'The court before which an action is brought concerning a disputed matter which is the subject of an arbitration agreement shall hold this action inadmissible provided that the respondent raises this objection before submitting any demand or defense on the substance of the dispute.' *Estatuto de Arbitraje National e Internacional* (Colombia) Law 1563/12, Article 70. 'A court before which an action is brought in a matter which is the subject of an arbitration agreement shall, if a party so requests, no later than when submitting his first statement on the substance of the dispute, refer the parties to arbitration.'

finding under Article 8(1) its proper meaning. As anticipated in (Chapter 3, section [E][3]), the Model Law's preparatory works carry a special interpretative significance and clarify UNCITRAL's drafting choice. Some of those drafting choices are analysed next.

[1] UNCITRAL's Drafting Choice

The drafting history of the Model Law appears to support a full judicial review of jurisdictional challenges. During the deliberations that led to the language of Article 8(1), a suggestion was made to add the words '*prima facie* finding' or similar phrasing that would direct a court to refer parties to arbitration unless it found that the agreement was *manifestly* null and void.[487] The explicit purpose of this addition was to support the position that gives arbitral tribunals chronological priority over national courts to rule on jurisdiction. But the Working Group rejected that proposal and decided to retain Article 8(1) as it reads today, which remains (conspicuously) silent on the required standard of court review.

That silence grows loud in the interpretation of Article 8 because after clear and specific debates, the drafters' prevailing view was that courts should not give priority to arbitral tribunals to deal with certain jurisdictional objections:

> [I]n the cases envisaged under paragraph (1) where the parties differed on the existence of a valid arbitration agreement, that issue should be settled by the court, without first referring the issue to an arbitral tribunal, which allegedly lacked jurisdiction.[488]

Authoritative commentary on the Model Law has noted that adding the word 'manifest' before 'null and void' would have limited judicial review to a *prima facie* finding that the arbitration agreement was valid.[489] Thus, it could be argued that by rejecting that proposal, the drafters clarified that courts should 'settle' disputes relating to the *existence* and *validity* of an agreement to arbitrate (not, e.g., its scope) before referring the parties to arbitration.[490] This understanding would be coherent with the fundamental premise that legitimises arbitration: the existence of a valid agreement to arbitrate. Therefore, without consent to arbitration, a party should not be forced to invest resources in arbitral proceedings and have to rely on setting aside actions or resist enforcement defences against an arbitral award.

However, the vagueness in the drafting that UNCITRAL chose permits Article 8 to cover and apply to a broader spectrum of situations (e.g., disputes related to the existence, validity, and scope of the arbitration agreement, etc.). It could also be argued that rather than a vague term, UNCITRAL used the word 'finds' in an intentionally ambiguous way to permit and include the two meanings discussed here (*prima facie*

487. Working Group Report A/CN.9/233, para. 77.
488. *Ibid.*
489. Howard M. Holtzmann et al., *A Guide to the Model Law* (n. 83), p. 303; *See also* Peter Binder, *International Commercial* (n. 96), para. 2-089, and the commentary of Julian D.M. Lew et al., *Comparative ICA* (n. 367), para. 14-61.
490. Holtzmann et al., *A Guide to the Model Law* (n. 83), p. 303.

and full review). Importantly, legal context and purpose help limit the vagueness (or ambiguity) of the term 'to find' in Article 8(1).

As will become evident throughout this work, the rejected wording proposal bears a narrower implication when considered in the larger scheme of the Model Law. Bearing in mind that one of the overarching purposes of the Model Law is 'fairness and efficiency' in dispute resolution,[491] the rejected text should not be interpreted to exclude the application of the *prima facie* approach completely. It simply rejects the idea of reading the law in binary terms by imposing or limiting the court review to the *prima facie* approach, *exclusively*, regardless of efficiency considerations in resolving the dispute at hand. It also reflects UNCITRAL's ideal for the Model Law to be a 'model' of broad international acceptance, providing States sufficient flexibility to deviate from its language when adopting it so as to limit the role of national courts to a *prima facie* standard of review if they prefer to.

Further, the drafting history of the Model Law is not conclusive regarding whether the *prima facie* approach should be adopted for jurisdictional challenges based on grounds other than the existence and validity of the agreement to arbitrate (e.g., scope, waiver, applicability, or capability of being performed).

The deliberations at UNCITRAL reveal another possible solution, not based on the Model Law, but on local procedural law. According to one view, given that the validity and enforceability of the arbitration agreement were dealt with in the Model Law, a court could only look to the Model Law, not to local law. This was at least the understanding of Sir Mustill, the representative of the United Kingdom, based on the language of Article 5 of the Model Law: 'In matters governed by this Law, no court shall intervene except where so provided in this Law.'[492]

However, the Chairman of the UNCITRAL meeting (Mr Loewe) thought it was too narrow a view of Article 8(1) and explained that Article 5 only limits the type of intervention. For those instances where court intervention is permitted, the Model Law did not impose a specific extent, like in the scenario discussed.[493]

A study of the Model Law's preparatory works reveals that the drafters considered (and rejected) other rules of priority. For example, in an early draft, the Working Group gave priority to the 'first seized forum'. If arbitration proceedings had been initiated, the subsequent court action should be stayed, and the judgment postponed until the arbitrators had made an award.[494]

A similar debate took place regarding the language of the second paragraph of Article 8 of the Model Law when addressing the powers of courts and arbitrators to deal with jurisdictional challenges. Concluding that Article 8(1) *imposes* a rule of priority would entail overlooking the language of Article 8(2), which explicitly *allows* concurrent proceedings. Article 8(2) is described and analysed below in section [F].

---

491. *See* Chapter 7 below.
492. Summary Records 312th Meeting, para. 8.
493. *Ibid.*, para. 9.
494. Working Papers of the Working Group on International Contract Practices at its Fourth Session, A/CN.9/WG.II/WP.38 (31 August 1982), p. 57, para. 54. *See also*, Working Papers of the Working Group on International Contract Practices at its Fifth Session, A/CN.9/WG.II/WP.40 (14 December 1982), p. 80, Article IV(83); and, the Commission Report A/40/17, para. 91.

None of these alternative rules of priority was approved or adopted in the final text of Article 8. The expert negotiators of the Model Law were aware of the nuances and implications that each of the debated alternatives would have for achieving the intended legislative purpose and coherence with other provisions (e.g., Article 16(1) – competence-competence, Article 5 – minimal court involvement).

The drafters were also mindful that the instrument was a *model* law and, therefore, deviations at the national level were possible. Reasonably, where a domestic legislator chooses to adopt the text as UNCITRAL drafted it, it will become difficult to justify that the meaning of its language differs from the one that its intellectual drafters explicitly intended.

As analysed next, what the Working Group drafted with *somewhat* more precision is the permitted grounds to prevent the enforcement of the parties' agreement to arbitrate.

[2] The Exceptions to the Enforcement

Like other contracts, arbitration agreements are enforceable unless a recognised legal ground is established for refusing enforcement.

The Model Law's non-enforceability provision (Article 8) is drafted at a high level of generality, as is Article II(3) of the New York Convention. It is silent regarding the specific defences a party could raise to resist a referral to arbitration. A party may, for example, contend that initiating the court action was justified because it never consented to arbitrate disputes and, therefore, no arbitration agreement exists.[495] In some instances, a party may argue that, even if an arbitration agreement exists, it is not a party to it. It may also resist the referral to arbitration on the basis that the dispute falls outside the scope of the arbitration agreement or that the relevant law does not allow the dispute to be resolved in arbitration. A party may also bring forward other arguments to resist the stay or dismissal of the case and its referral to arbitration.

However (and importantly), Article 8(1) provides for the *legal effect* that the defence raised produces, i.e., to render the arbitration agreement null and void, inoperative or incapable of being performed.

(a) Null and Void, Inoperative or Incapable of Being Performed

The Model Law does not set forth the grounds for the invalidity of the arbitration agreement. The term 'null and void' denotes an intrinsically defective contract and situations where the parties' consent to arbitrate was vitiated when concluding the agreement. It means that the arbitration agreement is 'devoid of legal effect.'[496] For

495. For example, because the discussions or negotiations about the dispute resolution clause never resulted in an agreement.

496. *Albon (t/a N A Carriage Co) v. Naza Motor Trading SDN BHD & Anor* [2007] EWHC 665 (Ch), England and Wales High Court, 29 March 2007, para. 18.

example, this would generally result from misrepresentation, illegality, incapacity of a party, mistake, duress, or undue influence.[497]

In his leading commentary on the New York Convention, Professor van den Berg explained that the term 'inoperative' in Article II(3) refers to initially valid agreements that have ceased to produce legal effects.[498] This could happen, for example, when the parties revoke their agreement or waive their right to pursue their claims in arbitration, either by agreeing to litigate them or through their conduct.

For instance, a court found the agreement to arbitrate had become inoperative through waiver. For almost a year, the defendant in the court action conducted itself in a way inconsistent with the right to arbitrate. It submitted substantive defences, served notices, sought to produce documents and requested injunctions. The court then concluded that the party's voluntary use of the 'machinery of litigation' rendered the arbitration agreement inoperative.[499]

Another court found that a party committed a repudiatory breach of the arbitration agreement by commencing litigation. For the court, the counterparty accepted the repudiatory breach by taking part in the proceedings without objecting to the court's jurisdiction.[500] Where a party has repudiated the arbitration agreement, it cannot rely on it in a later parallel proceeding to displace the court's jurisdiction. Correspondingly, the respondent who has accepted the court's jurisdiction despite the agreement to arbitrate, will be taken to have accepted the counterparty's repudiatory breach and lose the right to rely on the arbitration agreement.[501] Thus, the parties' agreement becomes inoperative.

Arbitration agreements are 'incapable of being performed' where obstacles prevent their setting in motion.[502] A court in India found that this wording 'signifies, in effect, frustration and the consequent discharge. If, after the making of the contract, the

497. *Rhone Mediterranee Compagnia Francese v. Lauro,* 712 F.2d 50, United States, US Court of Appeals, Third Circuit, 6 July 1983, pp. 3-4. (referring to Article II(3) of the New York Convention, the court held that 'null and void' encompasses only defences of duress, mistake, fraud, waiver and public policy). Also, Michael Pryles, The Kaplan Lecture 2009, 27 *Journal of International Arbitration,* no. 2 (2010) DOI: 10.54648/joia2010008. *See also,* Lew et al., *Comparative ICA* (n. 367), para. 14-42.

498. van den Berg, *The New York Arbitration Convention* (n. 11), p. 158. Also, Lew et al., *Comparative ICA* (n. 367), para. 14-45. *See also,* Peter Huber et al., 'Arbitration Agreement, § 1032 – Arbitration Agreement and Substantive Claim Before Court', in *Arbitration in Germany: The Model Law in Practice,* ed. Patricia Nacimiento, Stefan M. Kröll, et al. (Kluwer Law International, 2015), para. 19.

499. *Instagram v. Dialogue,* [2022] FCAFC 7, paras 86-88.

500. Under Article 4 of the Model Law, this situation constitutes a 'waiver of the right to object'.

501. *Marty Ltd v. Hualon Corporation (Malaysia) Sdn Bhd,* [2018] SGCA 63, Singapore Court of Appeal 10 October 2018.

502. van den Berg, *The New York Arbitration Convention,* n. 11), p. 159. Lew et al., *Comparative ICA* (n. 367), para. 14-47. *See also,* Huber et al., *Arbitration in Germany* (n. 498), para. 20; Stefan Kröll, 'The "Incapable of Being Performed" Exception in Article II(3) of the New York Convention', in *Enforcement of Arbitration Agreements and International Arbitral Awards: the New York Convention in Practice,* ed. Emmanuel Gaillard and Domenico di Pietro (Cameron May, 2008), pp. 326-330.

promise becomes incapable of being fulfilled or performed due to unforeseen contingencies, the contract is frustrated'.[503]

More concretely, a putative arbitration agreement may be incapable of being performed where the agreement is too vaguely worded to establish the parties' intention to arbitrate. Or when the arbitrator named in the agreement refuses to accept the nomination or the agreement names conflicting, binding forums or mechanisms to resolve the substantive disputes. Arguably, it would also be the case when the parties have agreed to arbitrate their disputes at an inexistent arbitral institution or one that no longer exists.[504]

(b) Arbitrability

Article 8 Model Law does not explicitly refer to issues of arbitrability. It could be argued that disputes related to non-arbitrable subject matters constitute a distinct exception to the enforceability of agreements to arbitrate.

The drafters of the Model Law discussed the possibility of including a list of non-arbitrable subject matters, either as an exhaustive list or as an open one to be supplemented by the adopting States. However, compiling such a list with an eye on international harmonisation proved impractical. Thus, the consensus was not to delimit non-arbitrable matters in the Model Law.[505]

The delegates also considered and rejected a proposal to include a general reference to arbitrability in terms similar to the language of the New York Convention. Its Article II(1) specifies that courts will recognise arbitration agreements *concerning a subject matter capable of settlement by arbitration.*[506]

The prevailing view, however, was that a non-arbitrable subject matter is only a ground for refusing to refer the parties to arbitration. The *effect* of non-arbitrable disputes, like other grounds, would be to render the arbitration agreement null and void.[507]

503. *Ramasamy Athapan and Nandakumar Athappan v. Secretariat of Court, International Chamber of Commerce*, A. No. 2671 of 2008, India, High Court of Madras, 29 October 2008, para. 22.
504. This was the decision in *Corporación LSR*, Exp. No. 2015-1181, Venezuela, Tribunal Supremo de Justicia (Supreme Court of Justice), 1 March 2016. Similarly, *Dregg v. Chr. Jensen Shipping A/S*, A/CN.9/SER.C/ABSTRACTS/153, p. 5, Supreme Court of Denmark, 22 June 2012 ('[T]he rules of the arbitration proceedings to be applied could not be determined with the necessary clarity and that arbitration proceedings could therefore not proceed'.). This is by no means a uniform outcome. Persuasive authority has concluded that where the parties have expressed the intention to arbitrate any dispute which may arise under their contract, the court should uphold them to their bargains even if the arbitration clause refers to a non-existent arbitration institution and rules. *See, e.g.*, Kaplan J's judgment in *Lucky-Golstar v. Ng Moo Kee*, [1993] HKCFI 14.
505. Working Group Report A/CN.9/216, paras 30-31.
506. Article II(1) New York Convention provides: 'Each Contracting State shall recognize an agreement in writing under which the parties undertake to submit to arbitration all or any differences which have arisen or which may arise between them in respect of a defined legal relationship, whether contractual or not, *concerning a subject matter capable of settlement by arbitration*' [emphasis added].
507. Working Group Report A/CN.9/245, para. 187; Working Group Report A/CN.9/246, para. 23. This was the stance of, e.g., the highest Malaysian court, which denied a stay request in

However, this (harsh) legal effect is debatable. That consequence (invalidity) may be unproblematic if the seat of the arbitration and the location where the Article 8 action takes place coincide. But that is not always the scenario of a dispute. Where it is not, it could well be that the substantive matter of the parties' dispute is arbitrable at the seat of the arbitration. It may also be the case that the parties chose a law to govern the arbitration agreement that does not exclude the arbitrability of the dispute.[508] Therefore, the arbitration agreement may not be enforceable in the Article 8 court's jurisdiction but remains valid. This solution would be more in line with the objectives of the Model Law, i.e., to promote and facilitate arbitration while respecting each State's prerogative to reserve specific subject matters to the authority of national courts.[509] For this reason, some court decisions have held that the legal effect of substantive non-arbitrability is to render the agreement inoperative or incapable of being performed.[510]

(c) Non-enforceability of the Future Award

A study of the Model Law's preparatory works also reveals that the drafters considered adding a specific ground for refusing the referral to arbitration. It would have required the court to look forward and consider whether the (future) arbitral award would be unenforceable in its State.[511]

Ultimately, the drafters rejected this proposal. Forecasting the enforceability of an award before it is rendered (or the proceedings even started) would have defeated legal certainty and undermined the promotion of arbitration. In any event, the arbitral award may still be enforceable in other States.

This is especially relevant because the arbitration may have no connection with the State where the Article 8 action is filed. The arbitration agreement's enforceability is universal (rather than territorial) as the parties can bring a substantive action in *any* State. As indicated in the introduction to this chapter, the Model Law made this explicit when defining its scope of application: 'The provisions of this Law, *except* articles 8 (…), apply only if the place of the arbitration is in the territory of this State.'[512]

In turn, this considered – but rejected – ground for refusing the referral to arbitration put the spotlight on another crucial issue: the law governing the validity of

---

foreclosure proceedings, which must be decided by national courts. Contracting out of this would be *void* as being contrary to public policy. *Arch Reinsurance Ltd v. Akay Holdings Sdn Bhd*, [2019] 1 CLJ 305, Federal Court of Malaysia, 29 January 2018.

508. *Anupam Mittal v. Westbridge Ventures*, [2023] SGCA 1, para. 55: 'the arbitrability of a dispute is, in the first instance, determined by the law that governs the arbitration agreement.'

509. Article 1(5) of the Model Law: 'This Law shall not affect any other law of this State by virtue of which certain disputes may not be submitted to arbitration or may be submitted to arbitration only according to provisions other than those of this Law.'

510. *See, e.g.*, *Tomolugen Holdings Ltd and another v. Silica Investors Ltd and other*, [2015] SGCA 57, Singapore Court of Appeal, 26 October 2015, para. 74; *Canada (Attorney General) v. Reliance Insurance Company*, 2007 CanLII 41899 (ON SC), Ontario Superior Court of Justice, 5 October 2007, para. 32.

511. Working Group Report A/CN.9/232, para. 51.

512. Article 1(2) Model Law.

the arbitration agreement. In short, by not allowing the court in an Article 8 action to weigh in the enforceability of the future award, the drafters of the Model Law curtailed the significance (or even the application) of the law of the forum over the enforceability of the arbitration agreement. As highlighted earlier (section [B]), considerations of the relevant law are crucial for determining the extent of court review under Article 8.

[F] ARTICLE 8(2): THE POWERS OF THE TRIBUNAL

A clear difference between the Model Law and the New York Convention is in the second paragraph of Article 8 of the Model Law. Unlike Article II(3) of the Convention, Article 8(2) explicitly tackles the risks and effects of dilatory tactics, dispelling the possibility of *lis pendens* defences.[513] According to its text, proceedings before a national court and an arbitral tribunal can coexist:

> Where an action referred to in paragraph (1) of this article has been brought, arbitral proceedings *may* nevertheless be commenced or continued, and an award may be made, while the issue is pending before the court. [Emphasis added]

Article 8(2) contributes to the Model Law's purpose of facilitating the *fair and efficient* resolution of disputes. It prevents parties from resorting to litigation to delay the resolution of the dispute in its proper forum.[514] That would be the result if the arbitrators had to wait until after a court determined the jurisdictional matter.

One of the two policies that appear to underpin the language of this paragraph is linked to the competence-competence principle, as the initiation of court proceedings does not trump the arbitrators' decision-making authority. Arbitrators are empowered to continue the proceedings while the question of their jurisdiction is pending before a court. In doing so, they can make decisions on their own jurisdiction and the substantive disputes. The other policy refers to the fundamental right of access to court justice, as parties have the right to request a court (in addition to arbitrators) to decide on the validity and enforceability of an arbitration agreement.[515]

The first policy aims to contribute to the prompt resolution of disputes in arbitration. If it appears that the arbitrators lack jurisdiction, the claimant will probably seek the suspension of the proceedings until the court decides the objection. Arguably, the second policy can contribute to the same aim. If it appears that the arbitrators lack

513. According to *lis pendens*, a court seized of an action should not entertain it if another court was seized first and the action is pending of determination, even if the second court is competent. In the European Union this is different, as the Brussels I Recast Regulation, Article 31(2) provides that: '[W]here a court of a Member State on which [a choice-of-court agreement] confers exclusive jurisdiction is seized, any court of another Member State shall stay the proceedings until such time as the court seized on the basis of the agreement declares that it has no jurisdiction under the agreement.'

514. Analytical Commentary (A/CN.9/264), p. 24, para. 25 ('The purpose of giving such discretion to the arbitral tribunal is to reduce the risk and effect of dilatory tactics of a party reneging on his commitment to arbitration.').

515. This was explicit during the drafting process; *see*, Working Group Report A/CN.9/245, para. 67.

jurisdiction, the judge may conclusively adjudicate the jurisdictional dispute instead of allowing the arbitrator to decide that matter first.

Distinctively, the permissive wording of Article 8(2) affords the parties and arbitral tribunals a degree of flexibility and discretion to commence or continue the arbitration.[516]

Arbitral tribunals are not obligated to continue the arbitral proceedings commenced and render an award. The language of the article provides that arbitral proceedings *may* - not must - be commenced or continued, and an award *may* - not must - be made.[517] Where the arbitral tribunal deems that the jurisdictional challenge has prospects of success, it may, for example, proceed to a preliminary determination of the jurisdictional issue (according to Article 16(3)) or, in exercising the discretion accorded by Article 8(2), may even suspend the proceedings and await the decision of the court.[518]

Drafting History

When paragraph 2 of Article 8 was incorporated (March 1984), the wording suggested was different. It is provided only for the continuation of arbitral proceedings, not for their commencement. This was the draft language:

> Where (...) arbitral proceedings have already commenced, the arbitral tribunal may continue the proceedings while the issue of its jurisdiction is pending with the court [unless the court orders a stay of the arbitral proceedings].[519]

Ultimately, the Working Group members agreed that the text should be amended to permit the parties to initiate arbitration while the matter was before a court.[520] This aimed at preventing parties from rushing to court with a lawsuit that would pave the way to a jurisdictional dispute, freezing out the initiation of the proper dispute resolution mechanism (arbitration).

During the deliberations, there were different opinions on whether there should be an order of priority (court or arbitral tribunal) to avoid parallel proceedings. Some delegates advocated a change to Article 8(2)'s draft text to exclude the possibility of jurisdictional disputes being concurrently discussed before an arbitral tribunal and a national court.[521]

516. Discretionary powers permeate arbitral authority in other instances of jurisdictional disputes. Specifically, under Article 16(1) of the Model Law, arbitrators are empowered, but not obliged, to decide jurisdictional matters. That discretion can be exercised in two ways: (a) to answer the jurisdictional question or await the result of the court determination in an Article 8(1) action; (b) If the arbitrators opt to exercise their decision-making powers, they can discretionally answer the jurisdictional question: (i) as a preliminary matter or (ii) together with making an award on the merits. *See* a further discussion related to the contextual meaning of Article 8 in Chapter 6; specifically, in relation to the competence-competence principle (section [C]).
517. This observation reflects the understanding of the Model Law's drafters. *See* Summary Records 312th Meeting, paras 32-33.
518. *See* Working Group Report A/CN.9/233, para. 80; Commission Report A/40/17, para. 92.
519. Working Group Report A/CN.9/246, para. 20.
520. Commission Report A/40/17, para. 90.
521. The intervention of Mr Ruzicka, the delegate of (then) Czechoslovakia at the Commission, is illustrative of that concern. He proposed 'that the court procedure should be completed before

In broad terms, the drafters discussed establishing the following rules of priority, assigning a decisive role to the forum entertained first:[522]

- Priority in favour of the arbitral tribunal: if the arbitral proceedings had already commenced, the court should postpone deciding the arbitral tribunal's jurisdiction until the award was made. That would prevent dilatory tactics by unnecessarily prolonging the arbitration proceedings.
- Priority in favour of the court: once the jurisdictional dispute is before the court, priority should be accorded to the court proceedings by empowering the court to order the stay of the arbitral proceedings or, at least, by precluding the arbitral tribunal from rendering the award.

The proposition of giving priority to the arbitral tribunal intended to follow Article VI(3) of the 1961 European Convention, which provides:

> Where either party to an arbitration agreement has initiated arbitration proceedings before any resort is had to a court, *courts* of Contracting States subsequently asked to deal with the same subject matter between the same parties or with the question whether the arbitration agreement was non-existent or null and void or had lapsed, *shall stay their ruling on the arbitrator's jurisdiction until the arbitral award is made, unless they have good and substantial reasons to the contrary.* [Emphasis added]

In terms of efficiency, moving forward with the arbitration without waiting for the court decision might translate into an unnecessary waste of resources if the court eventually rules against the arbitral jurisdiction.[523] But, for that same reason, some of the drafters of the Model Law advocated against the adjournment of a court decision on the preliminary jurisdictional objection.[524] Eventually, the prevailing view was not to establish a rule of priority in favour of either courts or arbitral tribunals in the Model Law.

Consequently, Article 8(2) does not empower courts to stay or suspend arbitral proceedings.[525] It was preferred to allow the possibility of arbitral proceedings to commence or to continue and an award to be rendered while the action is pending

continuing with the arbitral proceedings'. However, he confirmed that his delegation 'could accept the opposite view, namely that the tribunal should have precedence if that was the generally accepted view'. Summary Records 312th Meeting, para. 21.

522. A/CN.9/WG.II/WP.38, p. 57, para. 54; Secretariat Report (A/CN.9/263), p. 20, paras 23, 26; Summary Records 312th Meeting, paras 21, 35, 39-40; Add.3 Analytical Compilation of Comments by Governments and International Organizations on the Draft Text of a Model Law on International Commercial Arbitration. Report of the Secretary-General, 18th session, A/CN.9/263/Add.3 (31 July 1985), para. 26; and Commission Report A/40/17, para. 91.

523. This concern was the basis on which the Court of Appeal for Bermuda held that arbitral tribunals should normally await a decision by the court. However, the court emphasised that this should be the case where the court hearing on the jurisdictional issue is to be held shortly after the tribunal's decision on jurisdiction. *Christian Mutual Insurance Company & Central United Life Insurance Company & Connecticut Reassurance Corporation v. Ace Bermuda Insurance Limited*, [2002] Bda LR 56, Court of Appeal, Bermuda.

524. Commission Report A/40/17, para. 92.

525. For the deletion of the words 'unless the court orders a stay of the arbitral proceedings', *see* the Working Group Report A/CN.9/246, para. 21.

before the court (Article 8(2) of the Model Law). The understanding was that this flexibility would reduce the effects of dilatory tactics and, consequently, lead to an efficient resolution of the substantive dispute.[526]

The issue of simultaneous proceedings whilst the arbitration tribunal's jurisdiction is under judicial scrutiny was the topic of discussions also concerning the competence-competence principle (Article 16(1) of the Model Law). These will be analysed in the next chapter, which is dedicated to the contextual interpretation of Article 8(1).

[G] CONCLUSION

Article 8's silence on the extent of court review at the threshold of arbitration is not a drafting oversight. Experts of arbitration law and practice meticulously discussed its language, reflecting their drafting choice after debating whether to limit the review to a *prima facie* basis.[527] As a result, Article 8 does not *impose* such a limited review. Its text does not *require* it, and its drafting history explicitly rejected it. The crucial words in the previous sentences are 'impose' and 'require'. They are emphasised here to highlight their compulsory character as synonyms of demand, order, and a lack of a choice. As antonyms of *permit* or *allow*.

The Model Law's drafters debated adopting words or phrases of competing effects in other respects, too. Some were accepted, some were rejected, and others were moulded to operate coherently along with other provisions of the same instrument and the New York Convention.

For example, the drafters suggested, considered, and rejected the proposal to empower courts to refer parties to arbitration on their own motion. They have also considered and decided against empowering courts to suspend arbitral proceedings whilst deciding the jurisdictional question. The same happened regarding the idea of allowing declaratory actions on the validity of arbitration agreements or linking the assessment at the referral stage to the enforceability of the hypothetical and future award.

These approaches and remedies did not materialise in the text of the Model Law because its drafters decided against them and chose words and phrases that captured those decisions. Thus, it would be with discomfort to logic, if not impossible to argue, that even when the drafters decided against those alternatives, the rejected proposals can backdoor their way into practice through 'legal interpretation'. That understanding would undermine the certainty, predictability, and facilitation of arbitration goals that UNCITRAL set forth when adopting the Model Law. The same logic follows to reject the

526. *See* in particular the discussions in the Summary Records 312th Meeting, paras 14-41 (e.g., Mr Hjerner (Observer, International Chamber of Commerce) advocated that 'Article 8(2) ... should be retained in the interests of the efficiency of the arbitral proceedings, regardless of actions by one party in a local or foreign court to delay or prevent them.'; *see*, para. 15).

527. Similar to the rule in Article 31(4) of the Vienna Convention ('A special meaning shall be given to a term if it is established that the parties so intended.').

conclusion that Article 8(1) only authorises a *prima facie* review and judicial determination of arbitral jurisdiction.

Without clear and specific language in Article 8, its contextual reading becomes crucial as it might provide a determinative legal meaning to the extent of the court powers that it regulates. A contextual reading requires consideration of the synergic operation of other provisions of the Model Law and the instrument as a whole. The next chapter is devoted to that analysis.

CHAPTER 6

Legal Context

[A] INTRODUCTION

Article 8 of the Model Law is not a stand-alone provision. It forms part of a whole and operates in a context: in synergy with other provisions of the Model Law and in coherence with the New York Convention.

Context influences the outcome of legal interpretation. Given that context conditions court decisions, it is crucial to read Article 8(1) harmoniously within the Model Law framework so its language is interpreted in a way that is compatible with other provisions, not contradictory.

The language of Article 8 of the Model Law is often interpreted and applied in light of Article 16(1), which recognises the competence-competence principle. According to some scholars and case law, Article 16(1) establishes a rule of priority between arbitrators and judges that affects the reading of Article 8(1).[528]

Arguably, Article 5 of the Model Law also influences the interpretation of Article 8(1). Given that Article 5 imposes the general principle of minimal court intervention in arbitration, it is considered to support the view that Article 8(1) imposes a *prima facie* standard of review.

This chapter examines whether the national courts' review powers under Article 8(1) might be limited by the operation of Articles 5 and 16. This is based on an analysis of the language of those provisions and the deliberations at UNCITRAL leading to their text.

[B] COURT INVOLVEMENT

Court involvement under the Model Law framework is possible but limited. It is the exception, not the rule. Article 5 of the Model Law establishes the principle of limited court intervention by providing that:

528. At least where a party in an existing arbitration has already contested the jurisdiction of the tribunal.

> In matters governed by this Law, no court shall intervene except where so provided in this Law.

Clarity in circumscribing the term intervention is paramount, albeit challenging to theorise about. Conceptually, it is a mistake to confuse intervening with meddling in the arbitration proceedings. The latter has a negative effect and cannot be permitted. Conversely, a measured judicial intervention is welcomed.[529]

This work uses the term court *involvement* instead of intervention to avoid expanding in unnecessary distinctions and clarifications. This way, permitted court *involvement* in arbitration downplays the otherwise potentially negative connotation of 'intervention'.

The drafting history of Article 5 permits to conclude that this provision should not be taken to express hostility to court involvement in specific circumstances. A degree of court involvement has positively contributed to positioning arbitration as the preferred means for resolving international disputes. Some even recognise that the success of international commercial arbitration has only been possible with the safety net of court assistance and control in the background.[530] This idea reflects UNCITRAL's initial concern of ensuring that the Model Law balances the efficacy of parties' agreements with the legitimate interests of the legal system expected to recognise and give effect to those agreements.[531]

The purpose of Article 5 is to provide certainty about the instances in which court involvement is permitted.[532] Its immediate effect is to exclude any 'general or residual power' that national courts may enjoy and limits court involvement to the instances listed in the law.[533] In turn, this has the potential of fostering efficacy and efficiency in dispute resolution, whether a delay results from a dilatory tactic or, unintentionally, from multiple forum causes.

Article 5 also contributes to UNCITRAL's international legal unification and harmonisation goal. The broad acceptance and adoption of the Model Law neutralise

529. *See, e.g.*, Summary Records of the 309th Meeting, A/CN.9/246, annex; A/CN.9/263 Add.1-2, A/CN.9/264 (5 June 1985), UNCITRAL Yearbook, paras 22, 25, 40 ('Most delegations had agreed ... that [intervention] should be understood to cover assistance from the courts as well as judicial intervention proper.'), and Commission Report A/40/17, para. 63.

530. *See, e.g.*, Binder, *International Commercial Arbitration* (n. 96), p. 81 ('Regardless of attempts to free arbitration of all local restrictions, until arbitral tribunals gain court-like powers, arbitration remains ultimately dependent on the municipal courts for assistance during the proceedings and, especially, for the enforcement of awards.').

531. Secretariat Report A/CN.9/207, paras 19, 21.

532. Commission Report A/40/17, paras 62-63. Also, Holtzmann et al., *A Guide to the Model Law* (n. 83), p. 216.

533. A/CN.9/264, p. 18, para. 12. Courts have echoed this interpretation. *See, e.g., NCC International AB v. Alliance Concrete Singapore Pte Ltd,* [2008] SGCA 5, Supreme Court of Singapore; *LW Infrastructure Pte Ltd v. Lim Chin San Contractors Pte Ltd* [2012] SGCA 57, Singapore Court of Appeal, 16 August 2012 *Compagnie Nationale Air France v. Mbaye*, 2003 CanLII 35834 (QC CA), Quebec Court of Appeal, Canada, 31 March 2003; *Nigerian Agip Exploration Limited v. Nigerian National Petroleum Corporation and Oando, 125 & 134 Limited*, A/CN.9/SER.C/ABSTRACTS/153, p. 4, Nigeria Court of Appeal, Abuja Judicial Division 25 February 2014; *Rio Algom Limited v. Sammi Steel Co. Ltd. and Sammi Steel Canada Inc.*, A/CN.9/SER.C/ABSTRACTS/1, p. 11, Ontario Court of Justice, Canada, 1 March 1991.

the disparity between national approaches regarding the instances of court involvement.[534]

In addition to the situation that is the subject of this book (Article 8(1)), the Model Law provides for court involvement in arbitral proceedings in Article 9 (Interim Measures), Article 11 (Appointment of Arbitrators), Article 13 (Challenge Procedure), Article 14 (Failure or Impossibility To Act), Article 16(3) Competence of Arbitral Tribunals), Articles 17H and 17I (Recognition and Enforcement of Interim Measures), Article 27 (Court Assistance in Taking Evidence), Article 34 (Recourse Against Arbitral Awards), Articles 35 and 36 (Recognition and Enforcement of Awards).

In those instances, the difficulty lies in determining how much involvement is too much. Article 5 answers the *when* question (when is a court entitled to get involved in arbitration proceedings?). But, it does not offer any guidance to measure the *extent* of the court involvement when the law provides for it. Its drafters even recognised that this provision 'does not itself take a stand on the extent of court involvement.[535] Essentially, the article 'merely requires that any instance of court involvement be listed in the law.'[536]

Because the wording of the article does not define the extent of court involvement, Article 5 appears to give judges under Article 8(1) certain discretionary latitude.[537] At one of the discussions preceding the adoption of the Model Law, Mr Lowe, the representative of Austria and Chairman of the Working Group meeting, expressed this opinion:

> The court must accept an action and then decide whether the agreement was null and void; in that case, it would follow the *normal court procedure*. If it found that the agreement was valid, it would refer the parties to the arbitral tribunal. However, the details of court procedure could not be included in a uniform law, since they were a matter of civil procedure in each State. In article 5, only the type of intervention was limited.[538] [Emphasis added]

Although Article 5 does not indicate this, some read its language to refer not only to the limited instances of court involvement listed in the law but also to its extent. For example, in dealing with jurisdictional objections at the threshold of arbitration, the Federal Court of Malaysia held that judges should bear in mind the obligation of

534. Although it would be possible for the national legislator to list other situations of court involvement, in addition to those that the Model Law suggests.
535. Working Group Report A/CN.9/246, para. 187. Also, Summary Records 309th Meeting, p. 6 (Mr Herrmann (International Trade Law Branch)'s comment: ... '[C]lear understanding that the purpose of article 5 was not to deal with the extent of judicial control ...'); Summary Records 312th Meeting, para. 9 (Mr Loewe (Austria, and the Meeting's Chairman)'s comment at the Working Group meeting: 'In Article 5, only the type of intervention was limited.').
536. Analytical Commentary (A/CN.9/264), p. 18, para. 12.
537. This was the understanding of the Chairman of the UNCITRAL Working Group II meeting in 1985; Summary Records 309th Meeting, para. 40.
538. Model Law on International Commercial Arbitration, *Summary Records of the 312th meeting*, 6 June 1985, A/CN.9/246, annex; A/CN.9/263 ADD.1-2, A/CN.9/264 (6 June 1985), UNCITRAL Yearbook, para. 9.

'minimal intervention' that Article 5 imposes when determining the extent of review under Article 8(1) Model Law.[539]

The intention behind that approach is laudable, as it appears to be in line with one of the overarching aims of the Model Law: facilitation of arbitration. However, it does not find ground specifically in Article 5 and its preparatory history. This provision reflects the Model Law's theme of minimal court involvement but does not encapsulate the extent of the court's role. As mentioned, its wording is limited to the courts' opportunities to intervene to assist or control the arbitration process.

It is even debatable whether the Model Law exhaustively codifies all the instances in which court involvement is possible. In addition to the situations that the Mode Law explicitly lists, others may be governed *implicitly*.[540] It may be argued that others are not excluded from court involvement even though the matter is not regulated in the Model Law.[541]

Distinctively, there are situations in which the Model Law (in some way) does limit the extent of court involvement. For example, where arbitrators have determined as a preliminary matter that they have jurisdiction, the aggrieved party can immediately request a national court to decide the issue. Although the Model Law does not provide whether courts should give deference to the arbitrators' decision or decide the jurisdictional point *de novo*, Article 16(3) limits the judicial intervention to a single procedural instance:

> If the arbitral tribunal rules as a preliminary question that it has jurisdiction, any party may request, (...) the court (...) to decide the matter, *which decision shall be subject to no appeal* [emphasis added].

The Model Law takes a similar single-instance court involvement in challenges to arbitrators,[542] and where they fail to withdraw from office when they become *de jure* or *de facto* unable to perform their functions or act without undue delay.[543]

In all instances where the Model Law provides for court involvement (e.g., Article 8(1)), its extent should be discretionary rather than mechanical. The interpretative exercise should be guided by Article 2A of the Model Law and led by efficiency and effectiveness in resolving the *instant* dispute.

539. *Press Metal v. Etiqa Takaful*, [2016] 5 MLJ 417, paras 39-43. *See* further discussion and examples in Chapter 5.
540. Summary Records 309th Meeting, para. 7 (In regard to the question of express or implied provisions, it was impossible for the Model Law to deal expressly with every procedural instance that may arise in arbitral proceedings.).
541. Analytical Commentary (A/CN.9/264), p. 19, para. 15 (For example, issues of state immunity, the contractual relations between the parties and the arbitrators or arbitral institution, fees, costs, security for costs, breach of arbitration agreements, confidentiality of information, liability of arbitrators, enforceability of arbitral awards that have been set aside).
542. Article 13(3) of the Model Law ('... the challenging party may request, within thirty days after having received notice of the decision rejecting the challenge, the court or other authority specified in article 6 to decide on the challenge, *which decision shall be subject to no appeal*') [emphasis added].
543. Article 14(1) of the Model Law ('... if a controversy remains concerning any of these grounds, any party may request the court or other authority specified in article 6 to decide on the termination of the mandate, *which decision shall be subject to no appeal*.') [emphasis added].

[C] ARBITRAL COMPETENCE

Arguably, the arbitrators' power to rule on their jurisdiction (competence-competence) limits the extent of court involvement under Article 8 of the Model Law. As mentioned earlier, the Model Law recognises and adopts the competence-competence principle in Article 16(1). In broad and straightforward terms, that article provides that:

> The arbitral tribunal may rule on its own jurisdiction, including any objections with respect to the existence or validity of the arbitration agreement.

This text empowers arbitrators to decide any jurisdictional challenge, i.e., from disputes that question the very existence of the arbitration agreement to those related to its validity and scope.

That arbitrators enjoy competence to determine their jurisdiction is commonly known as the *positive* effect of the competence-competence principle. Although this effect is widely accepted and its valuable imprint is undisputed, it does not determine the extent of court involvement when deciding jurisdictional disputes at the referral stage (Article 8(1) Model Law). Questionably, its negative effect does. The critical question is whether competence-competence under Article 16(1) of the Model Law produces that effect. The following section addresses that question (and its heading anticipates the answer).

[1] The Model Law Does Not *Impose* the Negative Effect

The crucial feature of the negative dimension of the competence-competence principle is that it establishes a rule of priority in favour of arbitrators. As mentioned earlier,[544] the negative effect redirects the attention from the arbitral tribunal to national courts. It reflects the idea that the arbitrators' competence-competence necessarily strips national courts of the authority to *conclusively* determine jurisdictional questions *at the threshold* of arbitration (Article 8(1)).

Recognising this effect (or not) reflects policy considerations and a choice. Barcelo accurately explains it as a balancing exercise to resolve a dilemma between *arbitral efficacy*, on the one hand, and *fairness/procedural efficiency*, on the other.[545] The former aims to uphold the party's fundamental right to court access when it is disputed that the party is bound to a valid and enforceable arbitration agreement. The latter aims to prevent a party from obstructing or delaying arbitration. The challenge is in the practice of that balancing exercise – in identifying and weighing efficacy and efficiency when resolving a given dispute.

There are strong views that do not recognise the negative aspect of competence-competence. For example, Brekoulakis dismisses the negative effect and concludes that

544. *Ibid.*
545. John James Barcelo III, Kompetenz-Kompetenz and Its Negative Effect – A Comparative View, *Cornell Legal Studies Research Paper*, 17-40 (2017), p. 2.

competence-competence is limited to empowering arbitrators to decide any debate about their jurisdiction (positive effect) but not to curtail the powers of national courts.[546] In general terms, Paulsson seems to agree with Brekoulakis. He asserts that the arbitrators may decide disputes about their authority 'is all that is meant by "jurisdiction" to decide "jurisdiction".'[547] The principle's objective is *only* to avoid the paralysis of the arbitration as soon as a party raises a challenge.[548] Similarly, Bermann observes that competence-competence need not preclude a court from determining a jurisdictional challenge.[549]

Article 16 of the Model Law does not mention the negative dimension of competence-competence, nor does the text of Article 8. Yet, some authors have concluded that it forms part of the architecture of the Model Law as it 'best fits with the Model Law's drafting history, the basic structure and underlying principles'.[550]

It is difficult to accept that conclusion when Article 16(1) even uses permissive language to recognise its positive dimension. Exercising competence-competence is not an imposition without merits. It is a matter of discretion (based on judgment). Arbitrators *may*, but not *must*, rule on their jurisdiction. This provision affords arbitrators a (non-exclusive) prerogative but does not impose an obligation on them or direct arbitrators on how to exercise it.

The permissive language of Article 16 is in line with the arbitrators' role under Article 8(2) of the Model Law, which vests arbitral tribunals with discretionary decision-making powers to continue (or not) with arbitral proceedings whilst a jurisdictional question is pending in court (Article 8(1)).[551]

Arbitrators opting not to answer a jurisdictional question (or suspending proceedings) whilst a court is examining the point is an expression of arbitral authority, not the lack of it. Arbitrators do not have to rule on their jurisdiction simply because they have the power to do so. If they opt to do it, they can deal with the issue as a preliminary question or in an award on the merits (Article 16(3)).

Indisputably, Articles 8(2), 16(1), and 16(3) of the Model Law entrust arbitrators with power and procedural discretion. Discretion involves judgment. And judgment requires the arbitrators to assess when to exercise competence-competence and when not to.[552]

---

546. Brekoulakis, *The Negative Effect of Competence-Competence* (n. 12), p. 238.
547. Jan Paulsson, *The Idea of Arbitration* (Oxford University Press, 2013), p. 55.
548. *Ibid.*, pp. 55, 58.
549. George A Bermann, *International Arbitration and Private International Law: General Course on Private International Law* (Martinus Nijhoff, 2017), p. 15; Paulsson, *The Idea of Arbitration* (n. 547), p. 58 (The negative effect of competence-competence 'is not an inevitable corollary of allowing the arbitral tribunal to proceed when faced with a jurisdictional objection'.).
550. Bachand, *Article 8 of the Model Law* (n. 7), p. 465.
551. *See* the discussion in Chapter 6, section [C][2].
552. The words of John G. Roberts Jr, Chief Justice of the United States, are eloquence and pertinent here: 'It takes restraint to listen, instead of to speak, to consider, rather than to dismiss, to follow new wisdom, rather than the familiar doctrine'; at the HLS, Harvard Law School in the World | A Conversation with Six Justices of the US Supreme Court, YouTube (2017). Available at https://youtu.be/_EeU6Lo_i7I.

Therefore, the exercise of that discretion is not whimsical. It must be used to advance the policies that recognise arbitral authority.[553] Discretion is then linked to the arbitrators' overriding duty to enforce the parties' agreement and ensure efficiency. That duty is marked by the 'purpose' of the Model Law, the topic addressed in Chapter 7 below.[554]

Concluding that Article 16(1) necessarily dims courts' powers under Article 8(1) also undermines the meaning and the operation of Article 8(2):

> Where an action referred to in paragraph (1) of this article has been brought, arbitral proceedings may nevertheless be commenced or continued, and an award may be made while the issue is pending before the court.[555]

As mentioned earlier,[556] Article 8(2) brings about efficiency to arbitral proceedings, countering court actions intended (or not) to delay or prevent them.[557] It was envisioned to provide parties with the right to request a judicial determination on the enforceability of an arbitration agreement, in addition to lack of jurisdiction pleas during arbitral proceedings (Article 16(2)).[558]

If courts were *required* only to perform a limited (*prima facie*) review under Article 8(1), the solution that Article 8(2) offers would be of little relevance. To a great extent, the goal of discouraging dilatory tactics would be achieved by (erroneously) implying the term 'manifest' in Article 8(1), even where it is not present in it. Rather than commencing or continuing arbitration (Article 8(2)), the parties (and arbitrators) would have an incentive to wait for the court's *prima facie* ruling on the jurisdictional challenge.

The operation of Article 8(2) is more meaningful when a court under Article 8(1) undertakes a full examination of the jurisdictional dispute. In those situations, the text of Article 8(2) better serves the purpose that it carries and that its drafters intended for it to have.

It would be questionable to conclude that the drafters of the Model Law intended to couple only a *prima facie* review (Article 8(1)) to the possibility of parallel arbitral proceedings (Article 8(2)). Neither the text nor the drafting history of Article 8(1) and 8(2) supports that conclusion.

Therefore, put to a choice, courts should prefer interpretations that respect the meaning and harmonious operation of each term of paragraphs (1) and (2) of Article 8. Conversely, courts should avoid interpretations that ignore the text of some provisions, undermine their legal effects, or obstruct their effectiveness.

---

553. For Bingham, the rule of law requires decision-makers to always exercise the powers conferred on them in good faith, fairly, reasonably and with a view to advance the purpose for which the powers were granted, and avoid frustrating the policy and object of the law; Bingham, *The Rule of Law* (n. 475), pp. 60-65.
554. In a nutshell, that purpose is represented by a balancing exercise between the law's recognition and enforcement bias, and fairness and efficiency considerations in resolving the dispute.
555. Article 8(2) Model Law.
556. *See* Chapter 5, section [F].
557. Summary Records 312th Meeting, para. 15.
558. The drafters made this explicit during the discussions; *see* Working Group Report A/CN.9/245, para. 67.

[2] Concurrent Actions

The issue of simultaneous proceedings whilst the jurisdiction of the arbitration tribunal is under judicial scrutiny was a topic in the drafters' discussions also concerning the competence-competence principle.

As noted above, earlier drafts of the Model Law provided the possibility of resorting to national courts to obtain a declaration on the existence of a valid arbitration agreement. If adopted, that possibility could have been used at any time, even if arbitral proceedings were ongoing. The court enquiry would not have automatically stalled arbitration, but the court would have been empowered to order it. However, the text of draft Article 17 was silent about the possibility of initiating arbitration whilst a judge adjudicated the jurisdictional matter. The text of that draft article provided:

> **Article 17. Concurrent court control**
>
> (1) [Notwithstanding the provisions of article 16,] a party may [at any time] request the Court specified in article 6 to decide whether a valid arbitration agreement exists and [if arbitral proceedings have commenced,] whether the arbitral tribunal has jurisdiction [with regard to the dispute referred to it].
> (2) While such issue is pending with the Court, the arbitral tribunal may continue the proceedings [*unless the Court orders a stay of the arbitral proceedings*]. [emphasis added]

The Working Group decided to delete draft Article 17[559] because it conflicted with Article 16(3). At that time, in the drafting process, the wording of Article 16(3) provided the parties with more limited procedural avenues. Its current text allows any party to resort to a national court immediately after the arbitrators' favourable decision on jurisdiction. It also permits arbitration to continue and arbitrators to render an award.

At the Model Law's drafting stage, the idea of allowing concurrent proceedings was frowned upon. For that reason, the then draft Article 16(3) precluded a party from contesting an affirmative ruling by the arbitral tribunal on its jurisdiction until after the tribunal rendered the final award. The text of that draft article provided:

> **[Draft] Article 16. Competence to rule on own jurisdiction**
>
> (3) The arbitral tribunal may rule on a plea referred to in paragraph (2) either as a preliminary question or in an award on the merits. In either case, a ruling by the arbitral tribunal that it has jurisdiction may be contested by any party *only in an action for setting aside the arbitral award*. [emphasis added]

Allowing parties to resort to courts under draft Article 17 was also seen as an invitation for delaying tactics and obstruction. Further, it appeared to be in tension with 'the principle underlying article 16 that it was initially and primarily for the arbitral tribunal to decide on its competence, subject to ultimate court control.'[560]

559. Working Group Report, A/CN.9/246, para. 54.
560. *Ibid.*, para. 55.

The prevailing view was in favour of deleting draft Article 17 but still allowing court control (only) after the final award on the merits was made (draft Article 16(3)).[561] Yet, the delegates understood the benefits of devising an avenue for the parties (and the arbitrators) to obtain certainty on arbitral jurisdiction. Consequently, there were further deliberations on the divergent views as to when access to court control should be permitted after the arbitrators' ruling whilst preventing dilatory tactics.[562]

One of the several suggestions to achieve that result was reintroducing draft Article 17. In that case, access to court adjudication would have been available at any time. Therefore, including language in Article 16(3) would not be necessary to allow concurrent court control. In the end, UNCITRAL adopted the opposite view. The meetings report reveals that '[t]he Commission, after deliberation, decided not to reintroduce previous draft article 17 but to provide for instant court control in article 16(3)'.[563]

These deliberations have fuelled controversies on the role of national courts in enforcing arbitration agreements. This is mainly due to (mis)understanding that the explanation for not adopting draft Article 17 applies to Article 8(1). As noted three paragraphs above, the drafters had stated that it was for arbitrators to 'initially and primarily' decide jurisdictional challenges.

However, that explanation explicitly addressed the tension between draft Article 17 and the *then* draft Article 16(3). The quarrel was a matter of timing for court review *after* arbitral decisions on jurisdiction. Different opinions had advocated for court review either: (i) immediately (the current Article 16(3)), (ii) at the end of the arbitration (the *early* draft Article 16(3)), or (iii) at any time (draft Article 17).

It was not a discussion that questioned a court's powers when seized of a substantive claim allegedly covered by an arbitration agreement (Article 8(1)). The drafter's discussions on this scenario were about limiting it by potentially adding the term 'manifest', 'prima facie' or similar before the phrase 'unless the court finds that the arbitration agreement is null and void, inoperative or incapable of being performed.'

A proper analysis of the Model Law's preparatory works leads to the conclusion that the drafters decided against what Article 17 proposed to offer with the text adopted in Article 8.

First, they abandoned the possibility of mere judicial *declaratory actions* on jurisdictional questions (draft Article 17(1)). They preferred *jurisdictional defences*, at the request of a party, in the context of substantive actions (Article 8(1)). Second, the drafters decided against empowering courts to stay arbitral proceedings (draft Article 17(2)). On the contrary, Article 8(2) paves the way for concurrent proceedings, as Article 16(3) also does after preliminary arbitral determination of jurisdictional challenges.

561. *Ibid.*, para. 56.
562. Commission Report A/40/17, paras 157-159.
563. Working Group Report, A/CN.9/246, para. 161.

[3] Article 16's Drafting History

Nothing in the records of Article 16's preparatory works signals that the drafters of the Model Law intended competence-competence to produce and impose a negative effect on national courts. In fact, a study of the instrument's text and drafting history leads to the opposite conclusion.

The extensive reports and analytical commentaries reveal that the drafters presupposed and embraced the idea that a court *could* conclusively determine the existence and validity of the arbitration agreement at the referral stage. This is evident from the language of Article 8(1) and the drafters' discussions concerning judicial control after an arbitrator has ruled that it lacks jurisdiction, i.e., Article 16(3).

Arguably, Article 16(3) only triggers judicial control where arbitrators have assumed jurisdiction on a preliminary decision, but not when they lack jurisdiction to decide the substantive dispute:

> If the arbitral tribunal rules as a preliminary question that *it has jurisdiction*, any party may request, within thirty days after having received notice of that ruling, the court specified in article 6 to decide the matter which decision shall be subject to no appeal; while such a request is pending, the arbitral tribunal may continue the arbitral proceedings and make an award.[564] [emphasis added]

An early draft (in 1983) of Article 16(3) provided for court control (also) of arbitral determinations of lack of jurisdiction.[565] Ultimately, the Working Group decided not to use that language, making such arbitral decisions final. They did not accept the prospect of compelling arbitrators to continue with the arbitration if they believed they lacked jurisdiction.[566] However, the effect of such a negative jurisdictional decision is limited to terminating the proceedings. This leaves the jurisdictional question pending a conclusive answer.

The Working Group was aware that uncertainty would remain regarding the appropriate forum (litigation or arbitration) to settle the substantive dispute. However, and significantly for this study, the drafters explicitly noted that the claimant could bring its substantive claim to a court, 'which would then be able to rule on this issue [jurisdiction]'.[567] And at a more advanced stage in the drafting process of the Model

564. Article 13(3) of the Model Law adopts the same court control procedure and time frame for arbitral decisions in unsuccessful challenges against the members of the arbitral tribunal. ('… the challenging party may request, within thirty days after having received notice of the decision rejecting the challenge, the court or other authority specified in article 6 to decide on the challenge, which decision shall be subject to no appeal; while such a request is pending, the arbitral tribunal, including the challenged arbitrator, may continue the arbitral proceedings and make an award.').

565. Working Group Report, A/CN.9/245, p. 13, para. 58 ('A ruling by the arbitral tribunal that it has no jurisdiction may be contested by any party within 30 days before the Court specified in article [6].').

566. Summary Records of the 316th Meeting, A/CN.9/246, annex; A/CN.9/263 Add.1-2, A/CN.9/264 (10 June 1985), UNCITRAL Yearbook, paras 16-19.

567. Working Group Report, A/CN.9/245, para. 64. For example, Sir Mustill later noted that 'the party making the plea could then take the matter to the court. The question would then arise before the court whether the arbitration agreement was operative, and whether the matter should then be stayed under article 8.'; Summary Records 316th Meeting, para. 18.

Law, the Secretariat's Analytical Commentary confirmed that the inconclusively answered jurisdictional question could be dealt with *'by way of request in any substantive proceedings as referred to in article 8(1).'*[568]

Similarly, in August 1985, the Commission Report recognised that '... article 16(3) did not cover the case where the arbitral tribunal ruled that it had no jurisdiction. Consequently, in such a case, Article 16(3), read together with article 5, did not preclude resort to a court for obtaining a decision on whether a valid arbitration agreement existed.'[569]

Given all this, it is not possible to conclude that the text and drafting history of Article 16 produces a negative effect of competence-competence. This provision does not necessarily restrict the judiciary's powers in an Article 8(1) scenario, limiting it to a *prima facie* examination of jurisdictional objections. It is reasonable to expect that curtailing a power that the judiciary otherwise enjoys (by constitutional design or other sovereign structure) might require clear(er) statutory language, like that in some international and national arbitration instruments. Some of them are examined next.

[D] THE NEGATIVE EFFECT OF COMPETENCE-COMPETENCE IN POSITIVE LAW

The 1961 European Convention on International Commercial Arbitration is an early illustration of the codification of the negative effect of the competence-competence principle. According to the Convention, courts are banned from determining a disputed arbitration agreement's existence, validity, and effectiveness when arbitral proceedings have been initiated. Courts could, exceptionally, make such determination when they have 'good and substantial reasons'.[570] Conversely, the negative effect of competence-competence does not affect the court's powers where there is no arbitration in place.

At the national level, some laws have taken heed of this procedural wrangle and have passed similar legislative directions to codify the negative effect of the competence-competence principle.

French law is often cited as the ultimate representation of the negative effects of competence-competence.[571] France did not adopt the Model Law but is a State-party to

568. Analytical Commentary (A/CN.9/264), para. 15. Conscious of the fact that negotiated instrument was a 'model', the Commission noted that the issue could be dealt with differently based on local general law on arbitration or civil procedure (*ibid.*).
569. Commission Report A/40/17, para. 163.
570. European Convention on International Arbitration Article VI(3): 'Where either party to an arbitration agreement has initiated arbitration proceedings before any resort is had to a court, courts of Contracting States subsequently asked to deal with the same subject matter between the same parties or with the question whether the arbitration agreement was non-existent or null and void or had lapsed, shall stay their ruling on the arbitrator's jurisdiction until the arbitral award is made, unless they have good and substantial reasons to the contrary.'
571. It codifies the positive effect of competence-competence in its *Code of Civil Procedure, Book IV, Arbitration* (France) Decree No. 2011-48 (13 January 2011), Article 1465: 'The arbitral tribunal has exclusive jurisdiction to rule on objections to its jurisdiction.'

the New York Convention and, therefore, internationally bound to respect the text of Article II(3).

French law combines a deadline for court involvement and a limited extent of review. A court can only hear and determine a jurisdictional dispute where: (i) there is no arbitral tribunal in place, and (ii) the arbitration agreement is *manifestly* void or inapplicable.[572] The law provides that:

> When a dispute subject to an arbitration agreement is brought before a court, such court shall decline jurisdiction, except if an arbitral tribunal has not yet been seized of the dispute and if the arbitration agreement is manifestly void or manifestly not applicable.[573]

This approach signals a clear policy choice in favour of arbitration. Its rule-oriented basis advances predictability and arbitral efficacy, but it is not a choice without costs. The downside lies in its lack of discretionary judicial powers. Some scenarios would be suitable for a decisive interlocutory ruling in support of arbitral efficacy and efficiency, but French law does not provide for this.

For example, where a party lodges a court action before an arbitral tribunal has been seized of the dispute, French law gives the court a single option if the agreement's defect is not manifest: to decline jurisdiction (without determining the jurisdictional challenge). The parties then would have to move the substantive claim and the jurisdictional challenge to arbitration.

On the one hand, this risks creating odd scenarios. For example, the claimant would have to initiate arbitral proceedings relying on an agreement it believes is inexistent, void, or not applicable. The request for arbitration would have to include an objection to the arbitral tribunal's jurisdiction. The arbitral proceedings would aim to obtain a lack of jurisdiction decision.

The claimant would be entitled to litigate the substantive dispute only after successfully challenging the jurisdiction of the tribunal constituted upon its own request. The unnecessary waste of time and money in this scenario would do little to promote an efficient dispute resolution system and the reputation of arbitration.

On the other hand, it risks inviting a misuse of adjudicatory resources. In response to a request for arbitration, a party might file a substantive court action and

572. This rule of priority has influenced the approach adopted in other jurisdictions. For example, it served as the basis for the Argentine legislation to govern domestic arbitrations. Article 1656 of the National Civil and Commercial Code (2014) provides that a court shall grant a referral to arbitration request, 'except where the arbitral tribunal has not yet been constituted, and the agreement appears to be manifestly null or not applicable.'.

573. *French Arbitration Law 2011*, Article 1448. French courts have clarified that an arbitration agreement is 'manifestly inapplicability' when it is 'obvious, (...) detectable on a mere reading' and therefore 'excludes any interpretation relating to the will of the parties'; *SARL Pharmacie du Geant Casino v. SAS Brunet*, Case no. 19/01756, Poitiers, 11.02.2020, as cited in Laurence Kiffer, 'National Report for France', in *ICCA International Handbook on Commercial Arbitration*, ed. Lise Bosman, Supplement 114 (ICCA & Kluwer Law International, 2020), p. 15. *See also*, *Etablissement Lindgren Oy v. SARL Euro MC et autres*, [2016/56], Court of Appeal of Grenoble, France, 15 March 2016. (Where two applicable and conflicting arbitration agreements led the court concluded that it was impossible to determine the parties' will to arbitrate, and it concluded that the agreements were *manifestly* inapplicable.)

resist the potential referral to arbitration by relying on weak jurisdictional defences (e.g., not well-articulated, well-documented, or legally sound) against arbitration. They would be an (apparent) attempt to delay the resolution of the dispute and financially exhaust the opponent.

The action and its weak objections could be dismissed with the force of a conclusive judicial ruling. However, the French court would not be entitled to do so because the grounds for attacking the arbitration agreement do not raise to the level of the *manifest* (void or inapplicable) standard. Thus, the judge can only decline its jurisdiction and refer the parties to arbitration.

This would allow the party to try another round of challenges - this time before the arbitrators - based on the same (defective and disruptive) grounds. After hearing the parties' arguments and weighing the evidence, the arbitral tribunal could rule against the jurisdictional objections.

Undeterred by its unsuccessful endeavours, the losing party might exercise its right to recourse to the French courts, asking to decide the matter fully and conclusively. At this point, the court would be empowered to determine the jurisdictional challenge, putting an end to the dilatory manoeuvres. Given that the arbitral tribunal's findings do not limit the court's examination, this post-arbitral decision action could involve a significant investment of time and resources (a *de novo* examination).[574]

This three-act jurisdictional battle would be avoided had the court enjoyed some discretionary latitude and rejected the original jurisdictional dispute with prejudice. Disempowering national courts (to tackle mere dilatory tactics disguised as jurisdictional objections) counters efficiency. It risks paving the way to only-after-the-arbitrators-decision court access to strike down procedural manoeuvres that probably aim at exhausting the counterparty (financially or otherwise).[575]

Conversely, empowering courts to conclusively determine a (flimsy) jurisdictional challenge at the threshold stage heightens procedural efficiency and economy. If the initial substantive court action takes place at the seat of the arbitration, the court decision would produce *res judicata* effects. It would strongly disincentive the party from raising the same objections before the arbitral tribunal. And even if the party were to venture the same objection, the outcome would be predictable. As a result, arbitration may continue on a solid footing, as it would be futile to attack the (future) award on the same jurisdictional grounds (again).

Some national arbitration laws in Model Law jurisdictions also impose rules of priority by deviating from the language suggested in Article 8(1). They contemplate a qualified judicial finding by explicitly limiting the court's task to a *prima facie* review

574. Kiffer, *National Report for France* ('A firmly established line of case law states that, when reviewing the decision of the arbitral tribunal on its own jurisdiction, whether it accepted it or not, the court shall research all elements in law or in fact, allowing it to assess the scope of the arbitration agreement and to draw the consequences as to the respect by the arbitrators of the mission assigned to them.').

575. Professor Park aptly noted that the French approach has not gained widespread acceptance. 'Such across-the-board deference to arbitrators (or alleged arbitrators) commands no wide international consensus'; Park, *The Arbitrator's Jurisdiction* (n. 16), p. 28.

of jurisdictional objections. This avoids the court's hurdle of construing the extent of court involvement under Article 8(1) of the Model Law.

The Peruvian Arbitration Law is an example of such a legislative directive. It provides that courts shall refer the parties to arbitration unless the agreement is *manifestly* null and void and arbitration has yet to commence.[576] If the arbitration is international and the proceedings have not started, the court 'shall dismiss the objection only if it determines that the arbitration agreement is *manifestly* null and void (...)'.[577] If arbitration has commenced, the court 'shall dismiss the objection only if it determines that the subject matter *manifestly* violates international public policy'.[578]

The current Indian legislation uses a different language but to the same effect.[579] An Indian court shall grant the referral unless it *prima facie* finds that no agreement to arbitrate exists (section 8(1) – related to domestic arbitrations),[580] or such agreement is null and void, inoperative or incapable of being performed (section 45 – pertaining to international arbitrations).[581] A distinctive factor is that the limited court involvement is not conditional on the commencement of the arbitration or the constitution of the arbitral tribunal. Therefore, it might be incorrect (or at least conclusory) to affirm that the limited judicial power is a mirror effect of the arbitrators' competence-competence. It is an explicit statutory direction.

Germany and Denmark are also examples of jurisdictions whose arbitration laws considered and reflected some of these discussions when adopting the Model Law.

The Danish arbitration law does not specify whether the court should find *prima facie* or not whether an arbitration agreement is null and void, inoperative or incapable of being performed. However, where a party brings a substantive court action *after* the commencement of arbitral proceedings, the court is only permitted to decide matters of substantive arbitrability. This creates a rule of priority favouring arbitrators to determine other challenges that may affect an agreement's validity and enforceability. The Danish version of Article 8(1) provides that:

> A court before which an action is brought in a matter which is the subject of an arbitration agreement shall, if a party so requests, refer the parties to arbitration unless it finds that the agreement is null and void, inoperative or incapable of

576. *Arbitration Act 2008 (DL 1071)* (Peru), Article 16(13) ('The objection of the existence of an arbitration agreement, whether it is pleaded before or after the commencement of the arbitration, shall be admitted on the sole ground of the existence of the arbitration agreement, except in the first case, if the arbitration agreement is *manifestly* null and void.') [emphasis added].
577. *Ibid.*, Article 16(14). [emphasis added] ('However, if the arbitration agreement meets the requirements set forth by Peruvian law, the objection may not be dismissed.').
578. *Ibid.* [emphasis added].
579. *Arbitration and Conciliation Act* (India) Law 26 of 1996, and Amendment Acts 3/2016, 33/2019, 2/2021 (16 August 1996).
580. *Ibid.*, section 8(1): 'A judicial authority, before which an action is brought in a matter which is the subject of an arbitration agreement shall (...) refer the parties to arbitration unless it finds that prima facie no valid arbitration agreement exists.'
581. *Ibid.*, section 45: '[A] judicial authority, when seized of an action in a matter in respect of which the parties have made an agreement referred to in section 44, shall (...) refer the parties to arbitration, unless it prima facie finds that the said agreement is null and void, inoperative or incapable of being performed.'

> being performed. *However, if the action has been brought after the commencement of arbitral proceedings, the court shall have jurisdiction to rule on the jurisdiction of the arbitral tribunal only in respect of whether the subject matter of the dispute is capable of settlement by arbitration.*[582] [emphasis added]

In Germany, the timing element appears to trigger another (limited) version of the negative effect of competence-competence. The local policy choice reflects a rule-based pro-arbitration approach (French style) but is anchored to a general procedural efficiency stance.

Before the composition of the arbitral tribunal, a party to an arbitration agreement may seek judicial declaratory relief to determine whether arbitration is required and possible.[583] After the composition of the tribunal and in exercise of its competence-competence, it will be for the arbitrators to deal with the declaration sought.[584]

German law does not recognise the negative effect of competence-competence where the jurisdictional question is raised as a defence against a substantive claim. In this scenario, the German Arbitration Act does not specify the standard for reviewing jurisdictional questions. It does not provide for a clear rule of priority in favour of arbitrators either, regardless of the question being asked before or after the constitution of the tribunal. But despite this legislative silence, threshold questions are not answered on a *prima facie* basis.[585] The reason lies behind the twofold determination that the law imposes – a ruling on the court's jurisdiction and a declaration on the admissibility of the action.

This results from a significant textual deviation of the local legislation from the Model Law (Article 8(1)). According to section 1032(1) of the German Arbitration Act:

> A court before which an action is brought in a matter which is the subject of an arbitration agreement shall, if the respondent raises an objection prior to the beginning of the oral hearing on the substance of the dispute, *reject the action as inadmissible* unless the court finds that the arbitration agreement is null and void, inoperative or incapable of being performed.[586]

582. *Danish Arbitration Act 2005*, Article 8(1). It is not clear why Danish law made such a distinction, as the effect of non-arbitrability of a dispute would be to render the arbitration agreement null and void, or inoperative or incapable of being performed. *See* Chapter 6, section [D].
583. *German Arbitration Law 1998*, section 1032(1032): 'Prior to the composition of the arbitral tribunal, an application may be made to the court to declare whether or not arbitration is admissible.' According to section 1032(3), arbitral proceedings can still commence or continue, and the arbitral tribunal render an award.
584. *Ibid.*, section 1040(1041). After the arbitral tribunal's decision, a party could request a court to decide the jurisdictional issue (section 1040(3), (4)).
585. According to Kröll, '[i]n German arbitration law any challenge of the court's jurisdiction will lead to a full review by the court'; Stefan M. Kröll, 'National Report for Germany', in *ICCA International Handbook on Commercial Arbitration*, ed. Lise Bosman, no. Supplement 114 (ICCA & Kluwer Law International, 2020), p. 20.
586. *German Arbitration Law 1998* [emphasis added]. While the issue is pending before the court, arbitral proceedings to commence or continue, and the arbitral tribunal render an award (section 1032(3)).

To declare an action inadmissible, courts engage in a full review of the jurisdictional challenge, at least regarding the existence of a valid arbitration agreement.[587]

There are other examples of national legislation that limit the standard of court review at the referral stage. Regardless of the specific variations in its statutory reception, the crucial observation is that restricted court involvement is crystallised in the written law. Those illustrations of positive law represent a clear textual dissimilarity with the Model Law – a dissimilarity of significant legal consequence. In contrast with Article 8(1) of the Model Law, the explicit language of those positive laws directs the timing and extent of curial involvement. The limited court involvement is an imposed rule-based response to the commencement of the arbitral proceedings or the constitution of the arbitral tribunal rather than the interpretative result of a text that does not offer such explicit guidance (i.e., Article 8(1)).

It would be wrong to assume that this is (solely) a mirroring effect of recognising the arbitrators' powers to determine jurisdictional disputes. The policies behind the legislative choices may go beyond the arbitrators' competence-competence.

[E] CONCLUSION

The interplay of Article 8(1) with Articles 5, 8(2), and 16 does not produce or impose a negative effect of the competence-competence principle. Such an effect does not fit the Model Law's drafting history nor its basic structure, which does not impose it as a *necessary* consequence of the arbitrators' power to decide on their own jurisdiction.

The opposite conclusion would disregard the significance of textual dissimilarities. Some arbitration laws in Model Law jurisdictions have deviated from the model, explicitly limiting the court review to a *prima facie* standard of review. It would be questionable to impose the same effect when the text, context and preparatory works of Article 8(1) do not support it. The interpretative approach proposed in this book does not support this. Ultimately, it would threaten legal certainty and predictability.

Although decision-making powers must be exercised to advance the law's policies and purpose, '[p]olicy considerations cannot be permitted to distort the actual words of the statute, read harmoniously with the scheme of the statute, its object, and the intention of the legislature, so as to make [a legal provision] say something it does not'.[588]

Before any hard, final conclusions are drawn here, it is essential to analyse the last element of the interpretative exercise proposed in Chapter 3[E] above: legal purpose. That is the subject of the next chapter.

587. Huber et al., *Arbitration in Germany* (n. 498), p. 119.
588. *TELUS v. Wellman*, 2019 SCC 19 (CanLII), para. 79.

CHAPTER 7

Purpose: The Effective and Efficient Resolution of Disputes

[A] INTRODUCTION

The adjectives in the title of this chapter reveal the *purpose* of the Model Law. It relates to the effectiveness of arbitration agreements and arbitral awards and efficiency in dispute resolution.

Though 'purpose' is discussed here as the last element of the interpretative exercise proposed in Chapter 3 (section [E]), the order of its presentation does not matter. What matters is that purpose is ubiquitous, and the interpreter must identify it before pursuing it. It was present and relevant in the creation of UNCITRAL and in the adoption of the Model Law, and each of its provisions has a purpose that contributes to an overarching one.

In brief (the details are already presented in Chapter 2 above), the United Nations created UNCITRAL with the purpose of developing a unified and harmonious legal framework for doing business effectively, dissipating uncertainties in international trade. This aimed to contribute to global prosperity.[589] Arbitration is one of the legal areas within UNCITRAL's work programme to achieve that purpose.

The purpose of the Model Law is one step down the ladder of generality. This instrument's goal is to facilitate the resolution of disputes by encouraging, recognising, and safeguarding party autonomy in international trade.[590]

Stating that the purpose of the Model Law is to promote and facilitate arbitration is accurate yet an incomplete proposition. That relates only to the instrument's *efficacy* goal. But, the United Nations General Assembly recorded the purpose of the Model Law

589. A/RES/40/71, para. 6.
590. It is ancillary to *international* trade by design because it engineers a legislative system subjected to international rather than domestic rules; Bachand, *Judicial Internationalism* (n. 96), pp. 231-236.

in more comprehensive terms when adopting its text. Resolution 40/72 notes that the Model Law's objective is also to contribute to the *fair and efficient settlement of disputes* in international commercial relations.'[591] The words italicised complete the overarching purpose of the instrument and align it with the general purpose that the United Nations intended when establishing UNCITRAL.

Therefore, the Model Law does not seek solely to promote arbitration. Because the Model Law envisages arbitration as a supporting tool for expanding international commerce,[592] *fairness* and *efficiency* in resolving disputes are crucial to serving the needs of its users (the business community). As also noted in Chapter 2, this understanding was explicitly put as follows at the inception of the Model Law:

> [T]he paramount consideration in reviewing and revising the draft text [of the Model Law] should be the *efficient* functioning of international commercial arbitration. To that end, due account must be taken of the needs of those who in day-to-day practice would use the text and whom it was ultimately intended to serve.[593] [emphasis added]

The world's leading arbitration institution, amongst others, echoes this conclusion. In a recent publication, the ICC noted that '[a]rbitration is a valuable tool for the resolution of disputes. However, if it is to serve the needs of its users, it must be time and cost-effective.'[594]

This clarification of the broader view of the Model Law's purpose is significant because it exposes the instrument's combined pro-arbitration attitude to its interpretation and an efficiency-focused approach to its application.

If facilitating and promoting arbitration was the sole purpose of the Model Law, (any and) all referral to arbitration under Article 8(1) would accomplish the instrument's purpose. However, fairness and efficiency also form part of the instrument's purpose and should influence its interpretation and application. Therefore, faced with jurisdictional disputes in the context of Article 8(1), courts should interpret and apply that provision with a view to facilitating arbitration, having regard to fairness and efficiency considerations in the resolution of specific (jurisdictional) disputes.

Importantly, the court's task in facilitating arbitration is conditioned by the fundamental premise that legitimises the arbitration process: the parties consent to arbitrate.[595] Efficiency glosses the court's duty to balance legitimacy and the efficacy of

591. General Assembly A/RES/40/72, para. 4 [emphasis added]. *See* further comments in Chapter 2, section [B][3].
592. General Assembly A/34/17, paras 76-81. *See* further comments in Chapter 2, section [B][3].
593. Commission Report A/40/17, para. 15. This is not unique to the Model Law but deeply rooted in arbitration legislation generally. Cordero-Moss, for example, noted that '[e]ffectiveness and efficiency of arbitration are important principles of arbitration law and are at the origin of the widespread arbitration-friendly attitude that has characterised legislation and case law in the past decades'; Giuditta Cordero-Moss, 'The Alleged Failure of Arbitration to Address Due Process Concerns: Is Arbitration under Attack?', in *Stockholm Arbitration Yearbook*, ed. Axel Calissendorff and Patrik Schöldström, no. 3 (Kluwer Law International, 2021), p. 259.
594. Report of the ICC Commission on Arbitration and ADR Task Force on Reducing Time and Costs in Arbitration (2nd ed.), p. 4.
595. *See, e.g.*, Bermann, *The 'Gateway' Problem* (n. 13), pp. 2-3, where the author considers 'an arbitral regime to be legitimate (or to enjoy legitimacy) to the extent that the parties who were

the arbitration agreement. Accordingly, courts should avoid relying too heavily on equitable or policy considerations (e.g., avoidance of dilatory tactics) rather than party consent to justify a referral to arbitration.

This is where the purpose of Article 8(1) of the Model Law[596] gains relevance – to safeguard the *efficacy* of the parties' bargain to arbitrate their disputes. That article does so by recognising the agreement's binding effects, presuming its validity and encompassing scope, and subjecting its enforcement to limited exceptions.

The contextual operation of Article 8(1) and the overarching purpose of the Model Law seek to facilitate arbitration and infuse *fairness and efficiency* in the enforcement of the parties' agreement to arbitrate.

Before discussing 'efficiency' as an element of the purpose of the Model Law, the following section outlines the difficulties in defining the term at a high level of abstraction.

[B] FAIRNESS AND EFFICIENCY ARE RELATIVE, SUBJECTIVE AND DYNAMIC CONCEPTS

Fairness and efficiency are hard to define. There are illustrations of both concepts but not abstract, universal, or comprehensive definitions because they are relative and subjective concepts. To define fairness and efficiency (*ante facto*) would be to diminish them, for it risks confining their dynamic character.

In a nutshell, fairness and efficiency in international arbitration are closely linked to time and money. They are associated with the cost and duration of the arbitral process. Delays in the proceedings translate into an inefficient arbitration, whether those delays result from legitimate procedural steps or ill-intended tactics. Therefore, high costs and lengthy proceedings obstruct the achievement of the purpose of the Model Law (fair and efficient dispute resolution through arbitration).

Fairness shapes the contours of the arbitral proceeding and directs the arbitrators' actions. This materialises in (i) respecting the parties' fundamental rights to be treated equally and heard before the arbitrators decide their disputes, (ii) respecting the parties' procedural agreements and adopting procedures suitable to the circumstances of the case, (iii) arbitrators remaining independent and impartial throughout the proceedings, and keeping their decision-making within their mandate.

It could be argued that fairness is related to time because, as the legal maxim goes, 'justice delayed is justice denied'. Though efficiency could immediately be linked to money spent, the 'time' element cannot be divorced because time carries an investment of monetary resources.

---

compelled to arbitrate rather than litigate, and will be bound by the resulting arbitral award, consented to step outside the ordinary court system in favor of an arbitral tribunal as their dispute resolution forum.'

596. Like Article II(3) of the New York Convention, which, according to Woff, aims to 'facilitate and stabilize international business transactions by promoting the enforcement of arbitration agreements in international contracts'; Wolff, *New York Convention – Commentary*, p. 159 (n. 134), para. 192.

For some authors, efficiency is a relative value because it focuses on the perspectives of the arbitration actors.[597] For example, what might seem efficient for the parties may differ from the arbitral tribunal's view. Others associate arbitral inefficiency with the due process principle (fairness), as high costs may hinder low-funded parties' access to justice.[598] Other authorities have observed that, in virtually all cases, the increase in costs and delays is 'to the advantage of the party with deeper pockets rather than the more just cause.'[599] Hence, fairness requires a degree of efficiency; otherwise, lengthy proceedings may equate to a denial of justice.[600] And although the Model Law's ambition is to recognise and give effect to the parties' agreement to arbitrate and the greatest possible procedural freedom, its text was also envisioned to prevent or remedy instances of denial of justice.[601]

Fairness and efficiency cannot be measured in absolute terms; they are linked to the given dispute's specific circumstances. Save for rare exceptions, the complexities surrounding a dispute are unique. Although there may be factual and legal similarities between groups of disputes, each case presents its particularities. Even where the substantive law is the same for two cases, the facts, the parties, their legal relationship, arguments, and evidence differ in each dispute, as do the approaches and strategies of counsel and arbitrators. Between two alternatives for resolving an issue, one may be more efficient than the other, but none might encapsulate an ideal, abstract representation of efficiency (and fairness). Further, what parties in one dispute consider the most efficient alternative may find it inefficient under a different setting.

It is almost intuitive, then, that a dispute's fair and efficient resolution will require specific considerations and decisions. The same approach or solution may not be efficient when the particularities of cases differ. Consequently, efficiency in resolving a dispute involves assessment and judgment rather than ideal scenarios. And because balancing the risks of dilatory tactics versus the waste of resources is not an easy task

597. *See, e.g.*, Loukas Mistelis, 'Efficiency – What Else: Efficiency as the Emerging Defining Value of International Arbitration: Between Systems Theories and Party Autonomy', in *The Oxford Handbook of International Arbitration*, ed. Thomas Schultz and Federico Ortino (Oxford University Press, 2020), p. 375 ('[T]he content of [efficiency] varies depending on the different parties, actors, and factors involved in the arbitral process. [T]he assessment of various factors may lead to different concepts of efficiency').

598. *See, e.g.*, Cordero-Moss, *Due Process Concerns* (n. 593), p. 262. *See also*, Fabricio Fortese et al., Procedural Fairness and Efficiency in International Arbitration, 3 *Groningen Journal of International Law*, no. 1 (2015), p. 116 DOI: 10.21827/5a86a89d8e651 ('[F]airness requires some degree of efficiency, since justice too long delayed becomes justice denied. Equally, without fairness (...) proceedings could hardly be considered an efficient mechanism of dispute resolution.').

599. Justice Sundaresh Menon, Dispelling Due Process Paranoia: Fairness, Efficiency and the Rule of Law, 17 *Asian International Arbitration Journal*, no. 1 (2021), p. 7 DOI: 10.54648/aiaj2021001.

600. Cordero-Moss, *Due Process Concerns*, p. 262.

601. *See, e.g.*, Secretariat Report A/CN.9/207, paras 16-21 (Restrictions to the parties procedural freedoms 'would not be contrary to the interest of the parties, at least not of the weaker and disadvantaged one in a given case', at para. 21).

at a high level of abstraction,[602] no one-size-fits-all efficiency approach or solution can be proposed.

For that reason, the purpose of the Model Law is stated in assertive but broad terms, leaving considerable interpretative space for its application to concrete situations. It is no surprise that the purpose of the general and abstract norm (the Model Law) aims at 'efficiency *in dispute resolution*', and individual norms (court and arbitral decisions in each case) focus on 'efficiency in the resolution of *the dispute*' at hand.[603] In this sense, the Model Law provides courts with tools to facilitate the efficacy of agreements to arbitrate efficiently. Those tools have been discussed throughout this work but are briefly contextualised in the next section.

[C] EFFICACY AND EFFICIENCY AS ELEMENTS OF THE MODEL LAW'S PURPOSE

As discussed in greater detail in previous chapters, the Model Law lays out legislative tools that heighten the *efficacy* of agreements to arbitrate. For example, the *burden-shifting* presumption[604] encapsulated in Article 8(1) is in line with the Model Law's purpose of facilitating arbitration. The doctrine of *separability* is also closely related to the presumptive validity of arbitration agreements. Because an arbitration clause is considered a self-contained agreement, it enjoys legal autonomy even when it forms part of a substantive or underlying contract. Consequently, the invalidity of the underlying contract may not automatically invalidate the arbitration clause.

International arbitration practice and case law have adopted other interpretative tools that strengthen the efficacy of arbitration agreements. The *validation principle*, for example, enhances the presumptive validity of arbitration agreements and further supports the effectiveness of party autonomy. It is a rule of contract interpretation used to establish the parties' intention, in this case, to arbitrate disputes. Its application requires that the validity of arbitration agreements be based on any national law potentially applicable to it, which would render the arbitration agreement valid and effective. Article VII(1) of the New York Convention encapsulates this principle, which allows parties to rely on more lenient laws than the Convention.[605]

602. Analytical Commentary (A/CN.9/264), p. 41, para. 14 ('... the weight of these two conflicting concerns, i.e. fear of dilatory tactics and obstruction versus the waste of time and money, is difficult to assess at a general level imagining all possible cases. It seems that the assessment could better be made with respect to each particular case.').
603. This reflects Kelsen's distinction or norms: 'Norms may be abstract and general (e.g., statutes) or concrete and individual (e.g., judicial decisions) in character. Case law understands the law as a system of general and individual norms. Hans Kelsen, The Pure Theory of Law and Analytical Jurisprudence, 55 Harvard Law Review (1941), pp. 50-56 DOI: 10.2307/1334739.
604. The burden-shifting or presumptive validity principle of arbitration agreements was discussed in Chapter 5, section [D[4] above.
605. It provides that: 'The provisions of the present Convention shall not ... deprive any interested party of any right he may have to avail himself of an arbitral award in the manner and to the extent allowed by the law or the treaties of the country where such award is sought to be relied upon.' In 2006, UNCITRAL recommended the application of such provision to arbitration agreements; *see* A/61/17 (SUPP), pp. 61-62.

This principle assumes that the contracting parties must have intended to enter into a legally valid, effective and enforceable (rather than invalid, ineffective and unenforceable) contract, i.e., the arbitration agreement.

Relatedly, the relevant contract laws and their tenets of interpretation also apply to arbitration agreements.[606] Generally, contracts are interpreted with a view to respect and give full effect to the parties' intent. This is known as the principle of *effective interpretation*, which embraces a broad and liberal construction of agreements to arbitrate, favouring their enforcement even where they are poorly or vaguely drafted.[607] Likewise, questions related to the invalidity of arbitration contracts are interpreted narrowly.[608] Because arbitration agreements are presumed valid rather than invalid, a high threshold is commonly imposed to conclude that the parties' agreement to arbitrate is 'null and void, inoperative, and incapable of being performed'.[609] Similarly, where the language of a disputed arbitration clause bears two interpretations, courts prefer the one that honours arbitration.[610]

It is commonly understood that the principle of effective interpretation applies to issues related to the validity and scope of the arbitration agreement, not to those associated with the very formation and existence of the agreement to arbitrate.[611]

The effective interpretation approach is a general tenet of contract interpretation rather than a specific legislative device found in the Model Law. Its operation aligns with the Model Law's pro-arbitration attitude. It is naturally welcomed in jurisdictions that have adopted the New York Convention and Model Law as a clear policy choice in favour of arbitration.

The presumptive validity of arbitration agreements, the separability presumption, the validation principle, the broad and effective approach to interpreting arbitration agreements, and a narrow interpretative stance to jurisdictional objections form part of the pro-enforcement bias the Model Law offers to facilitate arbitration. A standard of full judicial review of jurisdictional challenges under Article 8(1) of the Model Law does not deny or rest effect to the operation of those pro-arbitration tools.

---

606. Born, *International Commercial Arbitration*, 1, pp. 684, 1426-1431 ('It is almost uniformly held or assumed that generally-applicable rules of contract construction apply to the interpretation of international arbitration agreements.', at p. 1426). *See, e.g., Insigma Technology Co Ltd v. Alstom Technology Ltd,* [2009] SGCA 24, Singapore Court of Appeal, para. 30: '[A]n arbitration agreement should be construed like any other form of commercial agreement.'; Also, *see* the discussion in Chapter 5, section [B] on the laws applicable to arbitration agreements.

607. *See* ICCA, *ICCA's Guide* (n. 407), p. 57, point IV.54.52. *See also*, Bermann, *International Arbitration* (n. 549), pp. 155-157. And, *Insigma v. Alstom*, [2009] SGCA 24, para. 34 ('[A]n arbitration agreement should ... not be interpreted restrictively or strictly.').

608. For example, *see Comandate Marine v. Pan Australia Shipping*, [2006] FCAFC 192, paras 209-214; *Albon v. Naza Motor*, [2007] EWHC 665 (Ch), para. 18.

609. Born, *International Commercial Arbitration* (n. 15), p. 697.

610. *Onex Corp. v. Ball Corp*, 1994 CanLII 7537 (ON SC), Ontario Supreme Court of Justice, 24 January 1994, para. 24 ('At the very least, where the language of an arbitration clause is capable of bearing two interpretations, and on one of those interpretations fairly provides for arbitration, the courts should lean towards honouring that option, given the recent developments in the law ...').

611. Lew et al., *Comparative ICA* (n. 367), para. 7-62; Fouchard et al., *Fouchard Gaillard Goldman on International Commercial Arbitration* (n. 9), paras 478, 481. Bermann, *International Arbitration* (n. 549), p. 156.

The same tools are equally available to arbitral tribunals and national courts. The challenging quest for a court when dealing with a referral to arbitration request relates to the second pillar of the Model Law's purpose: fairness and efficiency in the resolution of the dispute.

The Efficiency Tools in the Model Law

As also highlighted throughout the previous chapters, the text of the Model Law provides several avenues that reflect and facilitate its efficiency goal. One example is the waiver of the right to object for non-compliance with legal or procedural requirements (Article 4). The Drafting Group and the Commission understood that a general waiver rule for failing to raise objections promptly would help the arbitral process function efficiently and in good faith.[612] Another example is Article 11, which provides for court assistance in appointing arbitrators to avoid any deadlock or undue delay in the appointment process.[613]

Another example closely related to jurisdictional objections at the threshold of arbitration is Article 8(2) of the Model Law. As discussed earlier in this work, that provision vests arbitrators with powers to continue arbitral proceedings while the arbitration agreement's enforceability is challenged before a national court on a substantive action. If jurisdictional disputes arise during arbitral proceedings, Article 16(2) empowers arbitrators to rule on them either as a preliminary question or in an award on the merits. Such discretionary powers 'reduce the risk and effect of dilatory tactics of a party reneging on his commitment to arbitration'.[614]

Similarly, the Model Law seeks to anticipate dilatory tactics from respondents in arbitrations. To avoid stalling the proceedings by a non-participating respondent, the Model Law allows arbitrators to continue with the proceedings and render an award (Article 25(b)). The same solution applies when the claimant in the arbitration fails to appear at a hearing or produce documentary evidence (Article 25(c)).

Articles 13(3) and 16(3) relate to judicial control over arbitral decisions on challenges against arbitrators and their jurisdiction. Those articles include three features specifically envisioned to enhance efficiency and address the risk of delays. One of those features is the reasonably short period for requesting the competent court to decide the issue. As the Commission Report noted, allowing immediate court control, not only after the award on the merits, has a clear purpose: to 'prevent dilatory tactics and abuse of any immediate right to appeal that this solution was adopted'.[615] The second feature is the finality of the court decision, which is not subject to appeals. The third is the possibility of continuing arbitral proceedings whilst the court control is underway.[616]

612. Summary Records of the 308th Meeting, A/CN.9/246, annex; A/CN.9/263 Add.1-2, A/CN.9/264 (4 June 1985), UNCITRAL Yearbook, paras 27-65 and Commission Report A/40/17, para. 53.
613. Analytical Commentary (A/CN.9/264), p. 29, para. 24 ('Assistance by this Court is provided in order to avoid any deadlock or undue delay in the appointment process.').
614. *Ibid.*, p. 24, para. 25.
615. *Ibid.*, p. 41, para. 13.
616. *Ibid.*, p. 33, para. 36.

The wording of other provisions in the Model Law evidences its pro-efficiency stance in arbitration proceedings. However, that the Model Law seeks efficiency in arbitration does not mean that every arbitration is efficient. In fact, in recent years, arbitration users have criticised it for its inefficiency by pointing to increasing costs, lengthy and overregulated proceedings, and arbitrators progressively succumbing to 'due process paranoia'.[617,618]

Some UNCITRAL Member States channelled those concerns in a paper submitted to the Commission in 2018, noting that:

> Arbitration is increasingly under pressure and threatened to lose its role as the preferred means for dispute resolution for commercial disputes. Arbitration is under a double pressure: on the one hand, arbitral proceedings are getting increasingly complicated, and they expand both in terms of time frame and in terms of volume of documentation. This challenges one of the traditional advantages of arbitration as opposed to court litigation, namely efficiency.[619]

That paper included a proposal for amending UNCITRAL's Arbitration Rules (not the Model Law), which culminated in the adoption of the 2021 Expedited Rules.[620] These Rules aim to streamline arbitration processes of relatively less complex (or low-value) disputes and restore the perceived lost efficiency. Its Explanatory Note highlights that '[t]he Expedited Rules balance, on the one hand, the efficiency of the arbitral proceedings and on the other, the rights of the parties to due process and fair treatment.'[621]

The fact that UNCITRAL has been devoting significant workforces to discussing, developing and adopting instruments for the recognition and enforcement of other types of dispute resolution mechanisms (e.g., mediation)[622] is what a scholar described as 'a symptom of the declining hegemony of arbitration'.[623] UNCITRAL is currently working on legislative options for early dismissal and preliminary determination of disputes, amongst other topics.[624]

617. Due Process Paranoia refers to the arbitrators' deference to admitting the parties' (sometimes unreasonable) requests of new claims, evidence, extensions of times, etc., for fear of an attack to the arbitral award, based on violations of due process guarantees.
618. *See generally*, Mistelis, *Efficiency – What Else* (n. 597), pp. 349-376 ('[C]osts and duration have been identified as the factors that might endanger the existence of international arbitration itself', at p. 355). Similarly, Cordero-Moss, *Due Process Concerns* (n. 593), pp. 252-253, 265-266.
619. Proposal by the Governments of Italy, Norway and Spain: Future Work for Working Group II, A/CN.9/959 (30 April 2018), para. 5.
620. *See* Report of the Commission on its Fifty-fourth session, General Assembly A/76/17 Supp. 17 (28 June-16 July 2021), para. 189.
621. Draft Explanatory Note of the Secretariat on the UNCITRAL Expedited Arbitration Rules, A/CN.9/WG.II/WP.219 (28 July 2021), para. 1.
622. For example, the United Nations Convention on International Settlement Agreements Resulting from Mediation, A/RES/73/198 (20 December 2018), and the UNCITRAL Model Law on International Commercial Mediation and International Settlement Agreements Resulting from Mediation, A/RES/73/199 (20 December 2018).
623. Cordero-Moss, *Due Process Concerns* (n. 593), text in footnote 49.
624. *See* the Annotated provisional agenda for the Working Group II's meeting of 10-14 October 2022 (Vienna), A/CN.9/WG.II/WP.226.

The legal profession's responsive (or self-preserving) attitude towards the arbitration users' criticism contributes to devising potential soft-law solutions. For example, at the 2021 ICC Institute Annual Conference,[625] David W. Rivkin, a leading arbitration practitioner and former President of the International Bar Association, presented the 'Town Elder Arbitration Rules' (TEA Rules), which could supplement or amend the UNCITRAL Arbitration Rules. The TEA Rules propose using technology to develop a decision-tree approach for resolving matters issue by issue. This would facilitate the disposal of cases through early decisions on significant matters. It could even encourage a settlement, as the arbitrators' decisions could guide the parties on their prospects of full or partial success.

Other illustrations of the arbitration community's initiative to mend inefficiency are the Rules on the Efficient Conduct of Proceedings in International Arbitration (the Prague Rules).[626] The IBA Rules on the Taking of Evidence in International Arbitration also aim to standardise practices to streamline evidentiary matters.

The relevant point here is that soft-law instruments and practice complement the efficacy and efficiency tools that the Model Law offers. The synergy of laws, conventions, practice-driven rules, protocols, and guidelines contribute to building a solid normative framework for arbitration to become and remain a successful dispute resolution tool.

The broad language with which the Model Law words its purpose and lays out tools to achieve it requires a balancing exercise of competing but intertwined interests. That purpose is significant for interpreting Article 8(1) because it contributes to giving meaning to its terms and clarifies the court's role at the threshold of arbitration.

[D] THE TWO SIDES OF DILATORY TACTICS

Before discussing the courts' balancing exercise of efficacy and efficiency concerns, this section ponders on the courts' need to identify whether or not it is faced with a dilatory tactic.

Although filing a substantive court action in breach of an arbitration agreement may be a dilatory tactic or forum shopping, sometimes it is not. The reproach for the delays and higher costs is not always directed to the party that lodges the court action. It could be the respondent in the litigation rather than the claimant who embarks on an ill-intended tactic. As commented earlier, a respondent would do so by challenging the court's jurisdiction and requesting the referral to arbitration, taking advantage of the fact that the arbitration agreement's shortcomings are not *obvious* or *manifest*. The respondent would succeed in prolonging the dispute resolution if the court mechanically adopts the *prima facie* standard of review. Then, determining the agreement's (in)existence or (un)enforceability would involve an arbitral finding (Article 16(1) Model Law) and a subsequent court decision (Article 16(3) Model Law). The situation

625. Forty-First ICC Institute Annual Conference: Rethinking the Paradigms of International Arbitration (29 November 2021). *See* summary at: https://www.debevoise.com/news/2021/11/debevoise-partner-david-w-rivkin-discusses.
626. The Prague Rules were launched in 2018 and can be found at praguerules.com.

could become dire if no arbitral proceedings have even been set in motion. The delaying tactic could then extend to obstructing the selection of the members of the tribunal and challenging them before they can make a preliminary jurisdictional ruling.

So, suggesting that claimants initiate litigation in breach of arbitration agreements is a true statement as this one: defendants rely on invalid arbitration agreements to delay the resolution of the dispute. Although some authors might rely on first-hand experiences to make such statements, the fact is that no authority has conducted meaningful empirical research to substantiate either proposition. And the risk is that each side of the argument might be supported and influenced by sectorial preferences and their attitude or 'ratitute' (rat attitude)[627] towards arbitration.

Courts may *suspect* that commencing litigation is a dilatory tactic, but why *assume* it? Especially because breaching or ignoring an arbitration agreement is not without substantial risks and drawbacks. It could even be a 'tragedy'[628] for the claimant in the litigation if it gets what it seeks by disregarding the arbitration agreement: to avoid resolving its dispute in arbitration.

Commencing court proceedings as a mere dilatory tactic would involve a claimant not genuinely interested in promptly obtaining the relief it seeks. Or, at least, not in the most efficient manner. By putting the litigation in motion, sooner or later, the court will render its judgment on the substantive claim.

Notably, the claimant's court action might succeed in forcing a waste of resources but not necessarily in curtailing or delaying the opposing party's access to arbitration. Given the language of Article 8(2) of the Model Law, it cannot be suggested that the claimant benefits (procedurally) from commencing the court action in anticipation of the opposing party's imminent filing for arbitration. Litigation does not halt arbitration. Arbitral proceedings can commence or continue even where an action is pending before a court,[629] irrespective of the place of arbitration or the law governing the arbitration.[630]

A claimant commencing litigation as a dilatory tactic also assumes the risk that the respondent may not object to the court's jurisdiction, even if a valid and enforceable arbitration agreement exists. As courts cannot refer the parties to arbitration on

627. Justice Breyer of the US Supreme Court used the term 'ratitude' during oral arguments in *Badgerow v. Walters*, Case No. 20-1143 (U.S. S.Ct.), to describe a party's attitude against arbitration: '[I]f that's the main argument, what we're doing here normally is we are having, let's call him an arbitration rat. There is the guy who loves arbitration and then there is the rat who hates it, although he agreed to it, okay? Now he will express his ratitude in many different ways. First, he will not want to go in in the first place. Then, if you make him go in in the first place, he's not going to want the other guy to get any witnesses. And then, if you go and get that, he's not going to want anybody to enforce this thing which he lost in the third place. So, of course, these don't all just always follow. It depends on which of these provisions the guy can use and invoke in order to stop what he agreed to, which is the arbitration.' The transcript available at: https://www.supremecourt.gov/oral_arguments/argument_transcripts/2021/20-1143_f2ah.pdf.
628. As Wilde wittily put it, '[i]n this world there are only two tragedies. One is not getting what one wants, and the other is getting it. The last is much the worst; the last is a real tragedy!', Oscar Wilde, *Lady Windermere's Fan: A Play about a Good Woman* (1892) Mr Dumby, Act 3.
629. *See* discussion in Chapter 6, section [E].
630. A/CN.9/WG.II/WP.49, para. 19.

their own motion, the dispute would remain in the judicial forum. Therefore, no dilatory manoeuvre could be assumed from it.

This is linked to another risk that parties often try to avoid with arbitration: to litigate in an unfavourable jurisdiction or not 'neutral country',[631] i.e., a country that is not one of the parties' residence or place of business.[632]

By ignoring the arbitration agreement, the action would, generally, have to be commenced before the courts where the respondent is domiciled (or where the performance of the obligation in question takes place (e.g., where goods are delivered or the services rendered)).[633] *A priori*, this is not an attractive alternative for any claimant.

Further, the claimant's benefits in disregarding the agreement to arbitrate would have to outweigh the advantages of arbitration as a dispute resolution mechanism – for example, its high degree of procedural flexibility. In arbitration, parties can agree on the arbitration proceedings rather than complying with the rigid impositions of the domestic rules of procedure. This facilitates adjusting the proceedings to achieve greater expediency and lower the costs of resolving the dispute.

The fact that arbitral proceedings can be confidential is commonly perceived as another advantage over litigation, which is less restricted to public scrutiny. In arbitration, the parties can agree on the degree of privacy and confidentiality of the proceedings, the evidence produced, and the arbitral award. This could even extend to the very existence of the dispute. Commercial parties may have a legitimate interest in settling their disputes in open courts, but this is not always true.

Another commonly positive feature associated with arbitration is the right to select the decision-maker. Parties cannot choose the judge for their court proceedings, but they can select the members of the arbitral tribunal. That selection is based on the candidate's independence, impartiality, availability and expertise for the specific type of dispute. Given that arbitrators can be selected from different nationalities, the arbitral tribunal can be neutral from national (political, cultural, legal, social) influence. Although some judges' impartiality, independence and expertise might match the arbitrators', their appointment to the case does not depend on the parties' choice. Their

631. Nigel Blackaby et al., *Redfern and Hunter on International Arbitration*, 6th ed. (Oxford University Press, 2015), p. 29, para. 21.100 ('[A] reference to arbitration means that the dispute will be determined in a neutral place of arbitration, rather than on the home ground of one party or the other.'); Born, *International Commercial Arbitration* (n. 15), p. 71, §71.02[B][71] ('One of the central objectives of international arbitration agreements is to provide a neutral, even-handed forum for dispute resolution, detached from either the parties or their respective home state governments.').

632. Fouchard et al., *International Commercial Arbitration* (n. 9), p. 227, para. 433, and p. 235, para. 443. Gary B. Born, *International Commercial Arbitration*, 3rd ed., vol. 2 (Kluwer Law International, 2021), p. 2215, §2214.2202[A][2217] ('Parties frequently insist that the arbitral seat be "neutral" – that is, not the home jurisdiction of either party.').

633. This is the solution under, for example, the Regulation (EU) No. 1215/2012 of the European Parliament and of the Council of 12 December 2012 on Jurisdiction and the Recognition and Enforcement of Judgments in Civil and Commercial Matters (2012), Articles 4(1), and 7(1). Similarly, *see* the Convention on Jurisdiction and the Recognition and Enforcement of Judgments in Civil and Commercial Matters (2007), Article 2(1); *Federal Act on Private International Law (in force since 2017)* (Switzerland), Article 2.

availability and dedication to hearing the parties' case would be shared with the court's docket rather than with the more limited number of cases that arbitrators hear at a given time.

The finality of the arbitrators' award is highly significant, which – contrary to the first-instance judges' decisions – is not subject to the appeal mechanism of national court systems. Also, according to the New York Convention, the arbitral awards' worldwide enforceability means they are readily enforceable and only subjected to limited (but essential) protections.[634]

These are some considerations that judges should weigh in before *assuming* that a party initiated the court action for non-genuine purposes. It is reasonable to conclude that such an assumption is not easy to accept in the abstract without some indications or degree of evidence in the case. And where a court is persuaded that the purpose is non-genuine, the claimant risks facing the court's sanction powers, which are commonly more extensive than the ones arbitrators enjoy. That happens when the party opposing the enforcement of the arbitration brings a 'hopeless case',[635] advances a case 'wholly without any arguable merit',[636] or 'no reasonable prospect of success'.[637] Examples of sanctions are costs on an indemnity basis or as a cause of action that entitles the innocent party to seek compensation for damages.[638]

Considering the Model Law's purpose and the legislative tools available to achieve it, the following section focuses on the balancing exercise that courts need to undertake when applying Article 8(1). Admittedly, the following comments may appear to exceed the core inquiry of this work. That inquiry was whether the text, context and purpose of the Model Law require/impose courts to adopt either a *prima facie* or a full standard of review of jurisdictional disputes at the threshold of an arbitration. However, the next section is relevant as it explains why the Model Law calls for a more dynamic outlook to achieve its purpose, rather than rigidly and mechanically preferring one approach over the other in all cases.

[E] BALANCING EFFICACY AND EFFICIENCY

The competing-values dilemma or balancing exercise between efficacy and efficiency is not unique to jurisdictional disputes at the threshold of an arbitration. To a certain extent, courts may face a relatively similar balancing exercise at the post-award stage when deciding to adjourn the enforcement of arbitral awards that were challenged at

634. One hundred and seventy-two countries are party to the New York Convention. *Source*: UNCITRAL database, last accessed on 4 October 2023. Available at: https://uncitral.un.org/en/texts/arbitration/conventions/foreign_arbitral_awards/status2.
635. *Huntsman Chemical Co Australia Ltd and Another v. International Pools Australia Ltd and Others*, 36 NSWLR 242, Court of Appeal of New South Wales, Australia, 16 March 1995.
636. *Leonardus Gerardus Smits v. Dorothy Tabone*, [2007] QCA 337, Court of Appeal of the Supreme Court of Queensland, Australia, 12 October 2007, para. 48.
637. *Baillieu Knight Frank (NSW) Pty Ltd v. Ted Manny Real Estate Pty Ltd* (1992) 30 NSWLR 359, reported in *ibid.*, para. 45.
638. *See*, in general, Fortese, *Breach of Arbitration Agreements: Should Parties Be Disciplined with Indemnity Costs?* (n. 234), pp. 189-204.

the seat of the arbitration (Article 36(1) Model Law). The following section explores that situation.

The analysis of the balancing exercise after the arbitral award could have been dealt with in Chapter 6 above, with the contextual reading of Article 8. However, it is discussed here because its operation depends on identifying and understanding the 'purpose' of the Model Law.

Discussing the balancing exercise after the arbitral award was rendered serves as an introduction and inspiration for the discussion on the balancing exercise at the pre-award stage (section [E][2] below). The role of the court and the policies at play are not the same. However, the discussion seeks to show that arbitration's efficiency, efficacy, and legitimacy can be well served with a degree of judicial discretion and judgment.

[1] The Balancing Exercise after the Award

Because of its pro-arbitration emphasis, the Model Law presumes that arbitral awards (like arbitration agreements[639]) are valid and, therefore, readily enforceable. It does so by relieving the enforcing party of proving the award's validity, shifting the burden to the party resisting its enforcement.[640] At the same time, the Model Law *permits* courts to adjourn recognition or enforcement proceedings where the validity of the award is being litigated. Article 36(2) provides:

> If an application for setting aside or suspension of an award has been made (...), the court where recognition or enforcement is sought *may, if it considers it proper,* adjourn its decision and may also, on the application of the party claiming recognition or enforcement of the award, order the other party to provide appropriate security.

Notably, this article uses permissive language to describe discretion and judgment. The term '*may*' confers to the court the choice and right to do something: to adjourn the proceedings or not. The exercise of that discretion is not limitless. The court's discretion is legally constrained to avoid arbitrariness. The provision requires an appraisal of the particularities of the case and a judgment determining whether adjournment is proper or not.

If the court considers it improper, it has no discretion: it cannot suspend the recognition or enforcement proceedings. But if adjournment does appear appropriate, the court may or may not adjourn the proceedings. In assessing the determining factors, the purpose of the law guides the court. That is, the law's recognition and enforcement bias, along with fairness and efficiency considerations in resolving the dispute.

639. *See* Chapter 5, section [4].
640. Article 36(1), 'Recognition or enforcement of an arbitral award (...), may be refused only: (a) *at the request of the party against whom it is invoked,* if that party furnishes to the competent court where recognition or enforcement is sought proof that ...' [emphasis added].

The discretion this provision's permissive language (*may*) seems to afford is questionable in practice. It is difficult to accept that a court would find it proper to stay the (recognition or) enforcement proceedings but decide not to do so. It would be more likely that the court refuses to adjourn the proceedings because it is unpersuaded that doing otherwise is the proper course of action.

In any case, it is important to underline that suspending the recognition or enforcement of an award is an exceptional measure. It is not a direct and automatic consequence of the commencement of set-aside proceedings. The drafters of the Model Law discussed if that was a preferable legal effect but rejected it in the understanding that it would risk creating an incentive to disrupt the enforcement of awards.[641]

There is a similarity with the situation under Article 8(1) of the Model Law. As discussed above, the Model Law takes the same pro-efficacy and pro-efficiency stance in Article 8(2), allowing arbitral proceedings to advance or be suspended even where a jurisdictional dispute is pending before a national court.

Unlike Article 8(1) actions involving the enforcement of arbitration agreements, the award-enforcing court may consider adjourning its decision without a party's request.[642] Even where a party requests the adjournment, the court is not mandated to grant it. Given the provision's permissive language, the court could recognise or enforce the award even where the requested adjournment is based on an ongoing parallel setting aside proceedings.

Importantly, the court's appraisal of circumstances is ample but limited. It calls for a balancing of interests and policies exercise. Article 36(2) balances the Model Law's pro-recognition and enforcement objective with efficiency concerns. It permits avoiding concurrent control over the award and, consequently, prevents resource misuse. It also seeks to avoid the risk of conflicting decisions. Its drafting history reveals that Article 36(2):

> [C]an be used to avoid concurrent judicial review of the same grounds and possibly conflicting decisions, where this risk is not already excluded by the fact that the same court is seized with the application for setting aside and the other party's application for enforcement.[643]

The Model Law aligned its Article 36(2) with Article VI of the New York Convention, which also provides:

641. Working Group Report A/CN.9/246, paras 152-154. The drafters of the New York Convention had a similar concern when adopting Article VI; *see*, United Nations Conference on International Arbitration, Summary Records of the 17th Meeting, E/CONF.26/SR.17 (3 June 1958), p. 4. This distinguishes the New York Convention from its predecessor (Geneva Convention 1927), under which an application to set aside the award in the country where it was made, was sufficient to suspend its enforcement.
642. *See, e.g.*, Wolff, *New York Convention – Commentary* (n. 134), p. 465, para. 6 ('An accurate inference from the plain language of Article VI [New York Convention] is that the enforcement court can consider the adjournment not only upon a party's request but also of its own accord.').
643. Analytical Commentary (A/CN.9/264), p. 79, para. 75. *See also* Working Group Report A/CN.9/245, pp. 35-36, paras 156-158.

> If an application for the setting aside or suspension of the award has been made (...), the authority before which the award is sought to be relied upon may, if it considers it proper, adjourn the decision on the enforcement of the award and may also, on the application of the party claiming enforcement of the award, order the other party to give suitable security.

Referring to Article VI of the New York Convention, Professors Gaillard and Bermann have commented that it 'achieves a compromise between the two equally legitimate concerns of promoting the enforceability of foreign awards and preserving judicial oversight over awards'.[644] For Paulsson, Article VI is also a compromise between adequate safeguards to await the final decision in setting aside proceedings and the Convention's stance on preventing undue delay or obstruction of the enforcement of an award.[645]

While neither Article 36(2) of the Model Law nor Article VI of the New York Convention specify the legal standard or criteria by which the court should stay the proceedings, their language (and purpose) impose an evaluative judgment. It conditions the suspension of the award's enforcement to considerations of the efficacy of arbitral awards, efficiency in resolving the dispute, and the pervasive pro-arbitration policy that the Model Law and the New York Convention convey.[646]

Some authors have advanced comparable tests to explain when *it is proper* to stay enforcement proceedings. One of them, for example, suggests that the enforcing court ought to be satisfied that the arguments for setting aside the award *are with merit*.[647] Such a test embraces a contextual reading of Articles IV and V of the Convention and, with that, the Convention's presumptive validity of awards, which shifts the burden of proving otherwise to the respondent.[648] A similar test proposes that courts should adjourn enforcing proceedings if they are:

> [P]rima facie convinced that the request for the setting aside or suspension of the award in the country of origin is not made on account of dilatory tactics, but is based on rather reasonable grounds.[649]

When deciding on adjournment requests, courts have placed significant weight on:

- the Model Law and the New York Convention's general objective of facilitating the enforcement of awards;
- the likelihood of success in the setting aside proceedings;
- the duration of the setting aside proceedings;
- the potential hardship to the parties;

644. *See* the UNCITRAL Guide on the New York Convention (2016), p. 264.
645. Paulsson, *The NYC in Action* (n. 134), p. 213.
646. Wolff, for example, noted that 'virtually all courts weigh any factors supporting the adjournment against the NYC's main goal to facilitate and expedite the enforcement of foreign arbitral awards'; Wolff, *New York Convention – Commentary* (n. 134), pp. 465-466, para. 6.
647. Paulsson, *The NYC in Action* (n. 134), p. 214.
648. *Ibid.*, pp. 214-215. The other reason for courts to adjourn the enforcement of an award is that of international comity towards the courts of origin.
649. van den Berg, *The New York Arbitration Convention* (n. 11), p. 353.

- judicial efficiency;
- international comity;
- whether enforcement of the award would seriously prejudice the rights of one of the parties in a separate dispute.[650]

Because such decisions involve the courts' evaluative and discretionary powers, the exercise cannot be performed in the abstract. A Malaysian appellate court put it in clear terms and identified a similar (but more nuanced) test when it held that:

> How that discretion is to be exercised and what circumstances, conditions or situation may be said to be 'proper' for the exercise of discretion of suspension is, in our mind, a matter of judicial evaluation and scrutiny, having regard to all the facts and circumstances presented. The burden of proof is on the appellant to show on a *balance of probabilities* that the ground is satisfied.[651]

Other courts have considered 'the *strength of the argument* that the arbitral award was invalid'[652] and 'the ease or difficulty of enforcement of the Award and *whether it will be rendered more difficult if enforcement is delayed*, for example, by the movement of assets, improvident trading, and whether it is likely that there would be dissipation in the interim of the delay in enforcement.'[653]

In ordering the adjournment of an enforcement request, the Federal Court of Australia considered that the setting aside proceedings at the seat of the arbitration (i) was made *bona fide*, (ii) the arguments advanced were *not frivolous* but *plainly arguable*, and (iii) that there were no suggestions that the billion-dollar award debtor would dissipate assets to avoid paying the award.[654]

A Canadian Court phrased it differently but described a similar test when favouring an adjourning request. It concluded that the party resisting the award enforcement had shown that the arguments in the setting aside action were 'not frivolous'.[655] The Court was also persuaded to adjourn its enforcing decision because it found that doing so would '*not cause inordinate delay, nor will it create more difficulty* for Powerex [the Claimant] *to obtain payment*' in case the award was confirmed.[656]

In reaching the same outcome, the High Court of Hong Kong gave deference to the decision of the supervisory court and the strengths of the challenging party's position in the setting-aside proceedings. The court held that:

650. For example, a French court stayed the enforcement of an award based on the potential harm to a state party's sovereignty whilst that State faces an ongoing territorial dispute, *Fornan et al v. Malaysia (Sultan of Jolo v. Malaysia)*, RG 22-04007, Court of Appel of Paris, 12 July 2022, paras 27, 35.
651. *Malaysian Bio-Xcell Sdn Bhd v. Lebas Technologies Sdn Bhd and another*, Court of Appeal of Malaysia, 7 January 2020, para. 28.
652. *Dana Shipping and Trading SA v. Sino Channel Asia Ltd*, [2016] HKEC 599, Hong Kong Court of First Instance, 14 March 2016, para. 7.
653. *Ibid.*, para. 27.
654. *ESCO Corporation v. Bradken Resources Pty Ltd*, [2011] FCA 905, Federal Court of Australia, 9 August 2011, paras 86-88.
655. *Powerex Corp. v. Alcan Inc.*, 2003 BCSC 1096, Supreme Court of British Columbia, Canada, 4 July 2003, paras 11-12.
656. *Ibid.*

> Having reviewed the evidence and the 2 Awards, I am satisfied that *the application* made on the Mainland *to set aside* the 2nd Award *has real, i.e. realistic, prospects of success*.[657]

The passing of time between the commencement of setting aside and enforcement proceedings was crucial for the English Court of Appeals to decide against an adjournment. In IPCO, the court overturned the First Instance decision that had adjourned the enforcement of an award rendered in Nigeria. By the time the case reached the English Court of Appeals (in 2014), the award had been the object of setting aside proceedings before the Nigerian courts since 2004:

> If (...) we decline to order enforcement, the result is likely to be that IPCO, if the Award is upheld, will not be entitled to receive the fruits of it for a generation... That, in commercial terms, is absurd. It is inconsistent with the principles that underpin the New York Convention, which was intended to foster international trade by ensuring a relatively swift enforcement of awards and a degree of insulation from the vagaries of local legal systems.[658]

The estimated length of the setting aside proceedings may also play a significant role. This was the determining factor for granting adjournment in *Toyo v. Johan Holland*. In that case, the Supreme Court of Victoria reasoned that the parties probably knew whether or not the Singaporean court would set aside the award within two months. Therefore, the Australian court considered that the period of stay upon enforcement was so short that it 'should not put an obstacle in the way of the effective disposition of that application or in any way pre-empt it.'[659]

There are also examples of courts relying on a similar test but reaching the opposite outcome. For instance, a court refused to adjourn its enforcing decision because the resisting party failed to prove the existence of *a reasonable possibility* of annulment of the award.[660] Another court declined to suspend an enforcement decision because the defendants bore and failed to prove that 'there [was] *a prima facie or reasonably arguable case*' for invalidating the award in the Swedish courts, where the setting aside proceedings were taking place.[661] And the Parisian Court of Appeals has held that staying enforcement cannot simply depend on the merit of the annulment petition or the sizable economic burden on the award debtor.[662]

Yet another court held that in determining whether to adjourn enforcement proceedings under the New York Convention, courts should weigh in several factors:

657. *U v. S*, [2018] HKCFI 2086, Hong Kong Court of First Instance, 6 September 2018, para. 14 [emphasis added].
658. *IPCO (Nigeria) Ltd v. Nigerian National Petroleum Corporation*, [2015] EWCA Civ 1144, England and Wales Court of Appeals (Civ), 10 November 2015, para. 170.
659. *Toyo Engineering Corp v. John Holland Pty Ltd* [2000] VSC 553, Supreme Court of Victoria, Australia, 20 December 2000, paras 9-10.
660. *Inter-Arab Investment Guarantee Corp. v. Banque Arabe et Internationale d'Investissements*, Yearbook Commercial Arbitration, Volume XXII (van den Berg (ed.), ICCA & Kluwer Law International 1997) pp. 643-668, Court of Appeal of Brussels, 25 January 1996.
661. *Hallen v. Angledal*, [1999] NSWSC 552, Supreme Court of New South Wales, Australia, 10 June 1999, para. 50.
662. *Fornan et al v. Malaysia*, RG 22-04007, paras 25-28, 36-39.

- The general objectives of arbitration, expeditious resolution of disputes and avoidance of protracted and expensive litigation;
- The status of foreign proceedings and estimated time for those proceedings to be resolved;
- Whether the award sought to be enforced will receive greater scrutiny in foreign proceedings under a less deferential standard of review;
- The characteristics of foreign proceedings;[663]
- Balance of possible hardships to each party;
- Any other circumstances that could tend to shift the balance in favour of or against adjournment.[664]

These examples highlight the factors that national courts evaluate when deciding whether to enforce an award or wait until another court determines its validity. Enforcing courts enjoy the authority to make a conclusive determination in these matters. However, the 'purpose of the law' invites judges to *assess* whether the time is right to exercise that authority. A court's discretionary powers disappear where it finds that no proper circumstances justify suspending the enforcement of an arbitral award or where a party requests such a suspension without having challenged the award at the seat of the arbitration.

This resonates with the discretionary powers that arbitrators enjoy to continue with arbitral proceedings whilst their jurisdiction is contested in court (Article 8(2) and 16(3) Model Law). It also resonates with courts' assessment powers when deciding if an arbitration agreement is null and void, inoperative or incapable of being performed. The discretionary powers vanish if a court concludes that an agreement is valid and enforceable. In that scenario, it can only refer the parties to arbitration and decline to hear and decide the substantive claim (Article 8(1) Model Law).

The conclusion to highlight from these comments is that courts should perform evaluative judgments to determine their role and the timing to exercise their authority in each case instead of accepting and adopting pro-arbitration policies in the abstract. The contextual reading and the purpose of comparable provisions of the Model Law strengthen efficacy without seriously compromising efficiency and the legitimacy of arbitration.

[2] The Balancing Exercise at the Referral Stage

Nothing in the text of Article 8(1), its context and drafting background, imposes upon courts to adopt the *prima facie* approach to achieve the purpose of the Model Law. In

663. That is: (i) whether they were brought to enforce an award (which would tend to weigh in favour of a stay) or to set the award aside (which would tend to weigh in favour of enforcement); (ii) whether they were initiated before the underlying enforcement proceeding so as to raise concerns of international comity; (iii) whether they were initiated by the party now seeking to enforce the award in federal court; and (iv) whether they were initiated under circumstances indicating an intent to hinder or delay resolution of the dispute. *Europcar Italia, S.p.A. v. Maiellano Tours, Inc.*, 156 F.3d 310 (1998), United States Court of Appeals, Second Circuit, 2 September 1998, para. 8.
664. *Ibid.*

fact, from the previous chapters of this study, the conclusion appears to be the opposite. The wording of Article 8 was deliberately chosen and intended to exclude the sole application and operation of the *prima facie* standard of review. However, this does not mean that the Model Law rigidly imposes the full standard of review either. At least not for every jurisdictional challenge and in every case.

Nothing in the text, context, and purpose of the Model Law prevents courts from adopting either the *prima facie* or full review where doing so better serves the purpose of the Model Law in the given case.

The underlying idea is that pursuing procedural efficiency requires discretion and flexibility, not strict rules. To a certain extent, the Supreme Court of Canada's decision in the *Dell Computers* case is an example of flexibility. It held that even whilst national courts should typically settle certain jurisdictional matters (e.g., points of law), courts could allow arbitrators to rule on them first if this was best for the arbitration process.[665]

Two years later, the Ontario Court of Appeals accepted the flexible application of the rules of priority but in the inverse scenario. It held that some circumstances allow courts, rather than arbitrators, to address jurisdictional issues immediately. In doing so, 'the court must be satisfied that the application is not a delaying tactic and that an immediate court decision as to the arbitrator's jurisdiction would be best for the arbitration process'.[666] Another example of a flexible approach is the Full Federal Court of Australia in the *Comandate Marine* case. It held that where a credible case is made out, 'the Court should not grant a stay and should allow that issue to be heard by the Court before any arbitration.'[667] Years later, the same Federal Court recalled that 'any rigid taxonomy of approach is unhelpful, as are the labels "*prima facie*" and "merits" approach. How a judge deals with an application under section 8 of the C[ommercial] A[rbitration] A[ct] will depend significantly upon the issues and the context.'[668]

The case might warrant special attention where the seat of the arbitration and the place where the court action was lodged are the same. Given the seat court's supervisory powers and its decision's preclusive effects, it may be highly efficient for the resolution of the dispute if the court conclusively decides the objection at the earliest possible instance. Then, the arbitration of the substantive dispute would continue on a solid jurisdictional ground. It would provide efficiency by trumping the re-discussion of the same issue multiple times in two forums.[669]

In any case, settling jurisdictional objections early is crucial for efficiently resolving substantive disputes.[670] It is not a matter of *who* (judges or arbitrators) has the authority to determine the jurisdictional point. It is a matter of what forum should

665. *Dell Computer*, 2007 SCC 34, para. 86.
666. *Jean Estate v. Wires Jolley LLP*, [2009] ONCA 339, paras 104-106.
667. *Comandate Marine v. Pan Australia Shipping*, [2006] FCAFC 192, para. 217.
668. *Hancock v. Rinehart*, [2017] FCAFC 170, p. 145.
669. This was (e.g.) the understanding of the court decision in *UBS v. Harrison*, 2014 NBCA 26, para. 28, where the court held that the parties would suffer further costs and delays in having the matter resolved if they had to wait until an arbitration be initiated, the tribunal formed, and the jurisdictional point decided.
670. *Rakna Arakshaka Lanka Ltd v. Avant Garde Maritime Services (Private) Limited*, [2018] SGHC 78, Singapore High Court, para. 71 ('... settling the position at an early stage at the seat militate

decide it *first*. That may involve considering the arguments' probability of success (or even their plausibility), finality, certainty, practicality, and preventing delays and costs. In short, it is a matter of timing and policy. Timing is more a matter of efficiency than efficacy because it is uncontroversial that courts ultimately hold the key to recognising and enforcing an arbitration agreement (and an award).[671]

However, it is imperative to underline that courts must aim to honour the law's emphasis on the efficacy of agreements to arbitrate and the strong pro-arbitration stance. Though different jurisdictional issues may carry heavier 'efficacy weight' than others, favouring arbitration should be preferred over a degree of inefficiency.[672]

The point is that efficacy and efficiency need not be entirely or perfectly balanced out. The degree of the imbalance may differ depending on the jurisdictional ground. For example, compare jurisdictional disputes concerning the valid existence of the arbitration agreement to objections relating to its interpretation, the extent of the disputes it covers or the parties it binds. In both cases, the dispute involves a question of 'consent' to arbitrate. But the first group of jurisdictional matters is the premise or antecedent for discussing the second. This, in turn, justifies linking the assessment of consent to a rule of priority between courts and arbitrators in an Article 8(1) situation.

A visually clear image for assessing the question of consent comes from Professor Rau. He suggests looking at it in a series of concentric circles as a matter of degrees.[673] The point of departure is the core inner circle. This circle addresses the critical question: have the parties agreed to arbitrate *anything at all* concerning their legal relationship? After that, the inquiries can be about the precise scope of that agreement: with whom have the parties agreed to arbitrate (including non-signatories)? What dispute or type of dispute? Under what conditions (e.g., applicable arbitration rules, substantive law)? In short, any other question beyond the critical, primary question.[674]

Under Article 8(1) of the Model Law, courts should answer the first and critical question when asked to do so. The extent of review and degree of conclusiveness of their answer will depend on the circumstances of the case and the balancing exercise regarding the purposes of the law.

Where that core question is not asked or once it is clear that the parties have agreed to arbitrate 'something', there is no reason (in the abstract and for all cases) that the court be the first one drawing the fine lines as to the *what*, *with whom*, and under which *conditions* the parties consented to arbitrate. That is where the Model Law's and

against allowing a respondent to reserve its objections to the last minute and indulge in tactics which result in immense delays and cost.').

671. Julian D.M. Lew, Does National Court Involvement Undermine the International Arbitration Process, 24 *American University International Law Review* (2008), p. 535 DOI: 10.1093/icsidreview/23.2.260 ('[D]espite its autonomous character, international arbitration depends on national courts to provide effectiveness, support, and assistance for the process.').

672. This is in line with Wolff's commentary on Article II(3) of the New York Convention, for whom the *prima facie* approach seems more arbitration-friendly and, therefore, preferable. But the author admits that such a preference 'does not exclude that under the appropriate circumstances ..., a closer examination by the court is appropriate or even necessary'. Wolff, *New York Convention – Commentary* (n. 134), p. 189, para. 302.

673. Alan Scott Rau, Arbitral Jurisdiction and the Dimensions of 'Consent', 24 *Arbitration International*, no. 2 (2008), pp. 199-204 DOI: 10.1093/arbitration/24.2.199.

674. *Ibid.*, p. 204.

New York Convention's pro-arbitration bias, presumptions, and efficiency tools take full effect. The law's purpose of facilitating arbitration requires that the court defers the initial and preliminary decision of those jurisdictional issues to the arbitral tribunal. That efficacy purpose also overweighs considerations of efficiency.

This distinction accepts, reflects, and follows Professor Bermann's division between 'gateway' and 'non-gateway' issues. Bermann uses the term 'gateway issues' to designate only those jurisdictional matters that courts, rather than arbitrators, *may* decide (when asked to do so) at the outset of an arbitration.[675] Although 'non-gateway issues' are jurisdictional matters, too, they refer to those that national courts should reserve for initial determination by arbitrators.[676] Thus, both national courts and arbitral tribunals have the authority to determine gateway issues, whichever is asked first. The Model Law and New York Convention's pro-arbitration policies justify that arbitrators decide non-gateway issues in the first instance.[677]

It is worth repeating that the pro-arbitration policy and efficiency purpose may favour the *prima facie* approach even for gateway issues. The Model Law does not prevent national courts from doing so. Its scheme appears to trust that courts will do so in the appropriate circumstances to curb dilatory tactics. This is also incidental to the broad discretionary powers that national courts generally enjoy to control their docket (judicial economy). And it is analogous to the powers that the Model Law affords arbitrators in comparable situations. As discussed in previous chapters, Articles 8(2), 16(1), and 16(3) of the Model Law entrust arbitrators with procedural discretion to assess when to exercise their competence-competence.[678] In doing so, arbitrators (like courts)[679] should seek to enforce the parties' agreement to arbitrate and ensure efficiency in resolving the dispute. Ultimately, if the purpose is to counter delays and dilatory tactics, the court response in an Article 8(1) situation should be the one that more prominently achieves that purpose.

[F] CONCLUSION

The analysis in this chapter highlights that the Model Law seeks to achieve more than a single-layer purpose. The instrument combines a pro-arbitration attitude to its interpretation and an efficiency-focused approach to its application. It recognises arbitration as a means, not the end goal, of dispute resolution. It is not possible to reduce the purpose of the Model Law to promoting and facilitating arbitration.

675. Bermann, *The 'Gateway' Problem* (n. 13), pp. 7-8. For example, 'where it was alleged that the signature of one of the parties to the matrix contract had been forged, ... then this [is] a question going to whether there was any agreement ever reached and would be decided by the court'; David St John Sutton, *Russell on Arbitration*, 23rd ed. (Sweet & Maxwell, 2007), para. 2-012. Similarly, Lew et al., *Comparative ICA* (n. 367), para. 14-60.
676. Bermann, *The 'Gateway' Problem* (n. 13), pp. 7-8.
677. *Ibid.*, p. 8.
678. *See* the discussions in Chapter 6, section [C][1].
679. Born, *International Commercial Arbitration* (n. 15), p. 1177 ('[T]he procedural discretion afforded to the arbitrators with regard to jurisdictional matters under Article 8(2) (and Article 16(3)) should logically apply with equal force in national court proceedings.)'.

Arbitration is valuable as a dispute resolution tool if it serves the needs of its users. And resolving disputes through arbitration must be fair and efficient to serve their needs.

The rules and tools that the Model Law lays out facilitate arbitration and prevent dilatory tactics. They reveal a legislative design that puts the dispute's fair and efficient resolution upfront. An arbitration framework where resolving disputes is efficient promotes and facilitates arbitration as a system. But, if arbitration (as a system) is facilitated at a too-costly expense on its efficiency and legitimacy, it will not assist its development.[680]

That is why the Model Law's purpose can best be achieved by a well-balanced synergy between three critical components or factors: *legitimacy*, *efficacy*, and *efficiency*. Arbitration finds its legitimacy in the parties' consent to arbitrate their disputes. In facilitating arbitration, the law and the parties' contracts are best interpreted and applied with a view to giving efficacy to their agreement to arbitrate. In all cases, the law seeks to facilitate the resolution of the parties' disputes efficiently and fairly.

Early determination of jurisdictional objections is crucial for efficiently resolving the parties' substantive disputes. To that end, the role of national courts under Article 8(1) of the Model Law is to safeguard the efficacy of the parties' bargain to arbitrate their disputes fairly and efficiently. In fulfilling that role, the Model Law affords judges discretion and flexibility, not strict rules. Fairness and efficiency are relative, subjective and dynamic concepts that require specific considerations and decisions involving assessment and judgment rather than personal opinions and ideals on how to facilitate arbitration best.

Therefore, the Model Law does not rigidly impose one standard of review over the other for every jurisdictional objection and in every case. Nothing in the text and drafting background of Article 8(1) (and other provisions) of the Model Law imposes upon courts the obligation to adopt the *prima facie* approach to achieve its purpose. The Model Law does not prevent courts from adopting that approach either, nor from embarking on a full standard of review if it more efficiently settles the jurisdictional dispute in the case at hand. A robust judicial decision that conclusively settles the jurisdictional dispute may well contribute to the purpose of the Model Law, particularly if the full review and conclusive determination serve to dismiss non-meritorious jurisdictional claims or defences rather than mechanically referring parties to arbitration.

Therefore, Article 8(1) of the Model Law should be interpreted and applied to facilitate arbitration by favouring the efficacy of commitments to arbitrate. Where the parties dispute the existence, validity or extent of the agreement to arbitrate, courts need to assess and balance legitimacy and efficacy concerns, with a view to efficiency in resolving the dispute and a high degree of deference towards arbitration.

680. *See, e.g.*, Bermann, *The 'Gateway' Problem* (n. 13), p. 5, where the author explains that efficiency and efficacy cannot displace legality and legitimacy. A system that prioritises a fast resolution of the instant case without good legal support may jeopardise its legitimacy in the long run. The legitimacy of arbitration depends on the parties agreement to arbitrate.

CHAPTER 8

Conclusions

[A] INTRODUCTION

The objective of this book was to examine the timing of judicial determination of jurisdictional disputes in the presence of an arbitration agreement.

The analysis focused on Article 8(1) of the Model Law, which addresses the scenario where a party seeks to litigate a substantive dispute that should be arbitrated. In that scenario, Article 8 imposes the conditions and lays out the exceptions for national courts to discontinue the litigation and refer the parties to arbitration.

This work did not question *who* has the authority to settle jurisdictional disputes because under the Model Law, both judges and arbitrators enjoy such decision-making power (competence-competence). For an early settlement of jurisdictional disputes, the drafters of the Model Law breathed synergy -rather than jealousy- into the relationship between courts and arbitrators. The synergic dynamic between judicial and arbitral authorities serves to achieve the instrument's (legislative) purpose. That is, to facilitate the fair and efficient settlement of disputes in international commercial relations through arbitration.

The crucial question addressed here then was about '*when*' (timing) a court should exercise its authority with conclusive effects to settle jurisdictional disputes. That question arises because the interpretation and application of Article 8(1) are not uniform across jurisdictions. Some authorities have concluded that the Model Law *imposes* on national courts the obligation to undertake a limited (*prima facie*) review of the arbitration agreement and the objection to the arbitral tribunal's jurisdiction. The opposite interpretation and approach *require* that national courts fully examine the existence and validity of the arbitration agreement and ultimately decide the jurisdictional dispute. Intermediate positions stem from these two approaches and operate as exceptions for those main propositions.

This work examined and answered the '*when*' question from an autonomous legal interpretation perspective, detached from a given State's law, concepts, and rules.

Following the nuanced interpretative approach proposed here, this study's conclusions depart from previous publications, many of which rely on and reflect general policies and pragmatic solutions favouring arbitration. The main finding of this work is that the text of Article 8 (analysed in Chapter 5), read in its context (Chapter 6) and in light of its purpose (Chapter 7), does not *impose* or *require* one approach and excludes the other. On the contrary, this publication concludes that no approach is imposed; both are permitted. Applying one or the other approach is a matter of judgment (rather than opinion) based on the particularities of the case and aiming to achieve the fair and efficient resolution of the jurisdictional and substantive disputes.

This work further proposed applying the same interpretative strategy when interpreting national arbitration legislation that adopts the Model Law. In justifying that proposition, this work started by acknowledging the synergy in the relationship between UNCITRAL and State legislators. That relationship defines the Model Law's transition from soft to hard law. It reflects the operation of global legal pluralism in non-state-centred positivism. It recognises the non-state law and actors' crucial role as the normative source of states' legal positivism when incorporating (through statutes) norms generated outside their exclusive authority and territory (Model Law). UNCITRAL's efforts to harmonise and unify arbitration law rely on that cooperative interaction. This, in turn, fosters a paradigm shift in the way we interpret and apply 'national' arbitration laws (based on the Model Law).

Although this book did not engage in meaningful discussions to confirm or refute theories that present arbitration as an autonomous legal order, it shared some of its foundations and assumptions. This work builds upon the premise that national arbitration statutes that adopt the Model Law are instruments different from purely domestic laws. Not because those domestic arbitration laws are part of an 'autonomous legal order' or because arbitration constitutes a 'delocalised' system, but because they are *national laws of an international origin and character.*

In that understanding, this book has proposed that the Model Law and the domestic legislation that implements it deserve special interpretative considerations. Considerations that draw attention to and acknowledge their international origin, the purpose and principles on which they are based, and the uniformity goal they are directed to achieve. The interpretative approach proposed is based on Article 2A of the Model Law and *inspired* by the customary international interpretative guidelines codified in Articles 31-32 of the Vienna Convention.[681] The driving proposition is that a uniform interpretative framework for uniform law fosters its uniform application.

681. Through the New Convention and the Model Law, the United Nations and UNCITRAL created a legal ecosystem for international arbitration law. These instruments were designed to create a normative synergy to regulate matters in a unified way (*see* Chapter 2). This work then proposes that the New York Convention and the Model Law be interpreted in accordance with a consistent and coherent analytical framework (*see* Chapter 3).

[B] THE INTERPRETATIVE APPROACH PROPOSED

The interpretative approach proposed in this book focuses on the text, context, and purpose of the legal provision. Good faith as an element of legal interpretation plays a role, too. Not only because the Model Law (Article 2A) imposes it but also because it is embedded in international customary law to interpret treaties (e.g., the New York Convention). Here, good faith was associated with intellectual fidelity and constraint when reading the legal text. It guided the interpretative exercise to avoid giving Article 8 of the Model Law a meaning its words do not bear and relying on preconceptions, ideas, and ideals of procedural efficiency and best practices to prevent and curtail dilatory tactics.

Good faith interpretation was also understood here to feed the interaction between the legal instrument's text and purpose. Purpose guides the interpretative process where language may allow conflicting meanings. The good faith element directs purpose to support and confirm the meaning of the text (and avoid overriding it). In this understanding, good faith called for considering the context of the terms Article 8 of the Model Law uses, the instrument's purpose and the general principles the Model Law is based on.

The approach proposed in this work does not claim to be the final say or a top-down imposition but is part of an ongoing conversation. Other interpretative approaches may be suitable if they recognise and reflect the distinct nature of national laws that adopt the Model Law and the internationally uniform application goal UNCITRAL set. The approach advanced in this work bears that in mind and emphasises the interplay between the text, context and purpose of Article 8 of the Model Law and the entire instrument. It assumes and accepts that the instrument's pro-arbitration purpose and policies are embedded and communicated through its text.

Generally, issues of uniform legal interpretation and application become evident where there is a jurisdictional dispute, and judges and arbitrators must decide. Laws also guide parties in business dealings to identify their rights and obligations and avoid disputes.[682] Therefore, interpreting the Model Law is crucial not only for parties, judges and arbitrators but also for lawmakers. Comprehending the model's language and the extent of powers it affords to parties, judges and arbitrators is pivotal when deciding whether to adopt the Model Law with or without deviations.

Given the (i) textual similarities between Article II(3) of the New York Convention and Article 8(1) of the Model Law, and (ii) the symbiotic relationship between the Convention and the Model Law, it is safe to conclude that the interpretative result advanced in this book equally applies to the provisions of both instruments.

Where national legislators choose to adopt the Model Law without deviating from (in this case) Article 8(1), it is reasonably expected that the interpretation of such a provision and its equivalent in the national law will not differ. This conclusion is

682. As Lewis corrected noted, it cannot have been the intention of the drafters of the Model Law, that the success of their efforts was to be judged purely by the results of the decision-making of disputes; Lewis, *The Interpretation and Uniformity of the UNCITRAL Model Law* (n. 171), pp. 15-16.

respectful of drafting alternatives and mindful of the differences with statutes in Model Law jurisdictions that choose to deviate from the language proposed in Article 8(1) (e.g., Germany, Peru, India, Denmark).[683]

Once the Model Law is incorporated into local law, the judiciary plays a critical interpretative role because at the core of Article 8(1) is a court obligation. An obligation for courts to make an order, on a party request, if certain conditions are met.

Many authorities (case law and commentary) have concluded that Article 8 of the Model Law affords courts *only and exclusively* a *prima facie* standard of review. The benefits associated with this approach, expressed as pro-arbitration goals and policies, are often elevated to the sole statutory purpose. That single-minded purpose lacks a foundation in the wording of Article 8(1), its contextual design, and its drafting background. And, although decision-making powers must be exercised to advance the law's policies and purpose, policy considerations should not distort the text of the legal provision. Policy creation rests with the law-makers, not the decision-makers.

The drafters of the Model Law could have clearly and explicitly narrowed the standard of judicial review in Article 8(1) by including the term 'manifest' or 'prima facie' (or similar).[684] They could have done so, but they didn't. They considered it but decided against it. From that drafting choice, some authorities imply that the Model Law does not permit the *prima facie* approach and, therefore, requires a full judicial determination of the jurisdictional dispute.

In broad terms, the Model Law was not drafted to impose or exclude court determination of arbitral jurisdiction at the referral stage. The instrument simply provides tools to restrain court involvement[685] and circumscribe the court's role to limited legal grounds, subjecting the judicial inquiry to a party request[686] and within a time frame.

An automatic and across-the-board application of either approach (*prima facie* or full determination) might be an effective way to predict court decisions but at risk of inefficiency for the parties in dispute. Therefore, courts must assess and judge whether to conclusively settle the jurisdictional dispute or give priority to arbitrators according to the particularities of the case. Doing so requires balancing *efficacy*, *efficiency* and *legitimacy* concerns.

In general terms, the *prima facie* approach appears to be more promotion-of-arbitration driven. But, it may not always be equally suitable without assessing issues of efficiency and legitimacy. Efficiency in resolving a dispute is result-reliant, and legitimacy is always arbitration-agreement dependent.

---

683. *See* Chapter 6, section [D].
684. That solution would not have even been novel or untested in practice. It already existed, for example, in the 1981 French arbitration law and in the 1961 European Convention on International Commercial Arbitration.
685. For example, by recognising pro-arbitration presumptions, reversing the burden of proof, excluding powers to suspend arbitral proceedings, and affording explicit arbitral discretion to render awards whilst the jurisdictional dispute is pending in court.
686. The exception is where courts sua sponte refuse to refer the parties to arbitration on substantive arbitrability and public policy grounds.

In some cases, the success and good reputation of arbitration are praised compared to the higher levels of inefficiency of court litigation. At times, that has heavily weighed in the choice between '*prima facie*' and 'full review'. But that would make the choice a matter of convenience rather than conviction or legitimacy. And that has little to do with legal interpretation and even less with the rule of law.

The rule of law is above the convenience of a position or a doctrine because certainty and predictability are deeply ingrained in the rule of law. Certainty is crucial for the parties and important for the arbitrators. That is the idea of having a jurisdictional dispute be decided at the earliest stage possible. However, the certainty and predictability of the law being interpreted and applied properly rise above the interests of individual parties, courts, and arbitrators.

For this reason, in this work, the answer to the *timing* of conclusive court determinations of jurisdictional disputes is controlled by Article 8(1) and its proper interpretation (based on text, context, and purpose).

[C] THE INTERPRETATIVE RESULT

The language of Article 8(1) imposes a rule of procedure conditioned by substantive legal grounds. If the dispute between the parties is arbitrable and covered by the arbitration agreement, the court shall refer the parties to arbitration. Its text further subordinates the referral to the (formal and substantive) validity and enforceability of such agreement. The meaning of the terms that Article 8 uses is determined by their *context*.

The first paragraph of Article 8 is not directed to arbitrators, but the second one is, and so is Article 16(1). They vest arbitrators with the power to determine their own jurisdiction. They also trust them with discretion. Discretion involves judgment, which, in turn, requires arbitrators (and judges) to assess when to exercise their competence-competence and when not to.

The promoters of the *exclusivity* of the *prima facie* approach fail to recognise the limitations in the text of Article 8(1) to impose and justify it. They also fail to identify the stretch of the tools to prevent dilatory tactics that Article 8(2) offers. That courts would neutralise arbitral competence-competence, or 'usurp' the role of the arbitrators is to overlook the second paragraph of Article 8 (and 16(1)).

The relationship between Articles 8(1) and 16(1) is not about superiority. It is a matter of dialogue, not of isolated decision-making. It is not a clash of jurisdictional egos, but a contribution in favour of efficient procedural and dispute management. The powers of one are not curtailed by the other. In the order of things, courts have the final word. Not because they are 'superior' to arbitral tribunals but because the dispute resolution system requires a last stop. For jurisdictional issues, it is national courts. The final word rests with the arbitrators for substantive issues where their jurisdiction is secured. That is the system that the New York Convention and the Model Law envisioned. It may not be perfect, but the rule of law requires to respect it for as long as it is in place. Its modification for a better system is possible. It depends on practice, experience and decisive legislative action. Above all, it depends on the dialogue of the actors involved for the benefit of the users of arbitration as a dispute resolution tool to oil up international trade, prosperity and more egalitarian development.

Correctly understood, arbitral competence-competence is a legal device to tackle dilatory tactics. But, acknowledging and respecting competence-competence is not an end goal in itself. It is associated with 'efficiency' in dispute resolution. For this reason, competence-competence is not an obligation but a right. A power that arbitrators enjoy and must exercise with discretion to decide whether to stay or not proceedings until a court determines the jurisdictional objections under Article 8(1). If they find it proper to continue with the arbitral proceedings and make a jurisdictional determination, they enjoy discretion in deciding the jurisdictional dispute as a preliminary issue or with the merits (Article 16(2) Model Law).

That discretion is based on the particularities of the jurisdictional question, the opportunity when it is raised, and the risk of dilatory tactics and waste of resources. But those concerns are difficult to assess and balance at a general level, imagining all possible scenarios. The assessment must be made in each case.

Article 8(1) gives courts discretion.[687] That flexibility enables judges to assess in each case whether the risk of dilatory tactics is greater than the danger of wasting time and money. The effect of that danger is reduced by permitting the arbitration to commence or continue and for the arbitrators to render an award (Article 8(2)).

Undeniably, courts should avoid truncating or delaying arbitral proceedings. But an arbitration must first exist (or be required) to be delayed. If consent to arbitrate does not exist between the disputing parties, the court shall not refer the parties to arbitration. If it exists but is 'null and void, inoperative or incapable of being performed', the court shall not either.

The efficacy of (even putative) arbitration agreements and the parties' expectations are related. Parties that enter into an arbitration agreement expect their bargain to be respected. Article 8(1) of the Model Law affords efficacy to that expectation. However, just because a party has an expectation does not mean that it is a legitimate one.

Parties could not have expected that national courts would not control a jurisdictional issue. The flaw in that expectation is that neither the Model Law nor the New York Convention supports it. Both instruments are explicit about the judicial power to refuse recognition and enforcement of arbitration agreements and awards rendered on the basis of inexistent, invalid, or inoperative arbitration agreements. So, the point is in the *timing* of the court decision. The expectation then is (or should be) linked to the most efficient timing at which the jurisdictional dispute should be settled conclusively. That reflects one of the purposes of the Model Law.

As largely discussed in Chapter 7 above, *purpose* is an essential element of the interpretative strategy proposed in this book. It conditions the interpretation and

687. Only regarding the extent of court review to find whether the arbitration agreement is null and void, inoperative or incapable of being performed. Courts do not have discretion where there simply is arbitration agreement that covers the substantive court action. In this scenario, the judge *shall* refer the parties to arbitration.

application of Article 8(1) because its text and context do not limit, impose or require national courts always to apply the *prima facie* or full merits approach.

The analysis in this work emphasises that the Model Law seeks to achieve a combined purpose: to promote and facilitate arbitration, and fairness and efficiency in dispute resolution through arbitration. Therefore, purpose requires courts to resolve the dispute efficiently, with a view to favouring the enforcement of a commitment to arbitrate. To this end, the Model Law recognises some guiding principles and rules. Case law and arbitration literature have contributed other pro-arbitration guiding principles favouring the efficacy of agreements to arbitrate.[688]

For national courts, procedural economy and avoidance of dilatory tactics are not abstract concepts. In the ambit of a dispute under Article 8(1) of the Model Law, the decision of what is efficient results from a syllogistic exercise. It involves an interaction between the parties and the decision-maker. It burdens the parties with persuading the judge to decide the forum where the jurisdictional challenge should be thoroughly discussed and decided. It requires the court to ponder when to exercise the power within its authority and when not to. Whether it is appropriate – *under the circumstances of the case* – to exercise decision-making powers simply because it is the court to exercise it. The court's north star is in the purpose of the law, i.e., to facilitate, not impede, international arbitration. The balancing factor is that arbitration stands on a contractual basis.

That is why Article 8(1) does not place legitimacy (of arbitration), efficacy (of arbitration agreements), and efficiency (in resolving the jurisdictional dispute at hand) at opposing ends. On the contrary, it values their balanced interplay. Balancing those interests is a matter of appreciation and judgment that calls parties to advance persuasive arguments rather than rely on mechanical (and doctrinal) rules of priority.

Procedural fairness cannot flourish in an environment where a party is labelled as recalcitrant for the mere fact of commencing a court action rather than arbitral proceedings. Fairness can doubtfully be achieved without an open mind to consider arguments and evidence, discussions and reasoning, debate and doubt, rather than dismiss invalidity claims based on familiar doctrine.

Given the purpose of the Model Law, Article 8(1) should be interpreted as facilitating arbitration by favouring the efficacy of agreements to arbitrate. Where the parties dispute the existence, validity or extent of the agreement to arbitrate, courts need to assess and balance legitimacy and efficacy concerns, with a view on efficiency in resolving the dispute and deference towards arbitration.

If the resolution of jurisdictional disputes is efficient, the development of arbitration (as a system) is facilitated. But if arbitration is facilitated at a too-costly expense of its efficiency, it will not assist its advancement.

Adopting a *prima facie* or full review approach cannot be based only on a 'benefits' policy. It cannot be convincingly argued that either approach, in a pure form

688. For example, the separability presumption, the presumptive validity of arbitration agreements and its burden-of-proof shifting effect, the validation principle, cannons of contract of interpretation.

and excluding the other, is 'more efficient' or more closely achieves the Model Law's purpose.

Interpreting Article 8(1) as exclusively *imposing* either approach would be a static text-reading exercise, with minimum regard for the particularities of the dispute, the merits of the arguments and evidence, and the efficient resolution of the specific jurisdictional challenge.

Nothing in the text of Article 8 or the architecture of the Model Law (and Article II(3) New York Convention) supports that conclusion. Certainty and predictability are in the application of the text of the law – its breadth and boundaries are in its language, not in the interpreter's opinion. For what is the value of the text of the law if it will not be applied?[689] It cannot be accepted that portions of the legal text were drafted for no use. More uncertainty and unpredictability result from: (i) failing to give meaning and use to all the terms in the provision under interpretation, (ii) assigning a meaning to the text that it does not hold, (iii) adopting a meaning that contradicts the one that the drafters of the instrument explicitly intended, and (iv) preferring a meaning that selectively assumes a legal purpose that runs short from the one that UNCITRAL foresaw for the Model Law.

The breadth of the wording of Article 8 invites the view that its application can adapt to the given scenario and circumstances. Read in context and according to its purpose, Article 8 instructs courts to resolve the given jurisdictional dispute fairly and efficiently, with the strong, clear and compelling aim of facilitating and respecting party autonomy.

Hence, a robust judicial decision that conclusively settles the jurisdictional dispute does not necessarily reflect an anti-arbitration attitude. It may well contribute to the purpose of the Model Law (efficacy and efficiency of arbitration). Particularly where the full review and conclusive determination serve to dismiss non-meritorious jurisdictional claims or defences rather than mechanically referring the parties to arbitration, only to re-litigate the issue later on. The irony would be in creating inefficiency by assuming and avoiding a dilatory tactic that may not exist.

Efficiency is not a checklist with goals that can be ticked off in the abstract. It requires a measure of assessment, discretion and judgment to balance out the efficacy and efficiency purposes of the Model Law. In hard cases, the efficacy of the putative agreement to arbitration must prevail, and the referral to arbitration ordered, even at the cost of a slightly higher price for efficiency.

Essentially, the Model Law gives parties, courts, and arbitral tribunals discretion to advance or suspend the resolution of a dispute to tackle the effects of dilatory tactics. Flexibility and discretion should be exercised reasonably to ensure the most efficient and effective course of action for resolving the substantive disputes, adapted to the specific circumstances of the case at hand.

---

689. Referring to Article II(3) New York Convention, Professor Kessedjian noted that in some countries (e.g., France), its narrow (*prima facie* approach) interpretation has truncated *almost all potential for application*; Catherine Kessedjian, 'Is Arbitration a Service to Business or to the Legal Profession?', in *Contemporary Issues in International Arbitration and Mediation: The Fordham Papers (2009)* (Brill Nijhoff, 2010), p. 313.

After all, court determination of arbitral jurisdiction is not alien to the parties. Court involvement is an integral part of the arbitration system. Because jurisdiction directly affects the parties' fundamental right of access to justice, the Model Law, the New York Convention, academic writings and case law accept a full judicial examination of the legal grounds and factual circumstances that would exclude that right. Thus, whether a conclusive judicial determination under Article 8(1) takes place before or after the arbitrators have made their preliminary ruling should result from a balancing exercise between efficacy and efficiency, with a view of favouring arbitration.

Table of Cases

Index

INTERNATIONAL ARBITRATION LAW LIBRARY

1. Moshe Hirsch, *The Arbitration Mechanism of the International Center for the Settlement of Investment Disputes,* 1993 (ISBN 07-923-1993-1).
2. Aida B. Avanessian, *Iran-United States Claims Tribunal in Action,* 1993 (ISBN 18-533-3902-4).
3. Isaak I. Dore, *The UNCITRAL Framework for Arbitration in Contemporary Perspective,* 1993 (ISBN 18-533-3573-8).
4. Vesna Lazić, *Insolvency Proceedings and Commercial Arbitration,* 1998 (ISBN 90-411-1115-8).
5. Joachim Frick, *Arbitration in Complex International Contracts,* 2001 (ISBN 90-411-1662-1).
6. Katherine Lynch, *The Forces of Economic Globalization: Challenges to the Regime of International Commercial Arbitration,* 2003 (ISBN 90-411-1994-9).
7. Christoph Liebscher, *The Healthy Award: Challenge in International Commercial Arbitration,* 2003 (ISBN 90-411-2011-4).
8. Hamid G. Gharavi, *The International Effectiveness of the Annulment of an Arbitral Award,* 2003 (ISBN 90-411-1717-2).
9. Abdulhay Sayed, *Corruption in International Trade and Commercial Arbitration,* 2004 (ISBN 90-411-2236-2).
10. Gabrielle Kaufmann-Kohler & Thomas Schultz, *Online Dispute Resolution: Challenges for Contemporary Justice,* 2004 (ISBN 90-411-2318-0).
11. Christopher R. Drahozal & Richard W. Naimark (eds), *Towards a Science of International Arbitration: Collected Empirical Research,* 2005 (ISBN 90-411-2322-9).
12. Ali Yeşilirmak, *Provisional Measures in International Commercial Arbitration,* 2005 (ISBN 90-411-2353-9).
13. Christian Bühring-Uhle, *Arbitration and Mediation in International Business,* second revised edition, 2006 (ISBN 978-9-041-12256-8).
14. Bernard Hanotiau, *Complex Arbitrations: Multi-party, Multi-contract and Multi-issue – A Comparative Study*, Second Edition, 2020 (ISBN 978-94-035-1261-7).
15. Loukas A. Mistelis & Julian D.M. Lew (eds), *Pervasive Problems in International Arbitration,* 2006 (ISBN 978-9-041-12450-0).
16. Julian D.M. Lew & Loukas A. Mistelis (eds), *Arbitration Insights – Twenty Years of the Annual Lecture of the School of International Arbitration, Sponsored by Freshfields Bruckhaus Deringer,* 2006 (ISBN 978-9-041-12606-1).
17. Mark Kantor, *Valuation for Arbitration: Compensation Standards, Valuation Methods and Expert Evidence,* 2008 (ISBN 978-9-041-12735-8).
18. Christoph Brunner, *Force Majeure and Hardship under General Contract Principles: Exemption for Non-Performance in International Arbitration,* 2009 (ISBN 978-90-411-2792-1).

19. Loukas A. Mistelis & Stavros L. Brekoulakis (eds), *Arbitrability: International & Comparative Perspectives*, 2009 (ISBN 978-90-411-2730-3).
20. Sam Luttrell, *Bias Challenges in International Commercial Arbitration: The Need for a 'Real Danger' Test*, 2009 (ISBN 978-90-411-3191-1).
21. Monique Sasson, *Substantive Law in Investment Treaty Arbitration: The Unsettled Relationship Between International Law and Municipal Law*, Second Edition, 2017 (ISBN 978-90-411-6103-1).
22. Ileana M. Smeureanu, *Confidentiality in International Commercial Arbitration*, 2011 (ISBN 978-90-411-3226-0).
23. Won Kidane, *China-Africa Dispute Settlement: The Law, Economics and Culture of Arbitration*, 2011 (ISBN 978-90-411-3674-9).
24. Karel Daele, *Challenge and Disqualification of Arbitrators in International Arbitration*, 2012 (ISBN 978-90-411-3799-9).
25. Crina Baltag, *The Energy Charter Treaty: The Notion of Investor*, 2012 (ISBN 978-90-411-3428-8).
26. Alexandra Diehl, *The Core Standard of International Investment Protection: Fair and Equitable Treatment*, 2012 (ISBN 978-90-411-3869-9).
27. Manuel Indlekofer, *International Arbitration and the Permanent Court of Arbitration*, 2013 (ISBN 978-90-411-4766-0).
28. Günther J. Horvath & Stephan Wilske (eds), *Guerrilla Tactics in International Arbitration*, 2013 (ISBN 978-90-411-4002-9).
29. Albert Badia, *Piercing the Veil of State Enterprises in International Arbitration*, 2014 (ISBN 978-90-411-5162-9).
30. Nadja Erk, *Parallel Proceedings in International Arbitration: A Comparative European Perspective*, 2014 (ISBN 978-90-411-5264-0).
31. Simon Vorburger, *International Arbitration and Cross-Border Insolvency: Comparative Perspectives*, 2014 (ISBN 978-90-411-5419-4).
32. Ahmad Ali Ghouri, *Interaction and Conflict of Treaties in Investment Arbitration*, 2015 (ISBN 978-90-411-5417-0).
33. Reto Marghitola, *Document Production in International Arbitration*, 2015 (ISBN 978-90-411-5159-9).
34. Alfonso Gómez-Acebo, *Party-Appointed Arbitrators in International Commercial Arbitration*, 2016 (ISBN 978-90-411-6671-5).
35. Jonas von Goeler, *Third-Party Funding in International Arbitration and Its Impact on Procedure*, 2016 (ISBN 978-90-411-5015-8).
36. Dean Lewis, *The Interpretation and Uniformity of the UNCITRAL Model Law on International Commercial Arbitration: Focusing on Australia, Hong Kong and Singapore*, 2016 (ISBN 978-90-411-6700-2).
37. Stavros Brekoulakis, Julian D.M. Lew & Loukas Mistelis (eds), *The Evolution and Future of International Arbitration*, 2016 (ISBN 978-90-411-7004-0).
38. Rémy Gerbay, *The Functions of Arbitral Institutions*, 2016 (ISBN 978-90-411-6217-5).

39. Maximilian Clasmeier, *Arbitral Awards as Investments: Treaty Interpretation and the Dynamics of International Investment Law*, 2017 (ISBN 978-90-411-8357-6).
40. Tony Cole (ed.), *The Roles of Psychology in International Arbitration*, 2017 (ISBN 978-90-411-5921-2).
41. Pietro Ferrario, *The Adaptation of Long-Term Gas Sale Agreements by Arbitrators*, 2017 (ISBN 978-90-411-8232-6).
42. Jacob B. van de Velden, *Finality in Litigation: The Law and Practice of Preclusion – Res Judicata (Merger and Estoppel), Abuse of Process and Recognition of Foreign Judgments*, 2017 (ISBN 978-90-411-8342-2).
43. Dolores Bentolila, *Arbitrators as Lawmakers*, 2017 (ISBN 978-90-411-8354-5).
44. Giacomo Marchisio, *The Notion of Award in International Commercial Arbitration: A Comparative Analysis of French Law, English Law, and the UNCITRAL Model Law*, 2017 (ISBN 978-90-411-8391-0).
45. Csaba Kovács, *Attribution in International Investment Law*, 2018 (ISBN 978-90-411-9675-0).
46. Mary Mitsi, *The Decision-Making Process of Investor-State Arbitration Tribunals*, 2019 (ISBN 978-90-411-9600-2).
47. Ahmet Cemil Yıldırım, *Interpretation of Contracts in Comparative and Uniform Law*, 2019 (ISBN 978-94-035-1130-6).
48. Beata Gessel-Kalinowska vel Kalisz, *The Legal, Real and Converged Interest in Declaratory Relief*, 2019 (ISBN 978-94-035-1244-0).
49. Maximilian Pika, *Third-Party Effects of Arbitral Awards: Res Judicata Against Privies, Non-mutual Preclusion and Factual Effects*, 2019 (ISBN 978-94-035-1273-0).
50. Yulia Levashova, *The Right of States to Regulate in International Investment Law: The Search for Balance Between Public Interest and Fair and Equitable Treatment*, 2019 (ISBN 978-94-035-0931-0).
51. Flavia Marisi, *Environmental Interests in Investment Arbitration: Challenges and Directions*, 2020 (ISBN 978-94-035-1723-0).
52. Martina Magnarelli, *Privity of Contract in International Investment Arbitration: Original Sin or Useful Tool?*, 2020 (ISBN 978-94-035-2020-9).
53. Xu Qian, *Water Services Disputes in International Arbitration: Reconsidering the Nexus of Investment Protection, Environment, and Human Rights*, 2020 (ISBN 978-94-035-2203-6).
54. Nobumichi Teramura, Ex Aequo et Bono *as a Response to the 'Over-Judicialisation' of International Commercial Arbitration*, 2020 (ISBN 978-94-035-2073-5).
55. Bruno Guandalini, *Economic Analysis of the Arbitrator's Function*, 2020 (ISBN 978-94-035-2265-4).
56. Zena Prodromou, *The Public Order Exception in International Trade, Investment, Human Rights and Commercial Disputes*, 2020 (ISBN 978-94-035-2031-5).

57. Jürg Künzle, *Multiple Contracts and Coordination in International Construction Projects: A Swiss Law Analysis,* 2020 (ISBN 978-94-035-2024-7).
58. Cornel Marian, *The State's Power to Tax in the Investment Arbitration of Energy Disputes: Outer Limits and the Energy Charter Treaty*, 2020 (ISBN 978-94-035-1752-0).
59. Luke Nottage, Shahla Ali, Bruno Jetin & Nobumichi Teramura (eds.), *New Frontiers in Asia-Pacific International Arbitration and Dispute Resolution*, 2021 (ISBN 978-94-035-2855-7).
60. Eva Litina, *Theory, Law and Practice of Maritime Arbitration: The Case of International Contracts for the Carriage of Goods by Sea*, 2021 (ISBN 978-94-035-3035-2).
61. Franco Ferrari & Friedrich Rosenfeld (eds), *Autonomous Versus Domestic Concepts under the New York Convention*, 2021 (ISBN 978-94-035-3173-1).
62. Doğan Gültutan, *Moral Damages under International Investment Law: The Path Towards Convergence*, 2022 (ISBN 978-94-035-4025-2).
63. Simon Foote QC, *The Bona Fide Investor: Corporate Nationality and Treaty Shopping in Investment Treaty Law*, 2022 (ISBN 978-94-035-4185-3).
64. George A. Bermann, *Twilight Issues in International Arbitration: Latent Choice of Law Challenges*, 2023 (ISBN 978-94-035-1746-9).
65. Emmanuel Obiora Igbokwe, *Dealing with Bribery and Corruption in International Commercial Arbitration: To Probe or Not to Probe*, 2023 (ISBN 978-94-035-2066-7).
66. Peter Sester, *Contract Law in International Commercial Arbitration*, 2023 (ISBN 978-94-035-1036-1).
67. Julian Bickmann, *Fact-Finding in International Arbitration: The Emergence of a Transnational* Lex Evidentiae, 2023 (ISBN 978-94-035-1886-2).
68. Giovanna E. Gismondi, *International Environmental Law and International Human Rights Law in Investment Treaty Arbitration: The Contribution of Host States' Argumentation in Re-Shaping International Investment Law*, 2023 (ISBN 978-94-035-3047-5).
69. Fabricio Fortese, *Early Determination of Jurisdiction*, 2024 (ISBN 978-94-035-0268-7).

www.ingramcontent.com/pod-product-compliance
Lightning Source LLC
LaVergne TN
LVHW021726021026
849161LV00004BA/743
* 9 7 8 9 4 0 3 5 0 2 6 8 7 *